THRUXTON

The first 3

CW01081949

Motor racing at one of Britain's fastest circuits

1968 to 1997

by Paul Lawrence

Foreword by Derek Warwick

tfm publishing limited

Published by TFM Publishing Ltd
Brimstree View
Kemberton
Shifnal
Shropshire
TF11 9LL

Tel: 01952 583104
Fax: 01952 587654

First edition March 1998

ISBN 0 9530052 2 4

Printed by Frontier Print & Design, Cheltenham

Acknowledgements

A number of people have contributed greatly to this book and I am indebted to them for their assistance:

The many motorsport photographers for allowing their work to be reproduced.

The Visage Group for supporting the project.

Dennis Carter and the staff of the BARC for their help and encouragement.

Enid Smith, Press Officer for the BARC, for invaluable assistance throughout.

David Addison for data research and proof reading.

Don and Gwen Lawrence for historical research.

The many individuals who gave generously of their time to recount Thruxton memories, notably:

Peter Baldwin, John Burbidge, Dennis Carter, Bill Coombs, Charlie Cox, Tony Dickinson, Ian Flux, Michael Groves, Neville Hay, Ray Mallock, Kenneth Rainsbury, Fred Reeves, Tony Shaw, Tony Sugden, Graham White, Norman White and John Wickham.

Author's note

The Thruxton circuit had been open for a couple of seasons when I first went there as a young spectator. In later years, first as a marshal, then as a motor racing journalist, I have enjoyed countless race meetings in the Hampshire countryside. Close finishes are frequent at Thruxton and the last-lap dash into the Club Chicane has always produced some of the most exciting racing in the country.

The track is one of the most challenging in Britain and it's super-fast nature has regularly sorted the men from the boys. Many drivers never really master the daunting out-field section which remains virtually unchanged since it was created over the winter of 1967/68. But for everyone who has raced at Thruxton, whatever their result, goes my admiration.

Despite being dealt a crushing blow early in it's life as a race track due to planning problems, Thruxton has battled on and the efforts of the BARC and the land-owners to keep racing going should never be underestimated. Others with less determination would have been crushed by the events of the early 1970s.

I am now delighted to be able to recount the first 30 years of Thruxton history in this book. Whilst the words tell much, it is the photographs that will doubtless fire the memory banks of enthusiasts. This project was always intended to tell the story through the marvellous photographs of the BARC archive and I hope we have achieved that aim.

There are a number of people who have given freely of their time to assist with this project and to each of them I am indebted. Their memories and stories have helped put the flesh on the bones of a story that spans a period of enormous change within the sport.

Here's to the next 30 years at one of Britain's most demanding race tracks!

Paul Lawrence
Shropshire
March 1998

CONTENTS

A very special circuit

I'm very pleased to be able to write this foreword. Thruxton has always been a very special place for me and my family and it was always very much the circuit at which I wanted to do well. All my friends and family went to watch me race there and so it was always the most important race of the year for me. It was so close to home in Alresford that just about every marshal was a neighbour and I always got a very good welcome at Thruxton. It is still my home circuit.

It had a strong influence on my racing career as a racing driver as it was the first place where I had proper contact with circuit racing. When I started off racing in stock cars we went to spectate at the Formula 2 meetings and I remember watching drivers like Jochen Rindt and Graham Hill in the paddock. Then, after the race, we went into the bar and they were in there! That made a big impression on me as a youngster. Later in my career, my Uncle Stan kept an aircraft at Thruxton and we flew in and out of the circuit regularly.

I first raced at Thruxton in 1975 in a Hawke DL12 Formula Ford. I stayed in Formula Ford the following year in a Hawke DL15, then did two years in Formula 3. Through '79 and '80, I spent two years in Formula 2 when the Easter Monday meeting at Thruxton was the highlight of the season. I was fortunate enough to win the Formula Ford race at the 1976 Easter meeting and then the Formula 3 race at the 1978 Easter Formula 2 meeting. Those were very special wins for me.

It takes a very special set-up to do well at Thruxton and the bump at Church certainly sorts the men out from the boys. It is a very quick circuit. My brother Paul loved the place as well, and won his first Formula Ford championship race there in March 1986. The day before, at Silverstone, he had his first Formula Ford race and he won that as well! In fact, going to watch him race there in Formula 3 cost me a driving ban...

I'd been racing in Brazil over the weekend and flew back to Heathrow overnight to watch Paul in a Formula 3 race on a Bank Holiday Monday. I jumped into a hire car at Heathrow early on Monday morning and rushed down the M3. But I was caught by the police on the A303 doing a hundred and something and got banned!

In recent times I have worked with Dennis Carter of the BARC on RACMSA committees as part of the work that I do to improve safety at race circuits. I have a lot of respect for what people like Sidney Offord and Dennis have done for Thruxton.

Here's to the next 30 years!

Derek Warwick
Jersey
February 1998

CHAPTER ONE

The Brooklands and Goodwood Heritage

The roots of Thruxton are entwined with the history of the British Automobile Racing Club and the famous Goodwood circuit in Sussex. Although the airfield circuit at Thruxton hosted motorsport on both two and four wheels during the early 1950s, the story really began when the BARC needed a new home venue after the closure of Goodwood on safety grounds in 1966.

However, the origins of the BARC go right back to before the first World War. In 1912, a group of enthusiasts formed the Cycle Car Club for the growing number of rather fragile three-wheeled and four-wheeled devices that were popular at the time. Events were held at Brooklands, which had been completed in 1907, as well as rallies and touring trials on the open road.

Then, for four years, the Great War brought an end to any thought of motorsport as a generation of brave young men fought, and often died, on the battle-fields of Europe. But the spirit of the motoring pioneers lived on and the Club was re-formed soon after the war ended. To reflect the vehicles of the era, the Club name was changed to the Light Car Club and membership grew rapidly. As early as 1921, full-time staff were appointed to administer the Club which then underwent another change of identity when it became the Junior Car Club.

In 1921, the JCC organised the very first long-distance race in Britain when it inaugurated the 200 Mile Race around the outer circuit at Brooklands. The high-banking was a place for the abnormally brave and Henry Segrave was the first winner when he fought his 1487cc Talbot-Darracq around at an average speed of nearly 90mph! Over the next seven years, Segrave and Kenelm Lee Guinness made the JCC 200 Mile Race their own, and won it five times between them.

In 1929, the JCC planned to run a 24-hour race as its big event of Brooklands' season. However, local restrictions only permitted 12 hours of racing at a time and the Club was forced to change its original plan. Instead, it created the Double Twelve race which took over from the 200 Mile Race and in the first running of

this event, Giulio Ramponi completed over 1800 miles in his supercharged Alfa Romeo 6C. Two years later, the Earl of March and Chris Staniland won the handicap event in a diminutive 750cc MG Midget C-Type.

The JCC also ran a series of International Trophy events for Formula Libre cars at Brooklands through the 1930s, while the 200 Mile Race was revived in 1936 when the Donington circuit opened. Richard Seaman won the trophy that year in a 1500cc supercharged Delage but, even then, the clouds of war were starting to gather over Europe once more. Despite the growing threat from Nazi Germany, the JCC was still active and even organised an event called the British Rally to the United States and Canada in both 1936 and 1939!

Brooklands, August 1938. Prince Bira chases the Hon P Aitken during the 100 Mile Race.

Then, for the second time in the 20th century, Europe erupted into war and it was seven long years before motorsport emerged from the ravages of war-time. One of the many casualties of war was the Brooklands circuit, which was used an aircraft factory and lost for ever to the sport. Similarly, the Donington circuit was given over to wartime needs when it was requisitioned by the army. Ultimately, it would take the determination and money of Tom Wheatcroft before the circuit was finally re-opened for racing more than 30 years after the end of the war.

Through the 1930s, the Brooklands Automobile Racing Club had organised races at Brooklands, but was now without a home venue. An amalgamation with the Junior Car Club was arranged and the new club became the British Automobile Racing Club. Incredibly, as early as 1947, the newly-reformed Club organised its first race meeting when the Jersey Road Race was run over a 3.2-mile road circuit at St Helier on the island of Jersey. It was a fast circuit, and Reg Parnell averaged 84mph in his Maserati 4CL on his way to winning the 1947 race. The race was run for four years as a Formula 1 race before financial problems forced it to be abandoned. A single sportscar race was held in 1952 and won by Ian Stewart in a Jaguar XK120, but the circuit never again hosted race meetings.

However, the BARC had already found a new permanent home. The former Westhampnett airfield had been used during the war, adjacent to the Duke of Richmond and Gordon's Goodwood estate. The original idea came from Wing Commander Tony Gaze who recognised the possibility of creating a circuit on the airfield from which his brother flew his last war-time mission. Gaze mentioned the idea to Tommy Wisdom who immediately discussed the idea with the Duke. A 2.4-mile track was established on the airfield in just 12 months and opened for racing on September 18th 1948. This was a few weeks before the very first race at Silverstone and Goodwood was to become one of Britain's most popular circuits through its 18-year life.

Through the 1950s, the BARC hosted many major meetings at Goodwood and the calendar always featured at least one major international event. The best racing drivers from all over the world competed at the Sussex circuit and the BARC regularly ran a major meeting over the Easter weekend. Frequently, the Easter meeting would feature a non-championship Formula 1 race and, with a far less demanding grand prix schedule than the present day, most of the top teams and drivers would compete.

That was the start of a tradition that would carry on when the Club later moved to Thruxton, but in the 1950s, Goodwood was the home to many big races, including the Tourist Trophy and the BARC Nine Hours. This was one of the very first races to run into the hours of darkness in Britain and was first held in 1952 when Peter Collins and Pat Griffiths won in an Aston Martin DB3.

While the Club's activities centred on Goodwood, the BARC was also a prolific race organiser at other venues and ran meetings at Crystal Palace when the South London circuit re-opened to racing in 1953. When the British Grand Prix was held at Aintree in 1955, 1957, 1959, 1961 and 1962, the BARC was at the helm.

Goodwood was a tremendously popular venue with competitors and spectators alike, but as the 1960s arrived, all was not well. In 1962, Stirling Moss suffered extensive injuries in a dreadful, and unexplained, accident and, coupled to several other accidents and increasing noise objections from local residents, the circuit came under threat. Finally, concerns about spectator safety in the face of ever-increasing speeds at the venue proved the deciding factor for the Richmond family, and the circuit closed to racing in 1966. In April

Glorious Goodwood. Don Parker leads a group of 500cc cars through the Chicane.

of that year, restrictions were imposed by the Duke of Richmond and Gordon that would prevent the new 3-litre Grand Prix cars racing at Goodwood, along with sports and GT cars in excess of 3000cc.

Ironically, the Duke was also the BARC President and in May '66, he told the Club's AGM that there was no intention of closing the circuit. But his words were quickly overtaken by events and the curtain fell on the circuit with a BARC club meeting on July 2nd 1966. Without the revenue from the Easter International meeting, the racing income would not even support circuit maintenance.

After 18 years of international racing, glorious Goodwood closed its doors to racing. In the August issue of the BARC Gazette, the Duke explained the decision. 'The BARC will continue to promote top level racing at venues more spacious and adaptable to the speeds of the future.' A few months later, he elaborated on the situation. 'As speeds steadily rose, I knew we were shortly coming up against insuperable difficulties. The whole place was getting smaller and, in the end, performance would undoubtedly have burst it open at the seams.' It was a body blow to the BARC, but the key Club officials had been preparing for such news for some time. At the time, Grahame White and Barry Bland ran the Club's racing programme from Argyll Street in Central London and White would soon take over as Competitions Manager from Graham Macbeth.

The 1967 Easter International meeting was switched to Silverstone where a young Jochen Rindt won both parts of the WD & HO Wills Trophy Formula 2 race in a Roy Winkelmann-entered Brabham BT23. But this was only a temporary measure. Under the new chairmanship of Bill Paul, the BARC was pursuing all possible leads for a new home venue. By the autumn, plans were well under way for a completely new circuit, on the former airfield at Thruxton near Andover.

CHAPTER TWO

The creation of a race track

At the outbreak of the second World War, RAF Andover was deemed too small for the volume of aircraft it was required to handle. The Air Ministry surveyed local sites and the flat fields to the west of Thruxton village were requisitioned in 1940. The land was bought by the Air Ministry from the Thruxton Manor Estate and construction work on an airfield was quickly under way. The concrete runways of RAF Thruxton were tested by Blenheims on June 22nd 1941 but the rough surface resulted in three burst tyres and the opening of the airfield was delayed until August to allow time for tarmac to be laid.

A year later, Thruxton was central to the Dieppe raid on August 19th when large numbers of RAF personnel and aircraft gathered at the airfield, primarily for the purpose of smoke-laying in preparation for bombing attacks on the gun batteries flanking Dieppe.

Then, RAF Thruxton was increasingly used for launching troop-carrying gliders and a large number of aircraft took off from the airfield on the D-Day invasion of France. When glider operations ceased, the northern side of the airfield was used to store Horsas and late in 1945 more than 100 of the gliders were held in open storage before being broken up.

During 1944, American squadrons were also based at Thruxton with P47 Thunderbolt fighter-bombers flying missions from the airfield. But after the war, the airfield quickly became disused and was declared surplus in 1946. A year later, the airfield was leased by the Wiltshire School of Flying and this organisation was also responsible for converting Tiger Moths into Thruxton Jackaroos under a subsidiary company called Jackaroo Aircraft Ltd.

Three years later, in 1950, motorsport at Thruxton began when the airfield was first used for motorbike racing by the Southampton and District Motor Cycle Club. The first event was held on Easter Monday and the track was laid out on the runways, dodging the wartime gliders that still littered the airfield.

The original 1.89-mile course used a mixture of runways and perimeter road and was marked out by ropes. A second rope cordon kept the spectators back and the Southampton club set the venue up for each event, typically over Bank Holiday weekends. Fred Reeves, later to be Chief Marshal for the BARC at Thruxton for 20 years, was one of the early marshals. 'In those days, the paddock was on the outside of the circuit and the paddock entrance was off the back road,' recalls Reeves. 'About six feet back from the circuit on the grass, there was a stake about every six feet with a rope attached. That was the spectator barrier. I used to marshal on crowd control in those days and it was great. I was in front of everybody and I had somewhere to run if somebody came off!'

One of Murray Walker's earliest commentary assignments was to describe the racing in conjunction with his father. Murray vividly remembers commentating from the roof of a double-decker bus in driving rain!

The first meeting witnessed two wins for Geoff Duke, who also set the fastest lap of the day at an average speed of 72.15mph. The very first motorbike race at Thruxton was a non-experts race won by Ernie Barrett while amongst the competitors at that meeting was 16-year old John Surtees, who rode passenger to his father Jack in the sidecar race. The following year, Surtees was a racer in his own right and pressed Duke hard in both 500cc races. Also in 1951, the MV Augusta 500 made its UK debut in the hands of Les Graham and in those years, crowds in excess of 20,000 were commonplace at the temporary track.

The first of three car meetings of the era at Thruxton was held on August Bank Holiday Monday, 1952 on the original 1.89-mile circuit. John Coombs won twice in his Cooper 500 and also taking part in that very first meeting were Roy Salvadori, Arthur Mallock and Ivor Bueb. The meeting was jointly organised by the Bristol Motor Cycle and Light Car Club and the Sporting Owner Drivers Club. The circuit was substantially different to the present layout.

The runways that had been hastily constructed during the early months of the war were already starting to break up in places but it was a step between the runway and the perimeter track at what was called Windy Corner (now Segrave) that drew most criticism from drivers. From Segrave, the track followed the perimeter track through The Shelters (Noble) and Horizon Corner (Village) and round to Anchor Corner (Church). Here, the anchors were definitely needed, as the original circuit turned sharp right onto the runway before a fast left called Cross Roads led onto Ashton Straight which headed up towards the bottom of the present day paddock. This straight included the start and finish line before a tight right called Club Corner took the cars onto Home Straight and back out to Windy Corner.

That first meeting drew more than 60 cars and was headlined by some great sports-car battling between the Frazor Nash Bristols of Roy Salvadori and Ken Wharton and the HWM Jaguar of Oscar Moore. The big crowd enjoyed these battles so much that another impromptu race for sports cars was added to the end of the programme! Salvadori ended the day with three wins while John Coombs won two of the races for 500cc single seaters. The fastest lap of the day, and therefore the first Thruxton circuit record, fell to Moore in 1m28.4s, an average speed of 77.2mph.

The following season, 1953, a longer 2.76-mile layout hosted two meetings, including the most significant car meeting of the era when Tony Rolt won a Formula 2 race in his Connaught A Type on August Bank Holiday Monday (August 3rd). But before that event, the Bristol MC&LCC again combined with the Sporting ODC to run a club meeting on Whit Monday, May 25th. Following criticism of the bumpy track at the 1952 meeting, the lay-out was revised to produce a longer lap. This circuit started on the runway at the foot of the current paddock and ran out to what is now the Chicane (Club Corner). It then followed the perimeter track through what is now Allard and went all the way around the outside of the Complex before going through Kimpton Bends (Noble) and round to Anchor Corner (Church).

As before, the track then turned sharp right and this time followed the main runway (Farm Straight) almost back to the Complex before a sharp left called The Apex turned cars back onto the start/finish runway (Home Straight). The first race of the day was for 1200cc sports cars and was won by Archie Scott-Brown in his Tojeiro-JAP despite the efforts of a pursuing Arthur Mallock in his famous Austin 7-based special, WJ1515. Eric Fenning won the Formula 3 race in his rare Staride amongst opposition that included Ken Tyrrell in a Cooper-Norton. Later, Fenning's son John would be a rising star of the 1960s and then, after a long break from racing, a winner of Thoroughbred Grand Prix car races in the 1990s.

Back in May 1953, Sydney Allard used the Thruxton meeting to shake down his mighty Allard before the Le Mans 24-Hour race but could not match the pace of the Ecurie Ecosse C-Type Jaguars of Jimmy (elder brother of Jackie) and Ian Stewart. However, the bumpy surface meant that the circuit was left to the motorbikes at the end of 1953 and it would be 15 years before cars returned to Thruxton.

In 1957, the Air Ministry decided to sell the airfield and asked the planning authorities what use it should be put to. The planners decided that it should be used for flying and occasional racing, meaning no more than 28 days each year. The following year, the Ministry sold the circuit with this planning permission and motorbike racing continued.

Through the '50s, the wartime tarmac increasingly showed the strain of racing and the motorbike circuit layout was regularly changed to make use of the best remaining surface. Grass grew out of the tarmac in places and in the longer races such as the Thruxton Nine Hours, pot-holes would appear during the race. The organisers had prepared for this, however, and supplied the marshals with tarmac to fill in the pot-holes before the motorbikes came round on the next lap! Finally, in 1965, the condition of the runways became too bad and motorbike racing ended. But it was only to be a temporary halt.

In 1966, the Thruxton airfield was one of several venues under consideration by the BARC officials in their search to find a circuit to replace Goodwood.

Recognising that their time at Goodwood was limited, three BARC officials set about finding a new home. Kenneth Rainsbury, Sidney Allard and Tom Fisk started the search and recognised the potential of Thruxton. Ironically, they had actually considered the use of the venue for racing several years before Goodwood closed.

'In the early 1960s the Duke was getting very concerned at the speeds that were being attained at Goodwood and it became quite obvious, although nobody really wanted to admit it, that the writing was on the wall. I made enquiries of an area in Hampshire, which was War Office ground, to see if we could build a circuit there. We had no money, of course. It was just a green field site,' recalls Rainsbury.

'It became quite obvious after talking to the Ministry of Defence and one or two local people, that there would be an awful lot of objections on the grounds of noise. It was decided that the plan would be abandoned. Nothing happened for a few months but the next thing that did happen was that Sidney Allard, Tom Fisk and myself heard about Thruxton. We were all on the BARC Council at that time,' he continues.

'We could have bought the place, lock, stock and barrel for under £300,000. It was just an aerodrome then. We made a presentation to the BARC Council but the members felt that if we made desperate attempts to get Thruxton, this would upset our President, the Duke. They didn't feel that was the right thing to do. This was in the early 1960s,' explains Rainsbury.

Sadly, Allard, who had finished third at Le Mans and won the Monte Carlo Rally in cars of his own design, died in April 1966 aged 55 and would not see their work come to fruition. However, Fisk, who had co-driven for Allard on international rallies, saw the project to completion before returning to his native Australia at the end of 1971. Rainsbury, however, would go on to serve on the BARC Council over a remarkable unbroken run of more than 35 years.

'When Goodwood closed to racing, we had to make very, very big steps in trying to acquire somewhere to go motor racing. The only place that became obvious was Thruxton. We had lots of meetings and we made approaches to various people. The road system around the circuit didn't really exist then and the airfield was only a deteriorating perimeter track at the time,' says Rainsbury.

Prolonged and secret negotiations were opened with the owners of the airfield, Shonleigh Nominees Ltd, and by October 1967, the plans for the circuit were finalised and an ambitious deadline of March 1st 1968 set for the completion of the new circuit. In November, the first spadeful of earth was dug, barely a month after the first announcement of the circuit. However, warning bells were ringing right from the earliest days of the project when a small, but vociferous group of local people opposed the plans for the airfield.

As Competitions Manager of the BARC, Grahame White was heavily involved in the initial creation of the track. 'I was with the BARC during all the time we were getting Thruxton ready to race. I had run all the race meetings at Goodwood from about 1962 up to when it closed in July 1966. I used to be clerk of the course, secretary of the meeting and the starter! Geoffrey Woodhouse was the contact man who did all the arrangements for Henry Pelham at Thruxton. Bob Clarke and I were running the BARC and Bob's background was a little more away from motor racing. So he was the guy who actually went down there and controlled the building of the circuit,' recalls White.

The 2.356-mile layout followed the line of the original perimeter road, with slower sections incorporated at what became known as the Complex and the Club Chicane. The latter was designed to slow the cars before the pits and start/finish line. However, there was an initial plan to build the pits and paddock in a different location. 'My input was very much on the original plan and design of the circuit. The original plan was to have the start and finish and paddock in the hollow by the main hangars. I didn't feel that was as good as putting it right on the top of the hill where you could see a lot more of the circuit. It was also better from the access point of view,' says White.

Corner names were a mix of local features and significant names from within the sport. The first corner from the start took its name from Sidney Allard, while the next complex was named after speed record breakers Sir Malcolm Campbell, Donald Cobb and Sir Henry Segrave. Kimpton, Village, and Church were named from the local villages and features while Goodwood corner and the fast Brooklands sweep past the hangars were named in respect of the Club's early heritage. The Duke of Richmond and Gordon readily gave his permission for the use of the Goodwood name. The climb back up to towards the pits was christened Woodham Hill, possibly in recognition of the roles of Geoffrey Woodhouse and Henry Pelham, while the Club Chicane drew its name from the old control tower which remained in use to oversee airfield activity. Many years later, Kimpton would be re-named Noble in recognition of Richard Noble's World Land Speed record breaking successes.

With a mammoth effort by the contractors, the whole circuit was resurfaced, spectator banks constructed as far round the circuit as possible, marshals' posts built, telephones installed and race control buildings erected.

October 1967 at Thruxton. Construction work is underway as this shot looking back down the pit lane shows.

October 1967 at Thruxton. Looking towards Allard.

October 1967 at Thruxton. Earth banks lined the circuit for the early seasons.

October 1967 at Thruxton. Looking towards the control tower from what would become the pits entrance.

The opening meeting, March 17th 1968. Alistair McHardy on his way to winning the first race on the new circuit. Photo: Fred Clarke.

March 17th 1968. Ian Lowe (Imp), Ted Whitbourn (Anglia) and Chris Inch (Mini) battle into Campbell in front of a large crowd. Photo: John March

March 17th 1968. Ron Fry (Ford GT40) heads for Special GT victory. Photo: John March.

'The pits were just scaffold poles with corrugated iron on top and a wooden platform. The paddock was virtually as it is now but it wasn't surfaced. Race control was a room about six foot square,' remembers Rainsbury.

The teams worked right through the winter, their progress helped by good natural drainage on the chalk landscape. In early December, the construction team hit a snag when they dug through a water supply to the main hangar, but it was only a brief set-back. By December 29th, the 48ft wide track was ready for surfacing by Redland and work was well ahead of schedule.

While the teams worked, normal flying activity continued unaffected as Thruxton was, and continues to be, an active venue for light aircraft activity. Much of the credit for getting the circuit finished in such a short time went to Bob Clarke, the BARC General Manager who would also become Managing Director of British Racing Circuits Ltd, the company created to manage the venue. The initial round of expenditure was in the region of £75,000.

Just four and a half months after work started, the surface was complete and the BARC had defied the pundits who said it could not be done. Almost exactly on target, the first practice day was held on Saturday March 2nd when 100 entries were accepted. Many others were turned away as drivers were eager to try out the new circuit. Included among the single-seaters present that day were Formula 2 cars for Max Mosley and John Fenning. The honour of being first onto the circuit, however, fell to Ford Anglia racer Dave Rogers from Dorset.

Despite it being a cold and bleak March day, some quick

laps were still put in during the afternoon and fastest lap of the day went to Chris Lambert in his Formula 2 Brabham, who recorded a 1m22.8s lap. Tragically, the promising young racer lost his life later that year in an accident at Zandvoort in Holland. Others to test that day included Jenny Nadin (Beech Vee) who would later become Jenny Birrell and be a leading mover in the success of British Touring Car racing in the 1990s. Remarkably, some of the marshals present that day are still marshalling or officiating 30 years later.

March 17th 1968. Formula 3 winner Philip Tose leads Mike Keans.

They included Ron Scannell, Bob Lentell, Fred Reeves, Adam Holberton, Keith Lambert, David Taylor, Richard Fripp, Peter Cunnell, Stan Hunt and Ken Gibson.

After a trouble-free test day, the opening race meeting went ahead as intended two weeks later, with a BARC club meeting on Sunday March 17th 1968. As has so often been the case for Thruxton meetings in March, the day was cold, windy and, at times, wet! The circuit was inaugurated by the up to 1-litre Special Saloon car race which was won by Alistair McHardy in his Adcocks of Chichester-supported Hillman Imp after the Janspeed Mini of Geoff Mabbs was pushed off the grid with an oil leak. Other notable drivers of the era competing in that first meeting included Brian Cutting, Ron Fry, Jeremy Lord, Richard Longman and Brian Chatfield.

First day winners, apart from McHardy, were Ron Fry (GT), Brian Bull (Clubmans), Philip Tose (Formula 3), Alistair Cowin (Sportscars) and Ian Mitchell (Special Saloons over 1000cc). Only the Motoring News-backed GT race was a championship counter, all the others being non-championship events but the inaugural meeting still attracted a remarkable 10,000-strong crowd.

March 17 1968	
BARC meeting	
Special Saloons up to 1000cc	Alistair McHardy (Hillman Imp)
Special Saloons over 1000cc	Ian Mitchell (Mini Cooper S)
Motoring News Special GT	Ron Fry (Ford GT40)
Clubmans Sports	Brian Bull (Lotus 7)
Formula 3	Philip Tose (Brabham)
Sports Cars	Alistair Cowin (Jaguar E-Type)

The programme for that opening season comprised eight car meetings, including one organised by the Vintage Sports Car Club, and seven motorbike meetings. Incredibly, just four weeks after the first meeting, Thruxton hosted its first international meeting when the Easter Monday Formula 2 race was held on April 15th. The relatively late Easter that year was a major help to the circuit staff and contractors as they rushed to prepare the new circuit for the influx of spectators and international race teams. 'Running that first Formula 2 meeting was a very brave thing for the Club to have taken on,' reckons Rainsbury.

In readiness for the meeting, 4500 grandstand seats were built, although the last ones were only completed late on Sunday evening. But the hard work of the BARC was rewarded when at least 10,000 spectators paid 10 shillings each to watch the racing as well as a display from the Red Arrows. However, Ken Rainsbury considers that far more people than that were actually on site that day. 'We used to have chain-link fencing all the way along by the A303. People arrived with bolt croppers and on Good Friday we found great big holes cut in the wire so that people would be able to get in without paying. We wired it up on the Saturday but it was cut again overnight!'

'We had to rush everything forward to run the first meeting because the RAC weren't keen to give us a full licence to run international events on a brand new circuit,' says Grahame White.

'Everybody joined in and pulled their weight tremendously. It was an exciting time. I negotiated with all the Formula 2 teams to come and we had to have the circuit ready. The FIA stewards were on their way, so it had to happen. We had very few problems with the early meetings. We changed the positions of one or two marshals' posts as the cars got quicker. But all in all it used to run very well. The buildings weren't very luxurious but they worked perfectly well.'

The circuit was formally opened by the new BARC

March 17th 1968. Sports car winner Alistair Cowin (Jaguar E-Type) powers through the Complex. Photo: John March.

The grid for Heat 2 of the Formula 2 race, Easter Monday 1968. Jochen Rindt (Brabham BT23C) sits on pole (number 8) from Piers Courage (Brabham BT23C) and Jean-Pierre Beltoise (Matra MS7).

Easter 1968. Jenny Nadin spins her Formula Vee at the Chicane. Photo: Trevor Morgan.

Easter 1968. Barry Pearson two-wheels his Lotus Cortina through the Chicane. Photo: Trevor Morgan.

winner, learnt a hard lesson that summer in only his second season of racing.

'My first race at Thruxton was when Firestone had just come out with a ten inch tyre for the Mini. It was very early in my racing and these tyres had so much grip, I couldn't believe it. I only put two on the front and on the second lap of the race I was challenging for the lead. As we went through Kimpton the front had so much grip but the back was getting worse. It then let go completely and the car went sideways right across the grass and landed straight into the marshals' post on the right-hand side really hard. That was my first experience of Thruxton and I respected it much more after that! It made a bit of a mess of the car,' remembers Baldwin.

President, Lord Howe. The meeting, which featured a £9000 prize fund for the Formula 2 race, also marked the 60th anniversary of the first Brooklands Easter meeting. Sadly, the great Jim Clark was destined not to take part in that meeting after losing his life in an accident in the preceding Formula 2 race at Hockenheim in Germany a matter of days earlier.

April 15 1968	
European Formula 2 meeting	
Formula 2 Heat 1	Henri Pescarolo (Matra)
Formula 2 Heat 2	Jochen Rindt (Brabham BT23C)
Formula 2 Final	Jochen Rindt (Brabham BT23C)
European Formula Vee	Gerold Pankl (Austro)
British Saloons	Brian Muir (Ford Falcon)

Wearing an open-face helmet and goggles, and driving a Brabham BT23C, Jochen Rindt won the Formula 2 race and so began what would become a hat-trick of Thruxton Formula 2 victories for the mercurial Austrian. However, the 1968 win was not all plain sailing, as late in the race he slid off the track at Club, crashed through an Exide Batteries hoarding and bounced back onto the track, still leading! During the Easter race, Rindt established the first significant outright circuit record, with a best lap of 1m16.0s (111.60mph). After winning the 1969 and 1970 races, Rindt was tragically killed when qualifying for the 1970 Italian Grand Prix at Monza. However, he had scored sufficient points that season in the Gold Leaf-backed Lotus 49 and then, later in the new Lotus 72, to ensure that he became the only posthumous world champion in the history of the sport.

Through that first summer of racing, many club competitors quickly came to recognise just what a challenge the sweeping corners offered. Peter Baldwin, later to become a frequent and popular Special Saloon

May 19 1968	
BARC meeting	
Special GT	Jackie Oliver (Lotus 47)
Sports Cars	Jackie Oliver (Lotus 47)
Special Saloons up to 1000cc	Alistair McHardy (Hillman Imp)
Special Saloons over 1000cc	Don Currie (Mini Cooper S)
Formula Ford 1600	Brian Sharp (Merlyn MK11)

June 3 1968	
BARC meeting	
Osram GEC Special Saloons up to 1000cc	Peter Willcox (Mini)
Osram GEC Special Saloons over 1000cc	Richard Longman (Mini Cooper S)
Formula Vee	Mike Hayselden (Monaco Vee)
Special Sports	John Quick (Jaguar E-Type)
Formula 3	Norman Foulds (Brabham)
Historic Racing Cars	Hon Patrick Lindsay (Maserati 250F)

After a successful run of club meetings through the balance of the 1968 season, the racing season ended with the first of what would become the traditional Championship Finals meeting in October. In 1968, the key titles were clinched by Brian Bolton (V8 Cortina) in Special Saloons, Stewart Hands (Austin Healey 3000) in the Production Sports and Roger Nathan (Nathan Imp) in the GT championship. Nathan beat Bath garage-owner Ron Fry to the title when Fry's Ford GT40 retired with a broken fan belt.

Uniquely, the year ended with a visit from the RAC

Rally on November 16th. Having started in London, the crews had one forest stage in Surrey before arriving at Thruxton on Saturday afternoon on their way to the West Country forests. The circuit stage comprised five laps with cars starting at one-minute intervals and a maximum of 25 cars on the circuit at a time. A few drivers lost count and did more than five laps, but the fastest time went to Tony Fall's Porsche 911. Rallying was also to touch the BARC in December when Grahame White was seriously injured in a fall when competing in the London-Sydney Marathon. He was working on his BMC 1800 when he fell into a trench in Turkey and nearly died from internal bleeding as he was rushed 50 miles for an emergency operation. Thankfully, he later made a complete recovery.

The Formula 2 race was now established on the international calendar and the 1969 race would open the European Formula 2 Championship with continued backing from WD & HO Wills. However, as early as February '69, there were clouds gathering on the horizon as the motoring press reported rumours that an injunction could suspend racing at the new track.

Easter 1968. Beltoise points the Matra through Segrave.
Photo: Trevor Morgan.

Easter 1968. Rindt turns into the Chicane en route to victory.

July 7 1968	
BARC meeting	
Clubmans Sports	Joe Beavis (Mallock U2)
Special Saloons up to 1000cc	Martin Raymond (Mini)
Special Saloons over 1000cc	Richard Longman (Mini Cooper S)
Sports Cars	Eddie Nelson (Ford GT40)
Sports Cars	John Chatham (Austin Healey 3000)
Special GT	Tony Shaw (Jaguar E-Type)

August 4 1968	
BARC meeting	
FW Dixon Production Sports	Charles Blyth (TVR 1800S)
FW Dixon Production Sports	John Lewis (Jaguar E-Type)
Osram GEC Special Saloons up to 1000cc	Alistair McHardy (Hillman Imp)
Osram GEC Special Saloons over 1000cc	Roger Taylor (Ford Escort)
Formula Vee	Mike Haysey (Express Vee)
Motoring News Special GT	John Miles (Lotus 47)

September 14 1968	
Vintage Sports Car Club meeting	
Handicap	R Gilbert (Alvis)
Handicap	A Stirling (Frazer Nash)
Handicap	John Abson (Lagonda)
Spero & Voiturette Trophy	Geoff Coles (MG J4)
Historic Racing Cars	Bill Wilkes (Lotus 16)
Handicap	John Batt (Lagonda)
Handicap	Peter Walker (ERA)

September 29 1968	
BARC meeting	
Sports Cars	Tony Shaw (Jaguar E-Type)
Special Saloons up to 1000cc	Peter Willcox (Mini)
Specials Saloons over 1000cc	Richard Longman (Mini Cooper S)
Formula Vee	Nick Brittain (Austro)
Clubmans Sports	Joe Beavis (Mallock U2)
Sports/GT	Ron Fry (Ford GT40)

September 28 1968	
BARC Television meeting	
Special Saloons Heat 1	Mike Crabtree (Ford Escort)
Special Saloons Heat 2	Chris Inch (Mini)
Special Saloons Final	Richard Longman (Mini Cooper S)
Sports Cars	Tony Shaw (Jaguar E-Type)

October 13 1968	
Championship Finals meeting	
Osram GEC Special Saloons up to 1000cc	Laurie Hickman (Ford Anglia)
Osram GEC Special Saloons over 1000cc	John Blackburn (Ford Escort)
FW Dixon Production Sports	Warren Pearce (Jaguar E-Type)
Motoring News Special GT	Chris Skeaping (Chevron B6)

Brushing aside such concerns, the BARC started the season with a Formula 3 meeting in mid-March, and then organised a superb Easter meeting with nearly 40 entries for the feature race necessitating two heats and a final. As had already become traditional, qualifying was held on Saturday and racing on Monday. Although rather unique, this arrangement gave the teams a leisurely day on Sunday to re-fettle the cars and the whole weekend was blessed with warm sunshine.

Once again, Grahame White had assembled a fine entry with a smattering of grand prix drivers joining the Formula 2 stars. 'I was very much involved in the Formula 2 scene and I ran all the races in England. I was also a member of the Formula 2 organisers' committee and was a steward for a number of other meetings on the continent. It was good fun because you had all the Grand Prix drivers competing. One of the people I had to deal with was Bernie Ecclestone as he was manager of both Jochen Rindt and Graham Hill at the time.

'Pretty well all the competitors enjoyed driving there. It was quite quick and demanding. We got a tremendous entry together for that first Formula 2 race. I used to negotiate individually with each team and the graded drivers were the ones you had to pay start money to. These were the drivers who had scored world championship points in the previous season. There was no fixed fee, it was a case of negotiating with each driver or team. I was given a budget for that side of things and you'd start with the star names like Jochen Rindt and

Jackie Stewart. Formula 1 drivers were keen to do Formula 2 in those days. If they had a good car and a good team, they actually enjoyed it. The dates were sorted out so that there weren't any clashes,' remembers White.

'One year I had negotiated with Ferrari to come with its Formula 2 team and I went to Modena in the winter to make arrangements for it to enter. It was all agreed and it was great news because you could publicise that you had Ferrari coming. But the team withdrew about two weeks before the event. There was nothing I could do. It then entered the Crystal Palace Formula 2 race which we also ran over the Whitsun weekend at the end of May. Because Ferrari had upset us so much about Thruxton, I turned its entry down for Crystal Palace! I must be about the only person ever to turn down a Ferrari entry.'

Racing a Roy Winkelmann-tended Lotus 59 in the 1969 event, Rindt started from the eighth row of the grid, 19th place on the 3-2-3 format grid, for the final after picking up a puncture in his heat. But such a deficit made little difference to the outcome, as Jochen scythed through the field to take the lead on lap 19 of the 50-lap race. Rindt took the lead from Jackie Stewart's Matra MS7 with a move that started at Church and ended under braking for the Chicane, drawing rapturous applause from the packed grandstands. Rindt quickly pulled away from Stewart's Ken Tyrrell-entered Matra. The Scot would go on to win the first of his three world championships that year, but on Easter Monday he had

June 3rd 1968.
Terry Croker (Anglia)
gives Chris Buckton
(Mini) a scare at
Campbell.
Photo: Fred Clarke.

June 1968.
Brian Cutting
(Ford Mustang)
chases Barry
Hawkins' Mini.
Photo: John March.

June 1968.
Tony Merrick
(ERA R1A) leads into
the Complex from
Tony Hutchings (AFM)
and Patrick Marsh
(ERA R1B).
Photo: John March.

Championship Finals Meeting, October 13th 1968. Roger Nathan and his father celebrate winning the Motoring News Special GT championship with Roger's self-built Costin-Nathan. Photo: John March.

October 1968 Sports car grid. Warren Pearce's Jaguar E-Type is flanked by the Austin Healey 3000s of Stewart Hands and John Chatham. Photo: John March.

no answer to the pace of Rindt. The Lotus set a new outright circuit record on lap 26, when Rindt lapped in 1m14s (114.62mph). By the end of the race, he was nearly half a minute clear of Stewart with three more Matras completing the top five in the hands of Jean-Pierre Beltoise, Henri Pescarolo and Johnny Servoz-Gavin.

Though he did not feature in the finals results, motorbike racer Bill Ivy was another star of the 1969 event and made a great impression on Grahame White. 'They had given him a proper licence because he'd won a world championship on a motorbike. He was entered in a Brabham BT23C by Paul Watson and went out in practice and was quicker than all of them except Rindt!

'When he came in after practice he said, 'What's this mark against my name saying pole!' I said, 'well, you were the quickest and that means you're on pole position. He said, 'I don't want to be there. I haven't started one of these before. Put me in the middle, can you?' He was a super guy and we got on very well. Sadly he was killed on a motorbike a short time later, but he had showed so much natural flair,' says White.

A strong supporting programme featured race wins for Roy Pierpoint (Ford Falcon) and Brian Redman (Lola T70). The latter's Group 4 sports car victory was a narrow one as he spent the whole race battling with Jo Bonnier's similar car and Redman only grabbed the lead under braking for the Chicane with three laps to run.

With little restriction on circuit use, the 1969 season was one of the busiest that Thruxton was ever to witness, and 13 car meetings were held as smaller clubs like the Jaguar Drivers' Club took the opportunity to run its own meetings. After being set at 25

March 16 1969	
BARC meeting	
Production Sports	John Quick (Jaguar E-Type)
Osram GEC Saloons up to 1000cc	Bill McGovern (Sunbeam Imp)
Osram GEC Saloons over 1000cc	Richard Longman (Mini Cooper)
Les Leston Formula Ford 1600	Dave Walker (Lotus 61)
Motoring News Special GT	John Lepp (Chevron B8)
Chris Moore Memorial Trophy Formula 3	Alan Rollinson (Brabham BT21B)

April 5/7 1969	
Easter Monday Formula 2 meeting	
Formula 2 Heat 1	Jackie Stewart (Matra MS7)
Formula 2 Heat 2	Piers Courage (Brabham BT23C)
Wills Trophy International Formula 2	Jochen Rindt (Lotus 59)
RAC Saloons	Roy Pierpoint (Ford Falcon)
RAC Group 4 Sports	Brian Redman (Lola T70)

October 1968. The original pits and race control building. Photo: Trevor Morgan.

for the first season, the grid capacity was increased to 28 cars for 1969. The Austin Healey Car Club ran a 100-mile race for Production Sports race on July 26th with backing from the Southern Echo. The race was won by Tony Shaw in his well-known Comet Delltune Jaguar E-Type.

In that period, rapid E-Types proliferated and ranged against Shaw were drivers like John Quick, Mike Franey, John Burbidge and Warren Pearce. Burbidge and Shaw, in particular, lived very close to the circuit and were regular winners at Thruxton in those early seasons.

'I had this burning desire to drive cars,' recalls Shaw. Jaguar E-Type racer Mike Miles was a good friend and Shaw started racing in an E-Type in 1966 at Castle Combe. He built the car in his Dell Garage on the Salisbury road out of Andover and raced at Thruxton in 1968. 'Thruxton was the most demanding circuit I ever raced on. It sorts the men from the boys,' he says. Some support from the Comet fuel company led the to the car being run under the Comet Delltune banner.

The circuit had already hosted a mini-endurance race for club racers on May 26th when a round of the Osram GEC Special Saloon Championship (over 1000cc) was run over 100kms, which amounted to 27 laps. It was a new idea from the BARC and would become a regular feature of its national championships over the next few seasons. Another new idea was a Speed Fair held on June 15th, which featured three races as well as off-track competitions including an autocross, an autotest and a gymkhana. The event was originally suggested by Graham Hill as a fund-raiser for the Police Dependants' Trust. Highlight of the day was when Graham demonstrated his Lotus 49 Grand Prix car, though his lap times did not match Rindt's Formula 2 record.

The circuit was also used for sprints, and after two events in 1968, the first of seven events planned for '69 was held on March 24th over a one-mile course from Allard to Goodwood. The event proved to be a bitter-sweet day for local accountant Mike Miles who took best

Graham Hill chats to Jochen Rindt after the Austrian had won the Easter 1969 Formula 2 race. Photo: John March.

Piers Courage before the Formula 2 race, Easter 1969.
Photo: John March.

Ernesto Brambilla's
Ferrari Dino 166F2 at
Easter 1969 sporting
low-drag wheel trims.

Easter 1969. The start of the RAC Group 4 Sports race. Photo: John March.

April 27 1969
Mini Seven Racing Club meeting

Roger Taylor Trophy Formula Ford 1600	Tony Broster (Titan Mk4)
Mini Sevens	Paul Gaymer
Special Saloons up to 850cc	Roger Friend (Mini)
Special Saloons up to 1000cc	Roger Payne (Mini Cooper)
Special Saloons over 1000cc	Cyril Willmott (Mini Cooper)
Formula Libre	Dave Berry (Brabham BT16)

May 4 1969
BARC meeting

Formula 4	Robert Jarvis (Vixen Imp)
Production Sports	Warren Pearce (Jaguar E-Type)
Clubmans Sports	Charles Blyth (Lotus 7)
Motoring News Special GT	Alistair Cowin (McLaren M1C)
Special Saloons	Richard Longman (Mini Cooper)

May 26 1969
BARC meeting

FW Dixon Production Sports	John Quick (Jaguar E-Type)
Clubmans Sports	Charles Blyth (Lotus 7)
Osram GEC Saloons up to 1000cc	Bill McGovern (Sunbeam Imp)
Osram GEC Saloons over 1000cc	Richard Longman (Mini Cooper)
Motoring News Special GT	Willie Green (Chevron B5)
Historic Racing Cars	Neil Corner (Aston Martin DBR4)

June 15 1969
Speed Fair

Production Sports	Tony Shaw (Jaguar E-Type)
Financings Formula Vee	Steve Matchett (Austro)
Special Saloons	Terry Sanger (Ford Falcon)

July 6 1969
Jaguar Drivers' Club meeting

Special Saloons up to 1000cc	Peter Vann (Mini Cooper)
Special Saloons over 1000cc	Vince Woodman (Ford Escort)
Formula Ford 1600	Ian Foster (Merlyn MK11)
Production Sports	Tony Shaw (Jaguar E-Type)
Clubmans Sports/GT	Albert Powell (Nathan GT)
Formula Libre	Tony Roberts (Hawke DL2)

July 26 1969
Austin Healey Club meeting

Special GT	Jim Beach (Ford GT40)
Production Sports	Tony Shaw (Jaguar E-Type)
Special Saloons	Cyril Willmott (Mini Cooper)
Monoposto	Jim Yardley (Beagle)
Sports/Production Sports	Barry Wood (Austin Healey Sprite)

time of the day in his Jaguar E-Type and then wrote his car off when he crashed after the finish line. He was thrown out and sustained a broken leg.

In May 1969, Bob Clarke (General Manager and Secretary of BARC) resigned from the Club to return to industry. He had spent five years with the Club and played a central role in getting Thruxton built and running in such a short time. He was succeeded by the now recovered Grahame White.

But in that busy summer of 1969, all was not well behind the scenes. Local noise objectors were forming into a vociferous body and in August enforcement notices were served on the BARC by Hampshire County Council alleging that planning had not been gained for certain developments at the circuit. However, it was confirmed that racing would continue on at least the 28 days specified, for which planning permission had been granted a decade earlier.

In response, the BARC appealed to the Ministry of Housing against the two enforcement orders and in doing so, moved deeper into what was fast becoming a complex legal battle. The Club's contention was that the developments either did not need planning or else it was deemed to have been granted. Further, it claimed that the work was necessary for the safety and convenience of the public. This appeal stalled the enforcement notices and the 1969 racing programme continued as planned. However, the prospect of a public inquiry seemed to move a stage closer. The County Council's claim was that the construction of earth banks and ditches and the construction of marshals' boxes were among the 25 items that fell outside the planning permission. 'We are

August 9/10 1969	
Kodak Trophy meeting	
Group 4 Heat 1	Denny Hulme (Lola T70)
Group 4 Heat 2	Frank Gardner (Lola T70)
Kodak Super 8 Trophy for Group 4 Sports	Denny Hulme (Lola T70) (aggregate winner)
Group 5 Saloons	Dennis Leech (Ford Falcon)
Western Zone Formula Vee	Mikko Kazarowitsky (Veemax)

August 30 1969	
BBC TV Grandstand Trophy meeting	
Formula Ford 1600	Tom Walkinshaw (Hawke DL2)
Clubmans Sports	Robert Robertson (RLR P1)
FW Dixon Production Sports	John Quick (Jaguar E-Type)
Special GT	Alistair Cowin (McLaren M1B)
Special Saloons	Andy Elwin (Mini Cooper S)

September 13 1969	
Vintage Sports Car Club meeting	
Vintage and PVT Handicap	J D Martin (Austin Nippy)
Vintage and PVT Handicap	Frank Spencer (Bentley)
Spero and Voiturette Trophies	Geoff Coles (MG J4)
Vintage and PVT Handicap	A Cameron (Fiat Balilla)
Vintage Racing Cars	Neil Corner (Bugatti T35)
Vintage and PVT Handicap	Colin Readey (Riley)
Pre and Post-War Historic Racing Cars	Neil Corner (Aston Martin DBR4)
Vintage and PVT Handicap	R Elliott-Pyle (Lea Francis)
Vintage and PVT Handicap	Colin Readey (Riley)

September 21 1969	
BARC meeting	
FW Dixon Production Sports	Tony Shaw (Jaguar E-Type)
Clubmans Sports	Peter Wingfield (Mallock U2 MK5)
Special Saloons up to 1000cc	Peter Vann (Mini Cooper)
Special Saloons over 1000cc	Richard Longman (Mini Cooper)
Motoring News Special GT	Alistair Cowin (McLaren M1C)
Formula Ford 1600	Bryan Sharp (Merlyn MK11)

October 11 1969	
Championship Finals meeting	
Osram GEC Special Saloons up to 1000cc	Roger Williamson (Ford Anglia)
Osram GEC Special Saloons over 1000cc	Martin Birrane (Ford Falcon)
Financings Formula Vee	Steve Matchett (Veemax)
FW Dixon Production Sports	John Quick (Jaguar E-Type)
Motoring News Special GT	Roy Pike (Lotus 62)

seeking to bring the area under proper planning control,' said a spokesman for Hampshire County Council.

On August 10th the final round of British Group 4 championship was backed by Kodak and the spectators basked in warm sunshine. Two 25-lap heats were run to give an aggregate result for the evocative sportscars of the era. Denny Hulme, the 1967 Formula 1 world champion, drove Sid Taylor's Lola T70 and won narrowly from Frank Gardner (in Mike de Udy's car) who was slowed by overheating. Manchester jeweller and British sportscar ace, John Lepp won his class that day to claim the overall title with his Chevron B8. His car was then advertised for sale complete at £2650. Some 25 years later, similar cars were changing hands at more than £50,000! On the same programme was a European Formula Vee race which was won by former professional tennis player, Mikko Kazarowitsky.

Shortly after came the first Vintage Sports Car Club meeting at Thruxton on September 13th. Until circuit days became severely restricted, this meeting was an annual fixture on the calendar. The 1969 meeting is best remembered for a frightening accident that befell the Honourable Patrick Lindsay in his Maserati 250F. Lindsay, a virtuoso performer in a variety of classic and historic racing cars, lost his brakes as he raced into the Chicane. The front-engined Maserati, one of the all-time great Grand Prix racing cars, plunged backwards into the barriers and was very badly damaged. Lindsay was trapped in the wreckage for 30 minutes, but could perhaps count himself fortunate that his injuries were restricted to a broken leg and shoulder.

The season drew towards a close with the now-traditional Championship Finals meeting on October 11th when a 5000-strong crowd witnessed some good racing. Significant amongst the winners was young Roger Williamson, who won another Osram GEC Special Saloons (up to 1000cc) Championship race in his Ford Anglia. It was the start of a highly-promising career that would ultimately end in tragedy. Other winners that day included American Formula 3 racer Roy Pike who steered one of the rare Lotus 62s to victory in the Motoring News Special GT Championship race, John Quick (Jaguar E-Type) and Martin Birrane (Ford Falcon).

November 15 1969	
BARC Television meeting	
Formula 3	Emerson Fittipaldi (Lotus 59)
Special Saloons up to 1000cc	Peter Vann (Mini)
Special Saloons over 1000cc	Richard Longman (Mini Cooper S)

But there was one more race meeting still to be held as the 1969 season came to a close. A TV meeting was held on November 15th and, historically, featured in the first ever day of colour broadcasting on BBC TV. Just three races were held, to ensure they fitted in with TV schedules. Commentary for the BBC1 Grandstand Colour TV Meeting was by Murray Walker and 1968 world champion Graham Hill, who described two saloons events and a Formula 3 race.

At a similar meeting on September 28th 1968, Mini Cooper racer Ken Costello had carried a camera in his car. It was strapped in and wrapped in foam rubber, but the weight of the bulky camera was considerable and slowed the Mini so much that Costello didn't feature in the class results.

In the early seasons, normal race day commentary was carried out from the flying tower. But that brought an unexpected drama. Neville Hay was a regular circuit commentator in those early days. 'The only problem was that there was this big handle that set off the airfield alarm in case an aircraft was coming in with a problem. At one meeting, someone came to see us during the racing and caught the alarm handle and set it off. That caused a bit of excitement,' recalls Hay.

Later, the commentators moved to a perilous position in a tower close to the footbridge. That facility also brought its share of problems, however. 'There was a big Group 4 race with lots of Lola T70s and I had done a lot of research so that I could talk knowledgeably about the whole grid. My programme was up to date with lots of information and I was really ready to go.

I climbed up the ladder and as I got to the top I put my clipboard down on the platform. Just as I did that, a big gust of wind caught it and all my research was quickly scattered all over the circuit. I had to start commentating on the race without even a programme while someone went to fetch me another one!' remembers Hay.

In October, BARC News led with the headline: 'Thruxton - signs of a breakthrough?' An upbeat article suggested that preliminary discussions between solicitors for the circuit owners and those representing Hampshire County Council had taken place and it was suggested that real progress had been made. During those discussions, the Council also re-affirmed that it had no intention of stopping racing at Thruxton. Another encouraging piece of news was the completion of the A303 Andover by-pass and this removed one of the concerns about spectator access to the circuit. Apparently, when the circuit owners first met with the County Council to discuss their plans, they were asked not to run a Formula 1 race until the new by-pass had been opened!

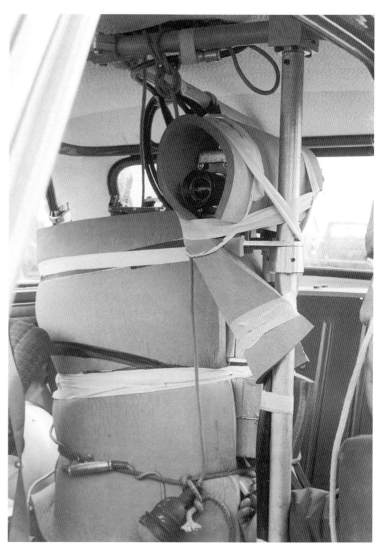

One of the early in-car cameras was an elaborate affair.
Ken Costello's Mini was fitted with this system in September 1968.
Photo: Trevor Morgan.

A further dimension to the legal situation came with news of an action by Kimpton Church of England Primary School in relation to noise from the circuit during school hours. Although practice and racing at weekends was not a problem, unsilenced testing during school hours in term time was a major problem. An offer to provide double glazing for the school was made but not accepted and the school governors sought an injunction in the High Court.

Then, three local residents, sponsored by the local Protection Society, applied to the local County Court for an injunction to restrain the use of the circuit for racing. To counter this, a Thruxton Circuit Local Supporters' Club was formed and reported that more than 500 local people supported the use of the circuit for racing, testing and research.

The Supporters' Club pointed out the great benefit that the use of the airfield had brought to the local area, with the creation of a number of permanent jobs. Also, the circuit had been responsible for the Norton Villiers motorbike business moving to Andover. The Club's letter to Andover Rural District Council also noted that: 'The circuit provides much-needed part-time employment in an area where wages are notoriously low.' In view of the pending High Court actions, the Rural Council's General Purposes committee decided to take no further action at this stage.

The Norton facility had been established in the hangars close to Woodham Hill soon after the circuit was completed. Norman White was the development rider and would go on to complete thousands of laps of the track. 'I went to Thruxton to join Norton as test and development rider in 1969. The Norton race shop was based at the circuit. After the road bikes had been assembled they were taken to the circuit and track tested. Every Commando was tested either on the circuit or the road. Nortons were always renowned for their handling and Thruxton was a lovely place to sort that out. I was employed there until it closed in 1975 and it meant lots of track miles,' says White.

The final news of 1969 was the formation of a new company called Thruxton (BARC) Ltd to manage all race meetings held at Thruxton. Richard Speakman was duly appointed as Company Manager.

CHAPTER THREE

The highs and lows of the early 1970s

As the new decade opened, uncertainty surrounded the future of the circuit. Undeterred, the BARC pressed ahead with a winter programme of improvements to the circuit's infrastructure with a new drivers' changing room and scrutineering bay for the competitors and better catering and toilets for the spectators. More good news for the fans was the completion of the A303 by-pass which would help relieve traffic congestion on race days.

However, in February 1970, the court case brought by the Kimpton school was successful in restricting week day circuit use. In the case of Kimpton Church of England Primary School v British Racing Circuits, an injunction was served to restrain use of circuit between 9am and 3.45pm during weekdays in term time. Racing at weekends not affected by this ruling.

March 8 1970	
BARC meeting	
Formula Ford 1600	Ian Foster (Merlyn MK11/11A)
Motoring News Special GT	Martin Raymond (Daren MK2)
Osram GEC Special Saloons up to 1000cc	Andy Holloway (Hillman Imp)
Osram GEC Special Saloons over 1000cc	Dave Minchin (Mini Cooper)
FW Dixon Modified Sports	Peter Kitchen (Austin Healey Sprite)
Chris Moore Memorial Trophy Formula 3	Mike Beuttler (Brabham BT28)

The 1970 racing season opened in sleet and rain on March 8th, with a club meeting delayed by an hour and a half due to ice on the circuit after a heavy overnight frost. Marshals drove their cars round the track to help clear the ice and when racing finally got underway Dave Minchin was a star winner in the Carmen Curlers Mini. During that era, Minchin frequently battled with Mini engine ace Richard Longman, who ran Downton Engineering near Fordingbridge. Longman did most of the winning, but Minchin won the first encounter of the new season.

At the end of March the weather was far kinder for the Wills Trophy meeting and a large crowd arrived for one of the best Formula 2 features the circuit would ever see. Two full grids were assembled for the 20-lap heats, from which the best 30 cars would go forward to the 30-lap final. Rindt had already earned the 'King of Thruxton'

tag and arrived at the Easter meeting with the latest Lotus 69 to be run by the newly-formed Jochen Rindt Racing team.

March 28/30 1970	
Easter Monday Formula 2 meeting	
Formula 2 Heat 1	Jackie Stewart (Brabham BT30/2)
Formula 2 Heat 2	Jochen Rindt (Lotus 69)
WD & HO Wills Trophy Formula 2	Jochen Rindt (Lotus 69)
Embassy Trophy Groups 5 and 6	Jo Siffert (Porsche 917)
Wills Three Castles Trophy Group 2	Frank Gardner (Ford Mustang)

Team patron John Coombs entered a Brabham BT30 for Jackie Stewart with backing from Ski Yoghurt while other leading Brabham entries included Tim Schenken, Derek Bell, Peter Gaydon and Carlos Reutemann. Jim Russell mechanic Ralph Firman (soon to start building racing cars in his own right) just completed a Lotus 69 in time for Emerson Fittipaldi to make his Formula 2 debut, while the fledgling March marque was represented by Chris Amon driving the first 702 Formula 2 design. Elsewhere in the entry were Jacky Ickx and Jo Siffert (BMWs), Jean-Pierre Jabouille in the French Pygmee and Francois Cevert and Clay Regazzoni in Tecnos. It was a superb entry, one of the best that Thruxton would ever host.

Stewart set a searing pace in qualifying and bettered Rindt's lap record to take pole for the first heat with a lap of 1m13.6s. Rindt responded with a 1m14.4s lap before heading off to London to get an aching tooth sorted out. On Monday, early morning rain gave way to a sunny day as Stewart and Rindt dominated their respective heats.

Rindt swept straight into the lead of the 46-lap final as Stewart led the chase. For the first few laps, Stewart kept pace with the flying Austrian, but gradually the gap increased and Rindt went on to complete his hat-trick of wins with a 12-second victory over Stewart. Local drivers Derek Bell and Rob Widdows were third and fourth in their Brabhams, but they were both a lap down on the winner. During the final, Rindt also matched his own existing circuit record with a 1m14s lap. Tragically, Jochen would never race at Thruxton again, but he had made his mark on the spectators and many of them would feel a great sense of loss when he died five months later.

As well as contesting the Formula 2 feature, Siffert also raced in the Group 5/6 sports car race in David Piper's glorious Porsche 917 and won at a canter, as he would do again the following season. Colourful Australian Frank Gardner completed a hat-trick of early season Group 2 saloon car wins in his Ford Boss Mustang.

Though the focus of racing at Thruxton was cars, the circuit's motorbike heritage was not ignored and in May the 500-mile Grand Prix d'Endurance was held for 60 bikes. Starting at 11am from a Le Mans-type start, the race lasted six hours. The circuit was also busy with frequent unsilenced mid-week testing. But time was running out for this particular element of circuit use.

Norman White, busy testing Norton Commandos, was lucky to survive that summer after a bizarre accident. 'On one occasion in 1970, myself and Peter Williams were out testing on a Wednesday afternoon. But I fell off and went down the ditch on the exit of the Complex. It was half an hour before somebody said, 'Where's Norman?' I knew nothing of this, of course. They sent a search party out and it was Tony Shaw who finally found me. The bike had fallen on top of me and I was out cold.

'It was a full hour after the accident before anyone found me. I'd been burnt by the exhaust, broken a bone in my neck and all sorts of things. I woke up several days later, convinced I'd been knocked over by a double-decker bus! I temporarily lost the power of speech,' recalls White.

Once recovered, White went on to make his mark on the motorbike endurance race. 'I didn't actually race at Thruxton until 1971 but I won my first race here. Of course, the reason I won it was that I knew every inch of the track! The following year John Player sponsored the works Norton team and I continued as a test rider and mechanic. In 1973 we had a busy schedule and there was a race in America on the same weekend as the Thruxton 500-mile race.

'The works Nortons had won the 500-mile race twice in a row and so the team manager asked me if I wanted to take the ride. I hadn't raced for almost two years but I teamed up with Reg Butcher and we won it. That was the last time a British motorbike won the 500-mile race. It was a very big event in those days. The following year I was leading on the first lap when the crankshaft snapped! In 1981, I came back and started my own

Tony Shaw (Jaguar E-Type) winning the Sports car race at the very first TV meeting, September 28th 1968. Photo: Hugh Bishop.

business on the airfield specialising in Nortons,' says White.

April 19 1970	
Mini Seven Racing Club meeting	
Formula Ford 1600	Reg James (Merlyn MK11A)
Mini Sevens	Len Brammer
Monoposto	Jim Yardley (Beagle)
Special Saloons up to 1000cc/ Mini Miglia	John Peachey-Austing (Mini Cooper)
Modified Sports/ GT/Special Saloons over 1000cc	Tony Shaw (Jaguar E-Type)
Formula Libre	Steve Thompson (Lola T60)

May 3 1970	
BARC meting	
Modified Sports	John Quick (Jaguar E-Type)
Formula Ford 1600/Formula 4	Robert Jarvis (Vixen Imp)
Osram GEC Special Saloons up to 1000cc	Andy Holloway (Hillman Imp)
Osram GEC Special Saloons over 1000cc	Gerry Marshall (Vauxhall Viva)
Gregor Grant Clubmans Sports	Rod Mansfield (Dino 6)
Vintage Handicap	Tim Blishen (Alvis)

May 24 1970	
BARC meeting	
Special Saloons up to 1000cc	John Turner (Hillman Imp)
Special Saloons over 1000cc	Richard Longman (Mini Cooper)
Formula Vee	Mike Hayselden (Monaco)
FW Dixon Modified Sports	Shaun Jackson (AC Cobra)
Forward Trust Formula 3	Richard Scott (Brabham BT28)
Motoring News Special GT	Alain de Cadenet (Porsche 908/2)

June 7 1970	
Jaguar Drivers' Club meeting	
Special Saloons	Mick Hill (Jaguar Anglia)
Formula Ford 1600	Andy Rouse (Dulon LD4C)
GT/Modified Sports	George Silverwood (Chevron B8)
Clubmans Sports	John Masters (Mallock U2 MK6B)
Jaguars	John Burbidge (Jaguar E-Type)
Lombank Formula 3	Carlos Pace (Lotus 59A)

June 14 1970	
Speed Fair	
FW Dixon Modified Sports	Ian Richardson (AC Cobra)
Les Leston Formula Ford 1600	Peter Lamplough (Palliser WDF2)
Special Saloons	Richard Longman (Mini Cooper)
Formula Ford 1600	Ronald Rossi (Lola T200)

For club car racing fans in 1970, a Thruxton favourite of the period was Tony Shaw in his Comet Delltune Jaguar E-Type. He was lucky to escape injury in May when the car was destroyed against the marshals' post at Church when the E-Types of Peter Archer and John Burbidge spun in front of him.

'I'd had oil pressure problems in the morning and started from the back of the grid. I drove through the field and as I came round towards Church on about the fourth lap I could see Shaun Jackson's Cobra in the lead. Down into Church, the yellow flags were out. The guys lying second and third were Burbidge and Archer in E-Types and when I arrived at Church they were spun

across the road,' says Shaw.

'In the end I elected to ease it over onto the grass but I just clipped the barrier in front of the passenger door. There was an almighty bang and the car bounced across the airfield minus a wheel. I thought it was going to roll but it finally came to a rest and I jumped out as quickly as possible. I looked back and there was a trail of debris. It was a big impact. I missed the other two cars but I wrote off my own car. We got a new shell and were back out in a couple of months,' he remembers.

While racing continued, the behind-the-scenes legal wrangles would not go away and as a result of complaints from local residents, it was announced that a public inquiry would be held, starting on July 9th. The BARC had already appealed against enforcement notices served by Hampshire County Council and sought support from the sport in the legal battle that was growing ever bigger. Joining the Club in appealing against the notices were British Racing Circuits Ltd, Norton Villiers and the Southampton Motor Cycle Club.

Graham Hill was one of the celebrities who gave evidence in support of the circuit during an inquiry that ran for 22 days. Hill told the inquiry: 'I believe Thruxton is one of the safest circuits in Europe. I think the design, which makes use of extensive run-off areas, incorporates a great deal of modern thinking about safety in motorsport.'

Norton Villiers told the inquiry that it had chosen to relocate its factory from Woolwich to Andover due to the availability of Thruxton as a test and development facility. However, Jeremiah Harman QC, counsel for Hampshire County Council suggested that the circuit owners had: 'Pursued a course both devious and energetic to obtain any advantage they could on the principle of 'gaining an inch and taking an airfield'.'

Harman continued that: 'Permission for motor racing on the circuit would be followed, in our submission, by organisation of Formula 1 grand prix racing. If that were to happen, we should be dealing here with crowds of 60,000, 80,000 even perhaps 100,000. The result of that on traffic, on disturbance in surrounding villages and disposal of litter and so on must inevitably have an extremely large impact on the airfield and the surrounding districts.'

Douglas Hockley, the Deputy County Planning Officer, gave evidence and local residents gave evidence about noise disturbance. Ian Glydewell QC, counsel for British Racing Circuits Ltd, said that the circuit management was prepared to limit racing to 28 days each year, with a maximum of 150 days unsilenced testing. But the speed of such inquiries is slow and it was adjourned on July 31st, resumed on September 24th and finally concluded on October 2nd.

In his closing speech, Denis Henry, counsel for the Thruxton Protection Society said: 'That for 175 days of the year, noise from the circuit makes life a misery for villagers. Motor racing enthusiasts - admirable people, lots of them - really are living in a completely different world, hopelessly out of touch with all modern thinking on conservation and pollution. If they cannot make their cars quieter they must take them and run them where villages and schools are not affected by them.' Henry did not dispute that Thruxton was a very good circuit for motor racing, but said: 'It only exists there because of wilful, deliberate and cynical defiance of planning laws. The circuit has already enjoyed three seasons of racing in defiance of planning laws and we say the time has come to stop.'

In his closing remarks for the BARC, George Dobry proposed a compromise. 'One of the most useful things revealed by the inquiry was the wholly uncompromising attitude of the Thruxton Protection Society members who will not accept any compromise.' He asked the Minister to consider giving the BARC permission to hold meetings on six days over Bank Holiday weekends and to allow racing on 20 other Saturdays or Sundays at the operators discretion. 'I do not see how you can go below that number - but probably you might not think 26 days excessive in number. Overall our attitude is that we would like the Minister to fix all these matters because we have got nowhere with the county council. They have given us no effective help over the years,' said Dobry.

Ian Glydewell QC, counsel for British Racing Circuits, submitted that in law the owners of the airfield held an existing users rights to stage motor racing and that the developments which had taken place there since 1968 were not an infringement of that right and did not constitute a material change of use. Commenting on allegations that the owners had ignored the planning authority, Glydewell continued: 'It is neither illegal nor morally wrong to carry out development without planning permission; it only becomes illegal if an enforcement notice is confirmed and one fails to comply with it. Still less is it wrong to go ahead with development when you take the view that you do not need planning permission when the use is not a change.' In closing the inquiry, the Inspector, A M Roberts, said he would shortly be visiting the site and that the Minister's decision would be made known later. It would, however, be more than 18 months before the outcome was finally announced.

With Grahame White now appointed General Manager of the BARC, there was plenty of good sport through the summer and autumn of 1970. On August 2nd, the BARC Surrey Centre ran another sprint in which fast lady Patsy Burt set best time of the day in her rare McLaren-Oldsmobile M3A.

A week later, more big single-seaters ventured onto the circuit in the first ever Formula 5000 race to be held at Thruxton. The meeting also marked the last Formula 5000 race for Peter Gethin before he stepped up to Formula 1. Just over a year later, he would become world-famous by winning the Italian Grand Prix for BRM in a race run at an average speed in excess of 150mph and in which the first five cars home were covered by just six-tenths of a second!

Back in August 1970, however, his McLaren M10B won one of the heats at Thruxton but lost out on the

aggregate result to the other heat winner Frank Gardner (Lola T190). Significantly, the mighty Formula 5000s also bettered the outright record set by the 1600cc Formula 2 cars and Gethin and Gardner jointly set the new mark at 1m13.6s (115.24mph). Other notable winners during the Kodak Trophy meeting were Bev Bond (Formula 3 Lotus 59A) and Dave Brodie who won the over 1000cc saloon car race in his Escort.

August 9 1970	
Kodak Trophy meeting	
Formula 5000 Heat 1	Peter Gethin (McLaren M10B)
Formula 5000 Heat 2	Frank Gardner (Lola T190)
Kodak Super 8 Trophy Formula 5000 - aggregate	Frank Gardner (Lola T190)
Kodak 135 Formula 3 Trophy	Bev Bond (Lotus 59A)
Western Zone Formula Vee	Lasse Sirvio (Austro)
Special Saloons over 1000cc	Dave Brodie (Ford Escort)
Special Saloons up to 1000cc	John Turner (Ford Anglia)

Two weeks later, the West Hants & Dorset Car Club organised a 100km Formula 3 race, preceded by two eight-lap heats. The feature race was supported by Formula 3 entrant Harry Stiller who also acted as Secretary of the Meeting. Incredibly, after 37 minutes of racing the race ended with a blanket finish as Brazilians Wilson Fittipaldi and Carlos Pace just beat a young Tom Walkinshaw (March 703) with their Lotus 59As.

The Formula 3 teams were back in September for the Yellow Pages European Formula 3 Cup. The late Gerry Birrell dominated the 40-lap race but the Swedes won the team award with Torsten Palm and Ulf Svensson. Closing the 1970 season was another TV meeting on November 14th during which Chris Skeaping won the final round of the Forward Trust Formula 3 Championship in his Chevron B17. Sadly, the year ended just as it had begun, in terrible weather.

With the outcome of the public inquiry still not announced, plans were made for the 1971 season and a mammoth 17-meeting programme was arranged. Having backed the European Formula 3 Cup in September 1970, Yellow Pages stepped in to become title sponsor of the Easter meeting. They also announced the commissioning of a Jochen Rindt Memorial Trophy. Rindt's skill and style had endeared him to the Thruxton crowds during a hat-trick of Easter Monday Formula 2 races and, in his memory, the magnificent trophy would be awarded to the winner of the Easter Formula 2 race. The trophy took the form of a racing steering wheel with the initials JR in the centre.

August 23 1970
West Hants & Dorset Echo Trophy meeting

Formula 3 Heat 1	Mike Beuttler (Brabham BT28)
Formula 3 Heat 2	Barrie Maskell (Chevron B17)
Echo Formula 3 Trophy	Wilson Fittipaldi (Lotus 59A)
Special Saloons up to 1000cc	John Routley (Mini Cooper)
Special Saloons over 1000cc	Richard Longman (Mini Cooper)
Modified Sports	Shaun Jackson (AC Cobra)
Formula Ford 1600	Andy Rouse (Dulon LD9)

August 30 1970
BARC meeting

Clubmans Sports	Mark Sharpley (U2 MK8B)
Osram GEC Special Saloons up to 1000cc	John Turner (Hillman Imp)
Osram GEC Special Saloons over 1000cc	Dave Brodie (Ford Escort)
Special GT	John Jordan (Ford GT40)
Formula Vee	Mike Hayselden (Monaco Vee)
FW Dixon Modified Sports	Norman Cuthbert (Lotus Elan)

September 12 1970
Vintage Sports Car Club meeting

Vintage and PVT Handicap	Tony Griffiths (Austin 7)
Vintage and PVT Handicap	Brian Mather (Frazer Nash)
Spero & Voiturette Trophies	Neville Farquhar (Brooklands Riley)
Vintage and PVT Handicap	M W Gibbs (Frazer Nash)
Vintage Racing Cars	Neil Corner (Bugatti T35)
Pre and Post War Historic Racing Cars	Neil Corner (Aston Martin DBR4)
Vintage and PVT Handicap	John Batt (Lagonda Rapier)
Vintage and PVT Handicap	Colin Readey (Riley)
Vintage and PVT Handicap	Patrick Marsh (ERA)

September 19/20 1970
Yellow Pages European Formula 3 Cup

Yellow Pages European Formula 3 Cup	Gerry Birrell (Brabham BT28)
Forward Trust Formula 3	Dave Walker (Lotus 59A)
Interserie	Jurgen Neuhaus (Porsche 917)
Special Saloons	Dennis Leech (Ford Mustang)

October 11 1970
Championship Finals meeting

Osram GEC Special Saloons up to 1000cc	John Turner (Hillman Imp)
Osram GEC Special Saloons over 1000cc	Colin Hawker (Ford Escort V6)
Formula Vee	Ronnie Grant (Austro)
FW Dixon Modified Sports	Norman Cuthbert (Lotus Elan)
Motoring News Special GT	Jeremy Lord (Astra RNR1)

November 14 1970
BARC Television meeting

Special Saloons up to 1000cc	Roger Williamson (Ford Anglia)
Special Saloons over 1000cc	Vince Woodman (Ford Escort)
Modified Sports	John Burbidge (Jaguar E-Type)
Forward Trust Formula 3	Chris Skeaping (Chevron B17)

March 14 1971
BARC meeting

Chevron Oil Modified Sports	John Burbidge (Jaguar E-Type)
Special Saloons up to 1000cc	John Turner (Hillman Imp)
Special Saloons over 1000cc	Vince Woodman (Ford Escort)
Clubmans Sports	Sid Marler (Ellova MK8B)
Motoring News Special GT	Jeremy Lord (Astra RNR1)
Formula Ford 1600	Tony Brise (Elden MK8)

Fittingly, the first name to go on the trophy was that of another world champion, Graham Hill. Having suffered major leg injuries in an accident during the American Grand Prix in the autumn of 1969, Hill was struggling to regain full fitness and arranged a Formula 2 programme with Ron Dennis' Rondel Racing team. He raced the latest Brabham BT36 alongside Tim Schenken while a strong March entry was headed by Jean-Pierre Jarier, Ronnie Peterson, Henri Pescarolo and a young Niki Lauda. A total of 41 cars (from an entry of 50) arrived at the circuit and were split into two heats, won by Hill and Pescarolo. However, the quickest qualifying time had been the 1m13.4s of Peterson in his Smog-backed works March. The final was played out in bright sunshine in front of a 40,000-strong crowd and proved to be another thriller.

Graham Hill (Brabham BT36) acknowledges the crowd after winning the 1971 Formula 2 Final. Photo: Trevor Morgan.

April 10/12 1971	
Yellow Pages Formula 2 meeting	
Formula 2 Heat 1	Graham Hill (Brabham BT36)
Formula 2 Heat 2	Henri Pescarolo (March 712M)
Jochen Rindt Memorial Trophy Formula 2	Graham Hill (Brabham BT36)
Formula Super Vee Heat 1	Erich Breinsburg (Austro Kaimann)
Formula Super Vee Heat 2	Jochen Mass (Austro Kaimann)
Yellow Pages Formula Super Vee Trophy Aggregate result	Erich Breinsburg (Austro Kaimann)
Yellow Pages Sports Car Trophy	Jo Siffert (Porsche 917)
Yellow Pages Saloon Car Trophy	Brian Muir (Chevrolet Camaro)

Hill led off the grid but was soon pushed back to second by Pescarolo who had just two laps of glory before his engine failed comprehensively. Hill regained control and built a small lead over Peterson as they lapped backmarkers for the first time. However, when they came round to lap the slower cars for a second time at two-thirds distance, Hill lost ground when badly baulked by Tetsu Ikuzawa into the Chicane. Hill also had

a broken exhaust which was costing him a few revs and Peterson hunted him down so that, with 17 laps still to run, the Brabham and March were nose to tail. Hill, of course, failed to be rattled by the presence of the young Swede and it seemed as though they would stay in formation to the flag.

Peterson, though, had other ideas. He kept his big effort until they rushed up Woodham Hill on the 48th lap of 50. With a big dive, he outbraked Hill and finally grabbed the lead. But it was not over yet. On the last lap, they came up to lap Jeremy Richardson's Brabham BT30 at Goodwood. Richardson saw them coming and started moving to the left, just as Peterson committed himself to the same line. Ronnie ended up on the grass and Hill quickly switched to the right of the track and passed both cars to win by six-tenths of a second as Peterson swiftly recovered from his moment on the grass. Their battle had also driven the lap record down further, with Peterson taking some consolation for losing the race by setting the new standard at 1m13.4s (115.55mph). Some 20 seconds behind the leading pair, Derek Bell was third for the second year in a row, this time in a Frank Williams-run March.

It was at a Formula 2 meeting of this era that a fresh noise complaint was raised by local residents. Traditionally, the Easter meeting featured qualifying on Saturday and racing on Monday, with Sunday being a quiet day. Fred Reeves takes up the story. 'One of our marshals at the time was a sergeant from the Metropolitan Police. When he was here for the weekend, on the Sunday he would go down to Andover police station to have a chat with his colleagues. He was in there one day when a local resident rang to complain about a racing engine being run at the circuit. The marshal volunteered to go and sort out the problem. When he got back to the circuit, there was a French Formula 2 car testing on the back road between the paddock entrance and the Complex. When challenged, the driver said, 'The papers say no engines on the circuit. We are not on the circuit!''

April 18 1971	
Mini Seven Racing Club meeting	
Formula Ford 1600	John Trevelyan (Crossle 20F)
Mini Sevens	Peter Drake
Monoposto	Brian Jordan (Brabham BT15)
Special Saloons up to 1000cc/ Mini Miglias	Les Nash (Ford Anglia)
Special Saloons over 1300cc	Brian Cutting (Ford Escort)
Formula Libre	Geoff Bremner (Chevron B15)

April 25 1971	
Nottingham Sports Car Club meeting	
Clubmans Sports	Ray Mallock (Mallock MK11)
Modified Sports	John Pearson (Jaguar XK120)
Formula Ford 1600	Richard Mallock (Mallock MK8B)
Special Saloons up to 1000cc	Andy Holloway (Hillman Imp)
Special Saloons over 1000cc	Mick Hill (Ford Boss Capri)
Formula Libre	Vern Schuppan (Palliser WD4)

May 2 1971	
BARC meeting	
Special Saloons up to 1000cc	Andy Holloway (Hillman Imp)
Special Saloons over 1000cc	Brian Cutting (Ford Escort)
Formula Libre/ Formula Ford 1600	George Whitehead (Gropa)
Motoring News GT	Jeremy Lord (Lola T212)
Formula Super Vee	John Wales (Royale RP9)
Group 1 Handicap	David Powers (Alfa Romeo)

After the excitement of the Formula 2 action, the rest of the season was a typical mix of club and national racing, although a couple of interesting experiments were tried. On May 2nd 1971, the BARC arranged a trial Group 1 race for standard cars. An encouraging 28-car grid assembled for a handicap race won by David Powers in an Alfa Romeo.

'We ran the very first Group 1 saloon car race for bog-standard cars. I rang all sorts of mates to get the entry together and most people entered something. I managed to get a Fiat 600 for one end of the grid and a Mercedes 600 with Adrian Hamilton at the other end,' remembers Grahame White. Though no one knew it at the time, it was the start of a movement that would radically change saloon car racing in Britain.

May 30 1971	
BARC meeting	
Osram GEC Special Saloons up to 850cc	Graeme Janzen (Mini)
Osram GEC Special Saloons 850-1000cc	Tony Dickinson (Mini)
Osram GEC Special Saloons over 1000cc	Gerry Marshall (Vauxhall Viva)
Modified Sports/GT	Alan Fowler (Mercury GT)
Formula Ford 1600/Formula 4	Chris Smith (Merlyn MK11A)
Clubmans Sports	Barry Foley (Lotus 7X)

June 6 1971	
Jaguar Drivers' Club meeting	
Modified Sports	John Burbidge (Jaguar E-Type)
Special Saloons	Brian Cutting (Ford Escort)
Formula Ford 1600	Jeremy Gambs (Lotus 61)
Historic Sports	Martin Morris (Jaguar D Type)
Lombank Clubmans Sports	Ray Mallock (Mallock MK11)
Jaguars	John Burbidge (Jaguar E-Type)

June 13 1971	
BARC meeting	
Formula Ford 1600/Formula 4	John Trevelyan (Crossle 16F)
Osram GEC Special Saloons up to 1000cc	Tony Dickinson (Mini)
Osram GEC Special Saloons over 1000cc	Dave Brodie (Ford Escort)
Chevron Oils Modified Sports	Dave Brodie (Lotus Elan)
Forward Trust Formula 3	Dave Morgan (Lotus 69)
Motoring News Special GT	Alan Fowler (Mercury)

June 1968. Brian Tarrant at speed in the Austin A40-Chevrolet. Photo: John March.

Rather less ground-breaking was a Fordson tractor race for celebrities held at the 'Stars for Spastics' meeting on June 6th, which was won by film actress Imogen Hassell. Sadly, the meeting was over-shadowed when Brian Tarrant crashed his brutish Chevrolet-powered Austin A40 Special Saloon on the exit of Kimpton. The car literally disintegrated and the race was stopped to allow the medical teams to attend the accident, but poor Tarrant died the next day from his injuries.

While the outcome of the public inquiry was awaited, mid-week testing continued through the spring and summer of 1971. On its way to Monaco for the Grand Prix, the Frank Williams team dropped in to put some miles on the March 711 they were running for Henri Pescarolo. The French journeyman knew the circuit well from his Formula 2 career, though the fast sweeps of Thruxton hardly seemed the ideal warm-up for the tight confines of the Monte Carlo circuit!

Relations with local residents were not always good, but on July 11th a BARC (North Thames Centre) sprint was organised to coincide with Andover carnival week. Fastest time of the day went to Peter Voigt in his Ginetta Imp, but this event was marred by an accident involving a light aircraft and a spectator's car! A month later, a round of the RAC Sprint Championship round was run by the Surrey Centre of the BARC and Spencer Elton (Brabham BT18) set the best time of the day.

The Formula 5000s returned on August 1st and a crowd of 10,000 spectators turned out for the Rothmans-supported meeting. They were rewarded with good weather, good racing and new lap records. Graham McRae won the feature race in his McLaren M10B while fellow Antipodean Dave Walker won the Formula 3 race under pressure from James Hunt and Roger Williamson. Frank Gardner (Formula 5000 Lola T300) sliced more than a second off Ronnie Peterson's outright record to leave the standard at 1m12.2s (117.47mph).

Two weeks later, the longest car race ever to be held at Thruxton was run on a Saturday when the 750 Motor Club moved its annual Birkett Six Hour Relay Race from Silverstone. This was the first time in its 21 year history that the relay had not been run at the Northamptonshire circuit. The team event was won by a squad of Alfa Romeos, including cars driven by Richard Pilkington and Jon Dooley. The Birkett stayed at Thruxton for 1972, before moving back to Silverstone and, most recently, Snetterton.

Another landmark event of 1971 was the creation of the Thruxton Saloon Car Racing Drivers' School. The first instructors were John Burbidge, Brian Cutting and Tony Shaw and, in September, they added two Formula Fords to the fleet of cars to be used by aspiring racers. At the end of the previous season Shaw had sold his E-Type to Mini racer Pino Scarpino and moved his business into a unit on the airfield. It was renamed Thruxton Racing Services and he worked on numerous racing Jaguars, including the successful E-Type of Burbidge.

Burbidge was very much a local hero, as at the time he lived in Thruxton village. A baker by profession, he was introduced to racing by Shaw. 'I bought Brian Cutting's Anglia and started racing at Castle Combe in 1967. That was a great mistake as the Anglia was built just for Brian! I'd never driven a car like it. But it was great fun. I wrote the Anglia off at Thruxton during practice for the television meeting in 1968. I came up into the Chicane and stuffed it straight into the barriers. I got it wrong and completely wrote it off,' recalls Burbidge.

'I didn't really get going until I bought the E-Type, which I first raced in 1970. Tony Shaw helped me tremendously,' recalls Burbidge. 'He used to build my engines for a packet of Guards and a Burbidge pasty! I lived in Thruxton village at the time and that caused a stir. I was pretty unpopular with some of the people in the village but I was young and I just wanted to go racing. It was marvellous for me to have the circuit on the doorstep,' says Burbidge.

'There were a lot of us out there in E-Types and Modified Sports was pretty competitive at the time. It was like driving a very fast furniture van. It was a real handful and when you got out of an E-Type, you knew you'd done it. Graham Hill narrated a film about driving around the circuits and I was an instructor at the early racing school at Thruxton. They were filming the school and Graham was doing some laps in a Formula 2 Brabham. Then he drove my E-Type for about 10 laps and said, 'That's impossible!' Though Hill had driven E-Types for John Coombs in the 1960s, that had been in the era of skinny tyres. Burbidge's modified car was running on monstrous 16 inch slicks.

Winning the TV race in November 1970 was a career highlight as the race was run in soaking wet conditions.

July 18 1971	
Austin Healey Club meeting	
Clubmans Sports	Andy Diamond (Gryphon)
Monoposto	Chris Featherstone (Lola T60)
Modified Sports	John Burbidge (Jaguar E-Type)
Special Saloons	Dave Minchin (Mini Cooper)
Formula Ford 1600	Mike Campbell-Cole (Merlyn MK11A)

August 1 1971	
Kodak BARC Formula 5000 meeting	
Rothmans Formula 5000	Graham McRae (McLaren M10B)
Forward Trust Formula 3	Dave Walker (Lotus 69)
Saloon Cars	Dennis Leech (Ford Mustang)
Saloon Cars	Martin Birrane (Ford Mustang)

August 15 1971	
750MC Birkett Six Hour Relay	
Won by Alfa Romeo team: Richard Pilkington, Jon Dooley, Ken Davis and Geoff Thomas	

August 22 1971	
West Hants & Dorset Echo Trophy meeting	
Echo Trophy for Formula 3	Roger Williamson (March 713M)
Clubmans Sports	Geoff Friswell (Mallock MK11)
Special Saloons up to 1000cc	Ray Payne (Hartwell Imp)
Special Saloons over 1000cc	Martin Thomas (Chevrolet Camaro)
Formula Ford 1600	Jeremy Gambs (Lotus 61)

August 29 1971	
BARC meeting	
GT/Clubmans Sports	John Jordan (McLaren M1C)
Special Saloons up to 1000cc	Tony Dickinson (Mini Cooper)
Special Saloons over 1000cc	Brian Cutting (Ford Escort)
Forward Trust Formula 3	Dave Walker (Lotus 69)
Chevron Oils Modified Sports	John Quick (Jaguar E-Type)
Production Saloons Handicap	Richard Leach (Toyota Celica)

'I was extremely lucky in that race because I built up an enormous lead and then backed right off. My pit crew missed this and Shaun Jackson nearly caught me in his AC Cobra. It would have broken my heart to lose that race in front of the TV cameras! I was tip-toeing round and he nearly caught me. I couldn't see a thing in my mirrors and then suddenly I saw his lights. He was coming up really quickly.'

'In the 100-mile race at Thruxton in 1971 I had a tremendous battle with John Harper in the Forward Engineering E-Type. We were about two yards apart for the whole race. It was a hot day and I must have lost about half a stone during the race. He was right behind me for 42 laps and then he spun on the last lap.'

Burbidge won the Chevron Oils Modified Sports class title in 1971 and scored 41 wins in total, before retiring from the sport in 1976 when the arrival of Porsches in Modified Sports signalled the beginning of the end of the E-Type era. 'My car was one of the best handling E-Types ever and it was really good in the wet. It took a long time but we got it right in the end,' says Burbidge. However, quick Lotus Elans in the hands of Norman Cuthbert, Jon Fletcher and Dave Brodie were always a threat to the more powerful cars.

'I had a tremendous scrap against David Purley at

Jon Fletcher's Modified Sports Lotus Elan was a regular performer at Thruxton during the 1970s. This is October 1973. Photo: John Gaisford.

Jean-Louis Lafosse (Brabham BT35) scatters the marshals at the Chicane, September 1971. Photo: Nigel Luckhurst.

John Miles (Chevron B19) during the RAC Sports Car race, September 19th 1971. Photo: Nigel Luckhurst.

A young Jody Scheckter on his way to winning the Iberia Trophy Formula 3 race in the rare Merlyn MK21, September 1971. Photo: Alan Ellis.

Thruxton. He was driving a works Porsche and I led him for about four laps. After the race he said to me that he didn't know you could get an E-Type as wide as that! I shut the door everywhere and it took him four laps to get by me. You had the power down the straight but it was under braking where they were streets ahead.'

'When I stopped racing I didn't go near the circuit for many years. Once I stopped, I didn't want to start wishing I was out there again.' However, his friendship with Mini ace Richard Longman kept Burbidge in touch with the sport and he is now an occasional visitor to race meetings.

Back in the closing stages of the 1971 season, another European Cup Formula 3 meeting was held in September. The major spoils were claimed by the French team of Pierre-Francois Rousselot and Jacques Coulon, while a non-championship Iberia Cup race was also held in two heats and a final. Winner of the final was rising South African star Jody Scheckter, who was starting to make a major impression with his raw speed in the rare but effective Merlyn MK21.

Over the winter of '71/72 there was another round of staff changes as Barry Bland left the BARC at end of February to join Motor Race Consultants. He was replaced by a young John Wickham, who had been marshalling with the Club, as Competitions Secretary. Grahame White remained General Manager and Club Secretary of BARC.

'I joined the BARC in 1972 when it was in Argyll Street. I was 22 at the time. Grahame White gave me the opportunity to get into racing and at the end of my first year Grahame left to go to Chevron. I was offered a job by John Surtees to

The Iberia Trophy drew Formula 3 entries from all over Europe. Here, Patrick Depailler heads Pierre-Francois Rousellot and Jochen Mass (car 23). Photo: Trevor Collins.

September 11 1971
Vintage Sports Car Club meeting

Handicap	Paul Cooper (Austin)
Vintage Sports Cars	Neville Farquhar (Riley)
Handicap	Harry Jones (Bentley)
Vintage and PVT Cars	Geoff Coles (MG)
Historic Racing Cars	Bill Wilkes (Lotus 16)
Handicap	John Batt (Lagonda Rapier)
Vintage Racing Cars	Hamish Moffatt (Bugatti T35B)
Handicap	Alain de Cadenet (Riley)
Handicap	John Venables-Llewellyn (ERA R4A)

September 18/19 1971
European Cup Formula 3 meeting

European Cup Formula 3	Pierre-Francois Rousselot (Brabham BT35)
Iberia Trophy Formula 3 Heat 1	Jody Scheckter (Merlyn MK21)
Iberia Trophy Formula 3 Heat 2	Barrie Maskell (Chevron B18)
Iberia Trophy Formula 3 Final	Jody Scheckter (Merlyn MK21)
RAC Sports	John Lepp (Chevron B19)
Special Saloons	Frank Gardner (Chevrolet Camaro)

September 26 1971
Monoposto Racing Club meeting

750 Formula	Mike Street (DC Plus)
Monoposto Formula	Brian Toft (Anco)
Mini Seven	Graham Wenham
Formula 1200	Peter Cooke (Lotus 7)
Mini Miglia	Len Brammer
Formula Libre	Richard Leach (Lola T200)

October 17 1971
BARC Championship Finals meeting

Osram Special Saloons up to 1000cc	John Turner (Sunbeam Imp)
Osram Special Saloons over 1000cc	Gerry Marshall (Vauxhall Viva)
Formula Vee	Brian Henton (Austro)
Chevron Oils Modified Sports	Dave Brodie (Lotus Elan)
Forward Trust Formula 3	Mike Walker (Ensign LN1)
Castrol/Motoring News Special GT	John Jordan (McLaren M6B)

administer the Formula 2 team, but at the end of 1973 I spoke to Sidney Offord and he gave me the chance to move to Thruxton and rejoin the Club,' recalls Wickham.

As the 1972 season started, Club officers were still waiting for the outcome of the public inquiry to be announced. A result had been expected by February 1971, but a year later, still nothing had been confirmed. However, the expectations were not good and a spate of rumours suggested that racing might be stopped completely. Brighter news came at Easter '72 when circuit manager Richard Speakman announced that the Hampshire County Council enforcement notices that the Club had appealed against had been quashed by the Minister. Racing would continue, but still the threat of the public inquiry hung over the track.

March 19 1972	
BARC meeting	
Chevron Oils Modified Sports	Tony Shaw (Jaguar E-Type)
Formula Super Vee	Tony Roberts (Royale RP14)
Special Saloons	Brian Cutting (Ford Escort)
Shell Clubmans Sports	Geoff Friswell (Mallock MK11B)
Castrol/Motoring News Special GT	Peter Brown (Ferrari 512M)
Britax Production Saloons	Roger Bell (BMW 2002)

April 1/3 1972	
Esso Uniflo Formula 2 Trophy meeting	
Formula 2 Heat 1	Niki Lauda (March 722)
Formula 2 Heat 2	Ronnie Peterson (March 722)
Formula 2 Final	Ronnie Peterson (March 722)
Wiggins Teape Group 2 Saloons	Frank Gardner (Chevrolet Camaro)
European Super Vee	Lasse Sirvio (Veemax MK5)

However, it was business as usual as the Easter Formula 2 fixture heralded the dawning of a new era. With Formula 3 engines having stepped up to 1600cc in 1971, Formula 2 badly needed a power hike and from the start of the 1972 season, the class changed to 2-litre production-based engines. Ironically, the Esso Uniflo-supported race was decimated by engine failures! In qualifying on Saturday, Argentinean Carlos Reutemann crashed heavily at Allard and badly broke his left ankle. The left rear stub axle failed on his Rondel Racing Brabham BT38 and pitched the car head-on into the barriers.

In the race, Ronnie Peterson dominated in the works STP March 722 to win the final by 25 seconds from Francois Cevert (Elf March). From an excellent 43-strong entry, there were 31 starters but just five cars finished the final after a spate of engine failures. The Thruxton race was the second round of European Championship, which had started at Mallory Park in March. It also comprised the third round of the short-lived John Player British Formula 2 Championship. While romping to victory, Peterson broke the outright circuit lap record and left it at 1m11.6s, (118.46mph).

Tragedy struck the circuit on April 22nd, when during a test session, speed-event competitor Bill Hedley-Matthews crashed his Ford Anglia and was killed when he went straight on at Campbell. A further tragedy was only narrowly avoided a week later during a Formula Vee race. Bill Titchen went off at Cobb and cleared the bank, clobbering well-known photographer John Gaisford in the process. Fortunately, Gaisford suffered only cuts and bruises.

April 23 1972	
BRSCC (SW) meeting	
International Super Vee	Brian Henton (Crossle 24F)
Castrol Mexico Challenge	Barrie Williams
West European Formula Vee	Tommy Brorsson (Hansen)
Special Saloons	Tony Pearce (Mini Cooper)
Formula Ford 1600	Richard Robinson (March 708)

April 30 1972	
BARC meeting	
Daily Express Formula Ford 1600 Heat 1	Derek Lawrence (Titan MK6)
Daily Express Formula Ford 1600 Heat 2	Ian Taylor (Dulon LD9)
Daily Express Formula Ford 1600 Final	Ian Taylor (Dulon LD9)
Special Saloons	Brian Cutting (Ford Escort)
Formula Vee	Mike Bailey (Austro)
STP Modified Sports	Ted Worswick (TVR Tuscan)
Lombard Formula 3	Rikki von Opel (Ensign LNF3)

May 14 1972	
750MC meeting	
750 Formula	Peter Ingham (Ingham GT)
Monoposto	Paul Weldon (Brabham BT15)
Mini Seven	Reg Armstrong
Formula 1200	Geoff Bremner (Mallock MK8)
Formula 4/ Formula Ford 1600	Syd Fox (Hawke DL9)
Mini Miglia/ Special Saloons	Roger Saunders (Sigma Mini)
Formula Ford 1600/ Formula Libre	Syd Fox (Hawke DL9)

May 21 1972	
Nottingham Sports Car Club meeting	
Modified Sports	Rod Forbes (Jaguar E-Type)
Formula Ford 1600	Dave Ferris (Merlyn MK20)
Clubmans Sports	Robert Glass (Mallock MK11B)
Special Saloons	Brian Cutting (Ford Escort)
Formula Libre	Bob Howlings (Brabham BT30/36)

May 28 1972	
BARC meeting	
Formula Ford 1600	Tiff Needell (Lotus 69)
Triplex Special Saloons up to 1000cc	Andy Holloway (Sunbeam Imp)
Triplex Special Saloons over 1000cc	Paddy Chambers (Mini Cooper)
Motoring News/ Castrol GT	Peter Brown (Ferrari 512M)
Formula Super Vee	Brian Henton (Crossle 24F)
Chevron Oils Modified Sports	Tony Shaw (Jaguar E-Type)

Finally, in May 1972, came the news that Thruxton's many supporters had been dreading. The Minister of the Environment, Peter Walker, announced the outcome of the public inquiry that had been held back in July 1970. On the positive side, his decision allowed racing to continue at Thruxton, quashing the enforcement notices served by Hampshire County Council. However, it only allowed racing and practising on 21 days a year subject to certain conditions. These included alterations to the entry gates, a tree planting scheme for the southern boundary and the painting of buildings. Also, the number of international meetings and the type of cars allowed had to be agreed with the local planning

authority. Though the inspector recommended that only 12 days of racing should be allowed, the Minister extended this to 21, but this would also include any practice days. An appeal was immediately lodged by the circuit promoters to increase this number but at least planning permission could now be applied for to allow the construction of permanent facilities.

Then, before May was out, came another threat. Following on almost immediately from the outcome of the public inquiry, a further action by three local objectors was brought against the circuit on noise grounds. This new challenge was potentially very serious as a decision against the circuit could force it to cease all noisy activities. Originally, when the case was taken to the High Court, the objectors could not continue due to the large cost that would probably be involved. However, they now appeared to have obtained considerable financial backing and the case would continue on June 6th. Equally, the financial burden of fighting the case would be a major problem for the Club. Further, the ramifications for the sport in general were massive if the case was lost.

At the last moment on the morning of the hearing, an out-of-court settlement was reached after hurried negotiations between the relevant lawyers. Fearing the very real prospect of complete closure of the track if the judge found against them, the circuit owners accepted an agreement for a maximum of 12 days racing and qualifying per year. The objectors also wanted a cut to six days for the balance of the 1972 season, but the circuit owners managed to raise this to nine which meant that only three meetings would have to be cancelled over the balance of the season, two for motorbikes and one for cars.

The agreement read: 'There shall not be more than two such days in any one month with the exception that in March or April of any year there may be three such days, not falling on three consecutive weekends. The duration of the racing shall be within the period 1pm to 6.30pm. Practice on the day of each race meeting may take place between 9am and 1pm, excluding church service hours. If there is no practice in the morning then racing may begin at 12 noon. Not more than three race meetings shall be preceded by practice on the day before the race or by practice on the Saturday before a Bank Holiday meeting.'

Testing was also drastically affected and it seemed that very few days of unsilenced testing would be allowed. The popular Saturday practice sessions were cancelled immediately, but the racing school would continue to operate on Fridays as the cars were fully silenced. A separate agreement was reached with Norton Villiers for their use of the circuit. It was a body-blow to the circuit, but not entirely unexpected by those close to the legal battles that had raged virtually since the circuit opened. The positive side to the solution was, at least, that racing could carry on, albeit at very reduced levels and that planning permission could be pursued to start upgrading facilities.

August 27th 1972, Stephen South (nearest camera) and Johnny Gerber retire at the Chicane after a Formula Ford incident.
Photo: Trevor Morgan.

their talents in Formula 1.

A surprise visitor to the '72 Finals meeting was film star Paul Newman, an amateur racer in his native America. It all started with an unlikely phone call to Grahame White in the BARC offices in London. 'I was in my office one afternoon and the receptionist said, 'There's an American guy wants to speak to you.' I picked up the phone the conversation went something like:

'Hi, is that Grahame White? It's Paul Newman here.'

'Fine, OK.'

'I understand you run the race meetings at Thruxton and this weekend there's a club meeting there. I'm just over here for a few days and I've nothing on at the weekend. I'd like to come down and have a look.'

'Yes, sure.'

'I'm staying at the Dorchester. Could you just tell me what time it starts.'

'Would you like me to send a couple of tickets over?'

'Well, yes, that would be great.'

'All the time I was thinking that someone was winding me up, but I sort of had to go along with it. I told him that when he got to the circuit to go to the tower and ring across for me and I'd go over and make sure he was OK. I sent these tickets to the Dorchester but thought nothing more of it. On the morning of the meeting I got a phone call from the building next to the entrance. The girl said, 'You're not going to believe this, but Paul Newman is here!'

'We spoke on the phone and he said he been at the circuit for a while watching practice and was really

In reacting to the events of May and June, Grahame White said that discussions would soon be taking place to see if the circuit was financially viable to continue. The next meeting on June 11th, went ahead but many people were saddened by the news and there was a general atmosphere of disappointment surrounding the club meeting run by the Monoposto Racing Club.

Several major Formula 3 races headlined the balance of the '72 season, including the July 30th round of the Forward Trust Championship which also included a round of the French Formula 3 championship. A massive 76-car entry needed two heats and a final, even though a dispute at the docks meant that not all of the French drivers arrived. Roger Williamson won the final, as he did many Formula 3 races that summer with his Tom Wheatcroft-entered GRD 372. Other winners that autumn included Tony Brise (Formula 3) and Tom Pryce (Formula Super Vee). This trio would surely have become the British Grand Prix stars of the second half of the decade had their careers not all been cut tragically short by three freak accidents just as they started to prove

Neville Hay interviews Formula 3 race winner Tony Brise, October 29th, 1972. Photo: John Gaisford.

enjoying it. I went and met him and organised lunch and so on. He asked if there was any time in the lunch break that he could go round the circuit with me just to have a look. I got hold of Richard Longman and asked if we could borrow his car. We found him a helmet and got him in the car so that he could do a few laps. He thoroughly enjoyed it and then went back to the control tower overlooking the Chicane and he spent the whole afternoon there. When he got back to London he phoned to say what a great day he'd had! He was just an enthusiast who wanted to come and see some racing,' recalls White.

Championship Finals Day 1972. Paul Newman takes Richard Longman's Mini for a few laps during the lunch break. Photo: John Gaisford.

The year closed with the announcement in November that White had resigned from the BARC after a disagreement with the Club's council over the future policy for the Club. White then joined Chevron Racing Cars as Director of Sales and Publicity. In the New Year, Sidney Offord from the Thames Estuary Automobile Club was appointed as replacement General Manager.

June 4 1972	
Jaguar Drivers' Club meeting	
Classic Sports	Peter Walker (Jaguar E-Type)
Formula Ford 1600	Syd Fox (Hawke DL9)
Thoroughbred Sports	Reg Woodcock (Triumph TR3)
Special Saloons	Brian Cutting (Ford Escort)
Historic Sports	John Harper (Lister Corvette)
Modified Sports	Dave Brodie (Lotus Elan)

June 11 1972	
Monoposto Racing Club meeting	
Monoposto	Brian Jordan (Brabham BT15)
Mini Seven	Reg Armstrong
Formula Ford 1600	Steve Coen (Palliser WDF2)
Special Saloons up to 1000cc	Andy Holloway (Hillman Imp)
Formula Libre	Martin Webb (Brabham BT30)
Allcomers	Martin Webb (Brabham BT30)

June 18 1972	
BARC meeting	
Chevron Oils Modified Sports	Ted Worswick (TVR Tuscan)
Forward Trust Special Saloons over 1000cc	Gerry Marshall (Vauxhall Firenza)
Forward Trust Special Saloons up to 1000cc	Len Brammer (Mini Cooper)
Forward Trust Formula 3	Rikki von Opel (Ensign LNF3)
Motoring News/ Castrol GT	Peter Brown (Ferrari 512M)
Formula Super Vee	Brian Henton (Crossle 24F)

July 9 1972	
BRSCC (SW) meeting	
Formula Ford 1600 Heat 1	Robert Cooper (Merlyn MK20A)
Formula Ford 1600 Heat 2	Dave Ferris (Merlyn MK20)
Formula Ford 1600 Final	Robert Cooper (Merlyn MK20A)
Clubmans Sports/ Modified Sports	John Burbidge (Jaguar E-Type)
Formula Vee	Graham Meek (McNamara)
Special Saloons	Martin Birrane (Ford Mustang)
Formula Libre	John Wingfield (Brabam BT21A)

July 30 1972
BARC meeting

Forward Trust Formula 3 Heat 1	Roger Williamson (GRD 372)
Forward Trust Formula 3 Heat 2	Mike Walker (Ensign LNF3)
Forward Trust Formula 3 Final	Roger Williamson (GRD 372)
Forward Trust Special Saloons	Gerry Marshall (Vauxhall Firenza)
Sunbeam Electric Formula Ford 1600	Dave Ferris (Merlyn MK20A)
European Formula Vee	Jaap Luyendyk (Karringer)

August 6 1972
West Hants & Dorset Echo Trophy meeting

Echo Trophy Formula 3	Jochen Mass (March 723)
Special Saloons up to 1000cc	David Gumm (Mini)
Special Saloons over 1000cc	Richard Longman (Mini Cooper)
Formula Ford	Richard Morgan (Lotus 61)
GT	Jeremy Lord (Astra RNR1)

August 13 1972
750MC Birkett Six-Hour Relay race

Winners: Porsche Club GB

Nick Faure, Eric Studer, W Hare, Edgar Valentine

August 28 1972
BARC meeting

BOC Formula Ford 1600	John Stevens (Merlyn MK17/20)
Special Saloons	Brian Cutting (Ford Escort)
Forward Trust Formula 3	Rikki von Opel (Ensign LNF3)
STP Modified Sports	John Fletcher (Lotus Elan)
Formula Super Vee	Tom Pryce (Royale RP14)
Formula Ford 1600	John Murphy (Hawke DL9)

September 9 1972
Vintage Sports Car Club meeting

Vintage Sports	David Llewellyn (Bentley)
Vintage cars up to 1100cc	Neville Farquhar (Riley)
Historic Racing Cars	Bill Wilkes (Lotus 16)
Vintage Racing Cars	David Llewellyn (Bentley)
Handicap race	Paul Cooper (Austin)
Handicap race	Chris Mann (Alfa Romeo)
Handicap race	Maurice Tomlin (Lagonda)
Handicap race	Dennis Barbet (Riley)
Handicap race	David Llewellyn (Bentley)

September 23/24 1972
BARC meeting

Forward Trust Formula 3 Heat 1	Mike Walker (Ensign LNF3)
Forward Trust Formula 3 Heat 2	Roger Williamson (GRD 372)
Forward Trust Formula 3 Final	Roger Williamson (GRD 372)
Sunbeam Electric Formula Ford 1600	Syd Fox (Hawke DL9)
Motoring News/ Castrol GT	John Burton (Chevron B21)

October 29 1972
BARC meeting

Forward Trust Special Saloons up to 1000cc	John Turner (Ford Anglia)
Forward Trust Special Saloons over 1000cc	Brian Cutting (Ford Escort)
Sunbeam Electric Formula Ford 1600	Derek Lawrence (Titan MK6)
Chevron Oils Modified Sports	John Burbidge (Jaguar E-Type)
Forward Trust Formula 3	Tony Brise (GRD 372)
Motoring News/ Castrol GT	Jeremy Lord (Astra RNR1)

CHAPTER FOUR

Fighting on with just 12 days of racing a year

Shrugging off gloomy predictions about the viability of a track allowed just 12 days of use each year, the BARC set about making the best use of what it had for the 1973 season and drew up a schedule of eight car race meetings, two of them over two days, and two motorbike meetings to use up the meagre 12-day ration.

Two of those precious days were, of course, allocated to the traditional Easter Formula 2 meeting, which was supported for a second year by Esso Uniflo. The final was a thriller, with constantly changing fortunes keeping the large crowd on the edge of its seat. Having been the star of Formula 3 in 1972, Roger Williamson graduated to Formula 2 and led the race in his GRD 273 until slowed by a puncture. Jacques Coulon (March 732) took over the lead but also retired, so Gerry Birrell's works Chevron B25 took the lead under pressure from Mike Beuttler's March 732. Two laps from the end they clashed at the Chicane and Formula 2 veteran Henri Pescarolo, who had been sitting right behind them, nipped through to win for the Rondel team and its self-styled Motul chassis. Team-mate Bob Wollek was second with Beuttler and Birrell recovering for third and fourth after a dramatic race. A new outright circuit record was shared three ways, between Coulon, Carlos Pace (Surtees TS15) and Jean-Pierre Jarier (March 732) at 1m11.2s (119.12mph).

April 21/23 1973	
Esso Uniflo Trophy Formula 2 meeting	
Formula 2 Heat 1	Patrick Depailler (Elf 2)
Formula 2 Heat 2	Roger Williamson (GRD 273)
Formula 2 Final	Henri Pescarolo (Motul M1)
RAC British Touring Cars	Frank Gardner (Chevrolet Camaro)
Vauxhall Firenzas	Frank Gardner
European Formula Vee	Mika Arpiainen (Veemax)

May 28 1973	
British Touring Car meeting	
RAC British Touring Car Championship	Frank Gardner (Chevrolet Camaro)
Modified Sports	Richard Jenvey (MG Midget)
Special Saloons	Gerry Marshall (Vauxhall Firenza)
Formula Atlantic	Ray Mallock (March 73B)
Historic Sports	John Harper (Lister Jaguar)
Wella for Men Formula Ford 1600	Roger Manning (Elden MK10)

March 25 1973	
BARC meeting	
Blue Circle Modified Sports	Jon Fletcher (Lotus Elan)
Blue Circle Modified Sports	Brian Hough (TVR Tuscan)
Forward Trust Special Saloons up to 1300cc	John Watts (Mini Cooper S)
Forward Trust Special Saloons over 1300cc	Brian Cutting (Ford Escort)
Motoring News/ Castrol GT	Jeremy Lord (Lola T212)
Britax Production Saloons	Roger Bell (BMW 2002)
Forward Trust Formula 3	Ian Taylor (March 733)

June 17 1973	
BARC meeting	
Esso Uniflo Special Saloons	Vince Woodman (Ford Escort)
Esso Uniflo Special Saloons	Andy Rouse (Ford Escort)
STP Formula Ford 1600	Derek Lawrence (Dulon MP15)
Formula Ford 1600	David Priddy (Lotus 51)
Clubmans Sports	Sid Marler (Gryphon C73)
Motoring News/ Castrol GT	Jeremy Lord (Lola T212)
Britax Production Saloons	Gordon Spice (Ford Capri)
Forward Trust Formula 3	Ian Taylor (March 733)

July 8 1973
BARC meeting

Forward Trust Special Saloons up to 1000cc	Ray Payne (Hillman Imp)
Forward Trust Special Saloons over 1000cc	Gerry Marshall (Vauxhall Firenza)
Blue Circle Modified Sports	Jon Fletcher (Lotus Elan)
Wella for Men Formula Ford 1600	Ted Wentz (Elden MK8)
Formula Super Vee	John Morrison (Super Nova)
Formula Ford 1600	Gerry Jolly (Titan MK6)
Modified Sports	Russell Bracegirdle (Triumph Spitfire)

August 5 1973
Alcoa European GT meeting

European GT	Claude Ballot-Lena (Porsche Carrera)
Forward Trust Formula 3 Heat 1	Mike Wilds (March 733)
Forward Trust Formula 3 Heat 2	Russell Wood (March 733)
Forward Trust Formula 3 Final	Michel Leclere (Alpine A364B)
Special Saloons	Brian Cutting (Ford Escort)
JCB Historic Cars	Nick Faure (Lister Jaguar)

September 16 1973
BARC meeting

Britax Production Saloons	Richard Lloyd (Chevrolet Camaro)
Britax Production Saloons	Ivan Dutton (Ford Escort)
Wella for Men Formula Ford 1600	Roger Manning (Elden MK10)
Forward Trust Special Saloons over 1000cc	Gerry Marshall (Vauxhall Firenza)
Forward Trust Special Saloons up to 1000cc	Ray Payne (Hillman Imp)
Forward Trust Formula 3	Tony Brise (March 733)
Thoroughbred Sports	John Harper (Jaguar XK120)
Formula Super Vee	Steve Tipping (Royale RP14)

October 28 1973
BARC Championship Finals meeting

Wella for Men Formula Ford 1600	Roger Manning (Elden MK10)
Britax Production Saloons	Richard Lloyd (Chevrolet Camaro)
Forward Trust Formula 3	Richard Robarts (March 733)
Blue Circle Modified Sports	John Pearson (Lotus Elan)
Forward Trust Special Saloons	Gerry Marshall (Vauxhall Firenza)
Motoring News/ Castrol GT	Jeremy Lord (Lola T212)

Roger Bell drifts his BMW into the Chicane in the Production Saloon race, March 25th 1973. Photo: Trevor Collins.

Easter 1973. Roger Williamson's GRD 273 won Heat 2 of the Formula 2 race and led the final until slowed by a puncture. Photo: MSPS Impact.

Easter 1973. Jean-Pierre Jarier's March 732 set a new outright circuit lap record but was destined not to finish the final. Photo: Trevor Morgan.

and Russell Wood but the final went to Michel Leclere (Alpine A364B).

The all-too-brief season ended with sadness at the October Championship Finals meeting when Merseyside TVR dealer Brian Hough was killed racing his ex-Ted Worswick TVR Tuscan. He was battling for the lead in the Blue Circle Modified Sportscar race when he went off backwards at Kimpton and was killed instantly. John Pearson (Lotus Elan) took a hollow victory while Gerry Marshall scooped one of many Special Saloon wins in his Vauxhall Firenza. Other winners that day were Richard Robarts (Formula 3) and Bournemouth solicitor Jeremy Lord who won the Castrol GT finale in his Lola T212.

After his season with the Surtees Formula 2 team, John Wickham rejoined the BARC in November 1973 as Assistant Manager. At the same time, the Club moved its offices from Argyll Street, London to Thruxton, making a saving of £3000 per year. The move took effect on December 17th 1973.

'I was Competitions Manager working with Sidney and he saw that the way to make the Club more financially successful was to run more races and take more entry fees. We actually introduced the open-ended timetable for race meetings. I understood what Sidney was trying to do for the Club and we had a fairly good relationship,' says Wickham.

'We got down to Thruxton and were put into the two Air Training Cadet huts just behind the control tower. They were incredibly damp and it was chaotic for the first couple of months. We had to get a lot of new staff in. I started off living in a caravan at Weyhill caravan park! During that first year we moved into the flying control tower which lasted for some time. I had the office facing out over the airfield with a balcony on the front, which was fantastic in the summer. We kept the two huts for storage for a while and gradually it all came together. Over the next three or four years my career developed slowly within the Club and I was clerk of the course at more and more races,' remembers Wickham.

The other two-day meeting of 1973 was in August when an Alcoa-sponsored meeting featured a round of the European GT Championship. It poured with rain and only 15 cars started the 40-lap race, 14 of them Porsches which were joined by the JCB Ferrari Daytona of Peter Brown. Claude Ballot-Lena (Porsche Carrera) splashed home to win the feature race while two heats and a final for the Forward Trust Formula 3 Championship produced heat wins for the March 733s of Mike Wilds

The start of the Formula 2 final, Easter 1973. Behind the leaders, a midfield shunt is just starting. Photo: Fred Taylor.

Over the winter £30,000 was to be spent on work at Thruxton to keep the circuit up to international specification and some of the money saved by moving out of expensive London offices would be ploughed back into the circuit. Finally, it was announced that the BARC would now organise all the meetings at Thruxton. Dates at the circuit were severely restricted, but the Club was determined to maximise those days and provide a venue that would be enjoyed by competitors and spectators alike.

The £30,000 investment was wisely spent over the winter months and in February '74, Sidney Offord proudly announced the changes that had been made. 'Work over the winter has included levelling run-off areas, all existing chalk banks have been faced with barriers, run-offs between Segrave and Cobb are now free of obstructions and spectator areas have been concentrated on the western side of circuit to provide space for 30,000 people,' he told the press. Prior to 1974, spectators had been allowed access beyond Segrave, but the area was denied public address due to the proximity of the village. By containing spectators between the Chicane and the Complex, existing facilities could be improved and the chalk banks raised considerably, so that fans could now see the majority of the circuit.

Sadly, after the completion of this major investment, the Formula 2 race had to be cancelled when the economic situation surrounding the fuel crisis, including a three-day working week for many, made it impossible to secure the title sponsor that was vital to the financial viability of the meeting. With much regret, in the first week of March '74, the BARC announced that the Formula 2 race was off. Shortly afterwards, came the news that the 2-litre sports-racing and GT events planned for later in the season had also been cancelled.

Providing light relief when the season opened on a typically cold and wet day in March was local driver Carl Jeanes from Stockbridge, who stripped off and ran through the paddock, much to the amusement and amazement of onlookers. His streak earned some cash for charity and he later raced in Formula Ford and Monoposto events under the pseudonym of 'The Streaker'!

The Easter meeting still went ahead with the British Touring Car Championship topping the bill, supported by a variety of national races as well as the first ever caravan race. Richard Lloyd won the main race in his Chevrolet Camaro, but the Formula 2 race, run over each of the six Easter weekends since the circuit opened, was sadly missed.

March 24 1974	
BARC meeting	
Wella Formula Ford 1600 Heat 1	Rupert Keegan (Hawke DL11)
Wella Formula Ford 1600 Heat 2	Richard Morgan (Ray 73F)
Wella Formula Ford 1600 Final	Richard Morgan (Ray 73F)
Forward Trust Special Saloons up to 1000cc	Ray Payne (Hillman Imp)
Forward Trust Special Saloons over 1000cc	John Elliott (Vauxhall Viva)
Tricentrol Sports GT	John Lepp (Chevron B26)
Forward Trust Formula 3	Brian Henton (March 743)
Britax Production Saloons	Nigel Stovin-Bradford (Chevrolet Camaro)

April 15 1974	
British Touring Car meeting	
Castrol Touring Cars	Richard Lloyd (Chevrolet Camaro)
Blue Circle Modified Sports	Jon Fletcher (Lotus Elan)
Tricentrol Sports GT	Jeremy Lord (Lola T280)
Wella Formula Ford 1600	Peter Orlando (Merlyn MK20A)
Historic Cars	Malcolm Clube (McLaren M1B)
Repco Caravan Race	Andrew Higton (Vauxhall VX4/90)

May 25/27 1974	
Formula 5000 meeting	
Rothmans Formula 5000	Ian Ashley (Lola T330)
Vauxhall Spring Cup	Barrie Williams
Castrol Touring Cars	Richard Lloyd (Chevrolet Camaro)
Forward Trust Special Saloons	Mick Hill (Ford Capri)

It was a cold day in March 1974 when Carl Jeanes stripped off and streaked through the Thruxton paddock for charity! Photo: Jeff Bloxham.

David Heale oversteers his Dulon MP15 Formula Ford through the Chicane in March 1974. Photo: Jeff Bloxham.

Ian Ashley en route to winning
the Formula 5000 race,
May 27th 1974.
Photo: Trevor Collins.

Mike Wilds vacates
the remains of his
Formula 5000 March
74A after a clash
with backmarker
Tony Dean
(Chevron B24) sent
them both off the
track on May 27th
1974.

Tony Stubbs gets it wrong at the
Chicane during 1974 in his
Production Saloon Moskvich.
Photo: Jeff Bloxham.

Instead, the honour of being the main event of the season at Thruxton fell to the Rothmans Formula 5000 Championship, which visited twice. In the May Bank Holiday meeting, Mike Wilds in the Dempster March 74A had a big shunt after touching Tony Dean's Chevron when lapping it into the Chicane. Wilds, who went on to race in Formula 1 for BRM, broke his wrist in the shunt. The race was won by Ian Ashley's Lola T300. The second Formula 5000 race was on August 18th and produced a new outright record when Australian Vern Schuppan lapped his Lola T332 in 1m11.0s (119.46mph). Schuppan had qualified in an incredible time of 1m10.2s, considerably over the 120mph barrier for the very first time. He then led the first five laps before falling oil pressure put the Sid Taylor entry out, leaving victory to Bob Evans' similar car.

In late October, the customary Championship Finals meeting featured the conclusion of a season-long battle for the Blue Circle Modified Sportscar Championship. Rochdale veteran Jon Fletcher started the race with a

50/50 chance of beating the nimble Davrian of Bob Jarvis to the title. However, when Fletcher planted his familiar Lotus Elan into the Chicane barriers, the matter was resolved! The year closed with a return of the TV meeting in November with support from Wella. But the Formula 2 race had been sorely missed in what proved to be a rather low-key season.

Jul 7 1974	
BARC meeting	
Shellsport Clubmans Sports	Richard Mallock (Mallock MK12/15)
Blue Circle Modified Sports	Jon Fletcher (Lotus Elan)
Blue Circle Modified Sports	Nick Faure (Porsche 911)
STP Formula Ford 1600	Richard Morgan (Crosslé 25F)
Esso Special Saloons up to 1000cc	Richard Longman (Mini Cooper)
Esso Special Saloons over 1000cc	Alec Poole (Ford Escort)
Formula Atlantic	Dave Morgan (Chevron B25)
Monoposto	Mike Bowers (Brabham BT21C)
Formula Ford 1600 non-qualifiers	Chris Woodcock (Dulon MP15B)

August 17/18 1974	
Formula 5000 meeting	
Rothmans Formula 5000	Bob Evans (Lola T332)
Forward Trust Formula 3	Brian Henton (March 743)
JCB Historic Cars	Neil Corner (BRM P25)
Britax Production Saloons	Brian Pepper (Chevrolet Camaro)

September 1 1974	
Vintage Sports Car Club meeting	
Vintage and PVT	David Fearnley (Frazer Nash)
Vintage Racing Cars	Peter Morley (Bentley Napier)
Handicap Race	David Llewellyn (Bentley)
Allcomers Race	John Roberts (Lotus 16)
Handicap Race	Mike Daniel (BMW)
Handicap Race	Ian Woolstenholme (Alvis)
Spero & Vioturette Trophy	David Fletcher-Jones (Lagonda)
Handicap Race	Simon Phillips (BMW 328)

September 22 1974	
BARC meeting	
Simoniz Special Saloons up to 1300cc	Jeff Ward (Hillman Imp)
Simoniz Special Saloons over 1300cc	John Turner (Skoda Coupe)
Tricentrol Sports GT	Pedro de Lamare (March 74S)
Triplex Production Saloons	Brian Pepper (Chevrolet Camaro)
Lombard Formula 3	Tony Rouff (GRD 373)
Tricentrol Super Saloons	Mick Hill (Ford Capri)

October 6 1974	
BARC meeting	
BP Formula 1300	Paul Webb (Delapena)
Clubmans Sports	Frank Sytner (Mallock MK12)
Formula Ford 1600	Tiff Needell (Elden MK10C)
Formula Ford 1600	John Skinner (Dulon MP15)
Modified Sports	John Burbidge (Jaguar E-Type)
Forward Trust Formula 3	Danny Sullivan (Modus M1)
Special Saloons	Brian Cutting (Ford Escort)

October 27 1974
BARC Championship Finals meeting

Tricentrol Sports GT	Jeremy Lord (Lola T280)
Wella Formula Ford 1600	Richard Morgan (Crossle 25F)
Britax Production Saloons	Bob Ridgard (Chevrolet Camaro)
Forward Trust Formula 3	Brian Henton (March 743)
Blue Circle Modified Sports	Alan Broad (Porsche 911)
Forward Trust Special Saloons	Mick Hill (Ford Capri)

November 16 1974
Wella Television meeting

Modified Sports	John Pearson (Jaguar XK120)
Formula Ford 1600	Richard Morgan (Crossle 25F)
Super Saloons	Mick Hill (Ford Capri)
Formula Atlantic	Stephen Choularton (March 73B)
Formula Ford 1600	Phil Dowsett (Titan MK6)

However, Offord and his team were not sitting still and were soon to announce the return of international racing to Thruxton for the 1975 season. Having successfully sponsored the BARC Formula Ford Championship for the previous two seasons, Wella had backed the '74 TV meeting. In January 1975, the BARC announced that Wella would be title sponsor for the Easter meeting which would be headlined by the welcome return of Formula 2. The hair-care organisation would also help American Ted Wentz to make his Formula 2 debut at the meeting, having backed him in Formula Atlantic during 1974.

The new season fired into life on March 2nd in appallingly wet weather but with bumper grids for most races. Over the winter, the RACMSA had approved an increase in the number of cars allowed to start at Thruxton, which was now up to 33 from 30. That first meeting also heralded major involvement from the Southern Organs company which was to become a prolific sponsor of both championships and drivers for a brief but spectacular period. It all ended dramatically with the sudden disappearance of company front-man Sidney Miller, and a number of drivers were left facing substantial debts as a result.

But at Thruxton, there was an air of anticipation as preparations were made for the first British Formula 2 meeting for two years. Further good news in the build up to the Easter race was the entry of Ronnie Peterson

in a March 752 run by Ron Dennis under the Project 3 banner. Peterson was racing with the Lotus Grand Prix team at the time, but was tempted back to Formula 2 for the race that he had won back in 1972.

March 2 1975
BARC meeting

BAF Formula Ford 1600	Geoff Lees (Royale RP21)
Forward Trust Special Saloons up to 1000cc	Jeff Ward (Greetham Imp)
Forward Trust Special Saloons over 1000cc	Dave Millington (Vauxhall Firenza)
National Organs Clubmans Sports	Noel Stanbury (Gryphon C4A)
Miller Organs Modified Sports	Dave Bettinson (Lotus 7)
Formula 3	Alex Ribeiro (March 753)
Formula Libre	Noel Stanbury (Gryphon C4A)

March 29/31 1975
Wella European Formula 2 Trophy meeting

Formula 2 Heat 1	Jacques Laffite (Martini MK16)
Formula 2 Heat 2	Vittorio Brambilla (March 752)
Aggregate winner	Jacques Laffite (Martini MK16)
BP Formula 3	Gunnar Nilsson (March 753)
Southern Organs Touring Cars	Richard Lloyd (Chevrolet Camaro)
BAF Formula Ford 1600	Frank Bayes (Merlyn MK17A)
Speed Merchants Historic Cars	Richard Thwaites (Elva MK7S)

However, the meeting was dominated by Jacques Laffite in the Martini MK16. He had also won in Portugal at the Estoril circuit three weeks earlier. The weather was very cold on Saturday but Monday was bright and mild, when the result was formed on the aggregate of two 30-lap parts. The race will long be remembered, however, as the year of the shunt after the chaos at the Chicane in the first part when Peter Williams spun his Formula Atlantic Chevron and stalled. The resulting shunt eliminated Hans Binder and Peterson who were unable to avoid the stricken car. Lamberto Leoni, Alberto Colombo and Ray Mallock all ploughed into the wreckage and were all eliminated, while Markus Hotz and Harald Ertl were also involved but managed to carry on. The Chicane looked like a battlefield but the race continued as the BARC marshals expertly moved the damaged cars.

John Wickham was one of those who witnessed the drama at close quarters. 'The Formula 2 shunt at the Chicane is a lasting memory. I was Secretary of the Meeting and once the race started I didn't really have any executive powers. So I went out over the bridge and I was just walking up to the marshals' post when it happened. We weren't quite as careful in those days in terms of race stoppages but the marshals got it cleared.'

British privateer Brian Henton drove superbly in his March to finish second in the first heat but struggled with tyre problems in the second part, so Patrick Tambay finished second on aggregate in a March 752. Henton and Laffite equalled Schuppan's outright record of 1m11.0s, though Laffite had qualified on pole in 1m10.1s, the fastest lap ever recorded at the circuit.

April 20 1975	
BARC meeting	
Mini Miglia	Alan Curnow
Formula 1300	John Allan (Allan Mk4)
Radio One Production Saloons	Jock Robertson (Mazda RX3)
Radio One Production Saloons	John Brindley (Chevrolet Camaro)
Thoroughbred Sports	John Harper (Jaguar XK120)
Forward Trust Special Saloons	Dave Millington (Vauxhall Firenza)
National Organs Clubmans Sports	Geoff Friswell (Mallock MK16)
Mini Seven	Graham Wenham

May 11 1975	
British Touring Car meeting	
Southern Organs Touring Cars	Stuart Graham (Chevrolet Camaro)
Allied Polymer Formula Ford 2000	Derek Lawrence (Crossle 31F)
Speed Merchants Historic Cars	Willie Green (Maserari 250F)
BAF Formula Ford 1600	Geoff Lees (Royale RP21)
Formula Ford Consolation race	Peter Owles (Merlyn MK11A)
National Organs Clubmans Sports	Geoff Friswell (Mallock MK16)
Simoniz Special Saloons	Nick Whiting (Ford Escort)

May 26 1975	
Formula 5000 meeting	
Shellsport Formula 5000	Ian Ashley (Lola T330/2)
BP Formula 3	Gunnar Nilsson (March 753)
Forward Trust Special Saloons up to 1000cc	Brian Prebble (Hillman Imp)
Forward Trust Special Saloons over 1000cc	Brian Cutting (Ford Escort)
Sports Cars	John Lepp (Lola T294)

On May Bank Holiday Monday, the Formula 5000 cars returned but the race was peppered with blown engines. Ian Ashley's engine let go comprehensively in the last 100 yards of the race, but he coasted over the line to win. During the race, Ashley had become the fourth driver to share the outright circuit record of 1m11.0s. Less fortunate were Richard Scott and Gordon Spice who also blew engines when lying second in their Lolas.

The headlines in July talked of a Formula 1 race for Thruxton. However, this seems to have been a storm in a tea cup that was sparked off when a foreign motorsport magazine listed the British Grand Prix at Thruxton. It was probably an error linked to the Formula 2 race.

August 17 1975	
Formula 5000 meeting	
Shellsport Formula 5000	Teddy Pilette (Lola T400)
BP Formula 3	Alex Ribeiro (March 753)
Brush Fusegear Formula Ford 1600	Tiff Needell (Crossle 25F)
Formula Ford 1600 Consolation race	Mike Blanchet (Lotus 61)
Speed Merchants Historic Cars	Willie Green (Maserati 250F)
Tricentrol Super Saloons	Gerry Marshall (Vauxhall Firenza)

The Formula 5000 series returned in mid-August and teams benefited from the first official test session since the planning restrictions had been imposed. With the local schools on summer holiday, a Friday afternoon session preceded the Formula 5000 meeting on August 17th and was limited to Formula 2, Formula 3, Formula 5000 and Formula Atlantic cars running between 1pm and 5pm at a price of £15 per car. No engines were permitted to be run before 1pm or after 5pm. Belgian Teddy Pilette (Team VDS Lola T400) won the race, but had to contend with a race-long chase from Alan Jones in the Ford V6-powered Thursdays/RAM March 751.

Then, on the penultimate lap, Jones had the rear wing collapse and he spun into the undergrowth on the approach to the Chicane, leaving the track at an alarming speed. Somehow, Jones dragged the battered car out of the ditch and finished third behind Richard Scott (Lola T400).

September 14 1975	
BARC meeting	
Monoposto	David Coombs (Manta 75)
Britax Production Saloons	John Brindley (Chevrolet Camaro)
National Organs Formula Ford 1600	Geoff Lees (Royale RP21)
Formula Ford 1600 Consolation race	Tim Wallwork (Titan Mk6A)
Miller Organs Modified Sports	John Evans (Lotus Elan)
Formula 1300	Bob Davis (Davis)
Esso Special Saloons	Phil Winter (Longman Mini)
Speed Merchants Historic Cars	Willie Green (Ferrari 250LM)

Championship Finals day was October 26th. Rising Swedish star Gunnar Nilsson had already sewn-up the BP Super Visco Formula 3 title and led the race until he ran wide and allowed works March team-mate Alex Ribeiro through to win. Nilsson chased back but then lost ground with another spin and finished seventh. In the supporting races, titles were clinched by Geoff Lees (BAF Formula Ford 1600) and Jock Robertson who added the Britax Production Saloon title to the Radio One title in his Mazda RX3. Lees had already won the Brush Fusegear title in his Royale RP21 in the season in which, against all odds he famously won all three major Formula Ford titles.

Three weeks later, the TV meeting enjoyed sponsorship from Forward Trust, a loyal backer of BARC championships. Gunnar Nilsson won the Formula 3 race once more to cap a fine season, while Gerry Marshall in the 5-litre Vauxhall Firenza affectionately known as 'Baby Bertha' won the saloon race after a pit stop. Gerry was simply playing to the audience and the TV cameras by running with Nick Whiting (Escort), Arthur Collier (Skoda), Tony Sugden (Escort) and Phil Winter (Mini).

Sugden, one of the stars of that race, was a frequent winner at Thruxton in a variety of Special Saloon cars over a career spanning nearly 50 years of competitive motorsport and over 400 race wins. Thruxton was generally a kind circuit to him. 'It was one of the few places where not a lot of things went wrong,' he reckons. The Escort that he raced that day had been built up from a crashed bodyshell that he acquired for £17 and equipped with a BRM twin-cam engine.

The 1975 TV meeting also marked the sad end of Hesketh Racing. Having failed to find the £300,000 they needed to continue in Formula 1, Lord Hesketh announced on TV from Thruxton that the team was pulling out of grand prix racing. James Hunt drove his Zandvoort-winning Hesketh 308 on an emotional parade lap of the track and Hesketh was presented with a BARC Gold Medal for his efforts in taking his private grand prix team to the very top of the sport.

Commentator Neville Hay also has cause to remember the 1975 season at Thruxton. Scaling the 50 foot tower on the outside of the circuit adjacent to the

Photographer John Gaisford in action at the 1975 TV meeting. Photo: Jeff Bloxham.

footbridge has struck terror into the hearts of many commentators over the years, but Hay had a couple of particularly dramatic moments while trying to keep the crowds entertained and informed.

'The first commentary tower built at Thruxton was a scaffold tower with scaffolding boards on top. And on top of the platform was this hut with insulation boards on the inside. It was a hell of a climb! Drivers like Graham McRae and Frank Gardner from Formula 5000 reckoned that climbing the tower was far more frightening than anything they ever experienced while they were racing,' says Hay.

'One Easter meeting I was trying to do the main commentary as well as the presentations. I climbed out of the box at one stage and my foot went straight through the scaffolding boards. I was left hanging by one arm and had to swing myself onto the ladder. When I told Sidney Offord about my gashed leg and torn trousers, he was more concerned about his scaffolding boards!

'The boards were soon replaced and on one occasion in the 1970s we had a longer race than was usual at Thruxton. Now, as is well known in motorsport, I smoke and when I finished my cigarette, I obviously hadn't put it out properly. The stub fell down behind the insulation boards and we didn't notice anything until the box started to fill up with smoke and flames! Now when you're 50 feet up in the air, there is nothing much to put a fire out with...'

Despite the fact that flames were licking around his feet, Neville stuck to his task and carried on commentating. His on-going description of the racing belied the drama that was unfolding around him and the 30-second break each lap while the commentator at the Complex took the reigns was a vital opportunity to tackle more pressing problems.

'We were left with only one option and that was to relieve ourselves on the fire and hope that was enough to put the fire out. My lap scorers were my son Richard and a chap called Philip Jones and it took the best efforts of all three of us to put the flames out. But now we had another problem, as we had created a good deal of steam and the whole box became a fog. So we had to open the door so that we could see out!' Undeterred, Hay had kept the commentary going and the drama went unnoticed by those lining the circuit.

In January 1976, following talks with the circuit owners, the BARC announced that it had taken control of the testing at the circuit and could offer up to 90 days of silenced testing and 10 days of unsilenced. Previously, this had been negotiated directly between organisations and the circuit owners. In the opening weeks of the year, everything looked good for the Easter fixture. DJM Records was confirmed as new title sponsors of the meeting. With artists like Elton John and The Tremoloes on their books, DJM was also supporting the BARC Formula Ford Championship that year.

Oct 12 1975
BARC meeting

Simoniz Special Saloons up to 1000cc	Jeff Ward (Hillman Imp)
Simoniz Special Saloons over 1000cc	Nick Whiting (Ford Escort)
Monoposto/ Super Vee	John Morrison (Super Nova)
Miller Organs Modified Sports	Richard Jenvey (Lotus Elan)
BAF Formula Ford 1600	Geoff Lees (Royale RP21)
Formula Ford 1600 Consolation race	Garrett Conklin (Hawke DL12)
Thoroughbred Sports	David Preece (Jaguar XK120)
Southern Organs Formula Atlantic	Gunnar Nilsson (Chevron B29)

October 26 1975
BARC Championship Finals meeting

BP Formula 3	Alex Ribeiro (March 753)
National Organs Clubmans Sports	Peter Cooke (Harrison MK7)
BAF Formula Ford 1600	Rod Bremner (Crossle 25F)
Forward Trust Special Saloons	Gerry Marshall (Vauxhall Firenza)
Miller Organs Modified Sports	John Cooper (Porsche 911)
Britax Production Saloons	Brian Rice (Chevrolet Camaro)

November 15 1975
Forward Trust Television meeting

Formula 3	Gunnar Nilsson (March 753)
Formula Ford 1600	Geoff Lees (Royale RP21)
Formula Ford 1600 Consolation race	David Wigdor (Merlyn MK20)
Modified Sports	Nick Faure (Porsche 911)
Special Saloons	Gerry Marshall (Vauxhall Firenza)

Gerry Marshall in typical pose with his Special Saloon Vauxhall Firenza, November 1974. Photo: Colin Taylor.

March 7 1976	
Formula 3 meeting	
BP Formula 3	Rupert Keegan (March 743)
Oceanair Clubmans Sports	Alex Ferrada (Mallock MK16B)
Forward Trust 1000 Plus Special Saloons	Tony Sugden (Ford Escort)
Forward Trust 1000 Special Saloons	John Homewood (Hillman Imp)
DJM Records Formula Ford 1600	Jim Walsh (Royale RP21)
Formula Ford 1600 Consolation race	David Toye (Royale RP21)
Modified Sports	Jonathan Palmer (Marcos GT)
Formula Libre	Val Musetti (March 752)

However, Formula 2 racing was becoming ever more expensive to organise and the 1976 meeting was expected to cost around £40,000 to stage, with the provision of a £25,000 prize and expense fund. The battle to make the meeting viable was getting ever harder despite the determination of the BARC to continue to host the meeting, Britain's only regular Formula 2 race of the season.

A further bombshell was soon to break, however. After agreeing a sponsorship deal based on guaranteed TV coverage, the BBC pulled out over a simmering dispute about the amount of advertising carried on the cars and around the circuit. With no TV, there was no sponsor and with no sponsor, the meeting was in jeopardy. Bravely, the BARC went ahead with the meeting and the consequent financial risk.

The crux of the dispute was that the BBC wanted the maximum sticker area on the cars to be 55 square inches, as it had been in 1968. It gave an ultimatum that, if this was not adhered to, they would not cover the meeting. However, the BARC's agreement with DJM Records was based on TV coverage on Grandstand. In an attempt to rescue the situation, Sidney Offord travelled to the preceding Formula 2 race at Hockenheim to try and get the teams to reduce the sizes of the stickers on their cars. But he met with a distinctly cool reception. The team managers, including Max Mosley of the March team, said no-way and the Thruxton race hung in the balance.

In the end, the BARC took the risk, which amounted to around £7000, and ran the meeting with no TV and no sponsor. It was a critical time for the survival of the Club, and the meeting's viability would now rest on the size of the crowd on raceday. Ironically, due to the increased publicity and good weather, the 16,000-strong crowd was large enough that the meeting just about broke even. But it had been a difficult and worrying time for all concerned and was an early warning of problems that would re-surface a decade later.

April 4 1976	
DJM Records Raceday	
Leyland Cars Mini 1275GT	Alan Curnow
DJM Records Formula Ford 1600	Frank Bayes (Image FF2B)
Formula Ford 1600 Consolation race	Graham Jones (Royale RP16)
Radio 1 Production Saloons	Brian Pepper (Opel Commodore)
Allied Polymer Group Formula Ford 2000	Geoff Friswell (Hawke DL14)
Esso Special Saloons	Tony Dickinson (Ford Escort)
Modified Sports	John Cooper (Porsche 911)
Leyland Cars Mini Miglia	John Hazell

Bespectacled Italian Maurizio Flammini won the race from pole position in the works March 762. Early in the race he nearly spun the car and actually stalled the engine at the Chicane but recovered well to win the 55-lap race by more than 25 seconds from Alex Ribeiro.

56

THRUXTON 1968 - 1997

The start of the 1976 Formula 2 race. Photo: Peter Tempest.

The 1976
Formula 2
pack pours
through Allard.
Photo: Fred
Taylor.

Bernard Devaney leaves
his crashed Formula Ford
Hawke, Easter 1976.
Photo: Fred Taylor.

A whole host of manufacturers had cars on the grid, including March, Elf, Wheatcroft, Martini, Ralt, Osella, Chevron, Lola, Minos, Modus, Boxer and Toj. Jean-Pierre Jabouille, who went on to give the Renault turbo grand prix engine its debut, set a new outright circuit record in his Elf 2J of 1m10.88s, (119.66mph). Though the magic 120mph barrier had been bettered in qualifying, it still remained tantalisingly out of reach in races.

A little piece of history was made on May 9th, when Tom Walkinshaw won two races at the same time at different circuits. He flew down to Thruxton to win the Touring Car race in his Capri after doing the first stint in the Silverstone Six Hour-winning BMW CSL that he shared with John Fitzpatrick! Walkinshaw's determination would later take him to the pinnacle of the sport as a team owner. Before later realising his own team management ambitions, John Wickham became Competitions Director of BARC that spring when Sidney Offord was made Executive Director of the BARC. More changes in the hierarchy came in June when Maurice Gorringe took over as Club chairman when Bill Paul retired after a nine-year term. Gorringe, who had raced at Brooklands before the war, was a director of Blue Circle and had arranged its sponsorship of the BARC Modified Sportscar Championship.

The summer of 1976 was not kind to Thruxton spectators. On May Bank Holiday Monday, 10,000 spectators watched David Purley (Chevron B30) win the Shellsport 5000 European Championship round in soaking rain. However, former skier Divina Galica won

the Alcoa Driver of the Meeting award for a charging drive to fourth place in a Formula 1 Surtees.

That meeting marked the first Formula Ford win at Thruxton for local superstox racer Derek Warwick. Having made the switch to circuit racing, the Alresford racer soon made an impression with his Warwick Trailers-backed Hawke DL15. The August Bank Holiday meeting also featured soaking rain and a non-

Brian Henton in the rare Boxer during the 1976 Formula 2 race. Photo: Didier Braillon.

championship Formula Ford race had to be abandoned. Earlier in August, the new grandstands at Club were used for the first time. They had been built during the long break in the racing calendar through June and July and increased the circuit's seating capacity from 550 to 900.

April 17/19 1976	
Jochen Rindt Memorial Trophy Formula 2 meeting	
European Formula 2	Maurizio Flammini (March 762)
Keith Prowse Touring Cars	Tom Walkinshaw (Ford Capri)
BP Formula 3	Rupert Keegan (March 743)
Ferraris	Willie Green (Ferrari 512S)
DJM Formula Ford 1600	Derek Warwick (Hawke DL15)
Thoroughbred Sports	David Preece (Jaguar XK120)

Ken Rainsbury presents Alex Ribeiro and Maurizio Flammini with the trophies after the 1976 Formula 2 race. Photo: Fred Taylor.

May 9 1976	
Formula 3 meeting	
BP Formula 3	Rupert Keegan (March 743)
Simoniz Special Saloons	Nick Whiting (Ford Escort)
Townsend Thoresen Formula Ford 1600	Derek Daly (Hawke DL15)
Formula Ford 1600 Consolation race	Trevor van Rooyen (Royale RP21)
Britax Production Saloons	Tony Lanfranchi (Opel Commodore)
Clubmans Sports	Nick Adams (Mallock MK18)
Keith Prowse Touring Cars	Tom Walkinshaw (Ford Capri)

May 31 1976	
Shellsport 5000 meeting	
Shellsport 5000	David Purley (Chevron B30)
Oceanair Clubmans Sports	Guy Woodward (Mallock MK14)
Forward Trust Special Saloons up to 1000cc	Ginger Marshall (Mini Clubman)
Forward Trust Special Saloons over 1000cc	Nick Whiting (Ford Escort)
Rochas Classic Cars	Woody Harris (Ford GT40)
DJM Formula Ford 1600	Derek Warwick (Hawke DL15)

August 8 1976	
Indylantic meeting	
Indylantic Heat 1	Ted Wentz (Lola T460)
Indylantic Heat 2	Ted Wentz (Lola T460)
Indylantic Heat 3	Jeremy Rossiter (Chevron B29)
Indylantic Final	Phil Dowsett (Chevron B29)
RAC Formula Ford 1600	Kenny Gray (Royale RP21)
Clubmans Sports	Malcolm Jackson (Mallock MK14)
Britax Production Saloons	Gerry Marshall (Ford Capri)
DJM Formula Ford 1600	Rod Bremner (Crossle 30F)
Formula Ford 1600 Consolation race	Ashley Ward (Van Diemen RF76)

August 29/30 1976	
BARC meeting	
Monoposto	'The Streaker' (Lotus 35)
DJM Formula Ford 1600	Rod Bremner (Crossle 30F)
Mini Miglia	Alan Curnow
Formula Super Vee	John Morrison (Lola T326)
RAC 2-litre Sports	Tony Charnell (Chevron B31)
Hitachi Special Saloons	Jeff Ward (Hillman Imp)
Oceanair Clubmans Sports	Steve Farthing (Mallock MK16)

Actor Denis Waterman (centre) presents Derek Warwick with the awards after the DJM Records Formula Ford race at Easter 1976. Photo: Fred Taylor.

The Shellsport Formula 5000 series returned in September but it was a race hit by tragedy. Gentleman racer John Wingfield crashed violently when his Formula 2 Ralt RT1 slewed sideways into the marshals' post at Village on the first lap of the race. The race continued while the rescue crews worked tirelessly to save him, but his injuries proved too severe. It was an accident made all the more tragic by the fact that his brother Peter had been killed in a similar accident in 1969 when his Mallock U2 hit a marshals' post at the Croft circuit. To complete the awful tragedy, the Thruxton Shellsport race winner was Brian McGuire in a Williams FW04, who later lost his life in a racing accident at Brands Hatch.

The 1976 championship season ended with one of the most enduring controversies ever to hit the circuit. In the BP Super Visco Formula 3 Championship, it was the year of the season-long battle between Rupert Keegan in the car backed by his father's British Air Ferries concern and Italian Bruno Giacomelli. Arriving at Thruxton for the final race, Giacomelli needed to win with fastest lap to beat Keegan to the title. Keegan simply needed to prevent his rival winning.

September 12 1976	
Shellsport 5000 meeting	
Shellsport 5000	Brian McGuire (Williams FW04)
BP Formula 3	Bruno Giacomelli (March 763)
DJM Formula Ford 1600 Heat 1	Jim Walsh (Royale RP21)
DJM Formula Ford 1600 Heat 2	Rod Bremner (Crossle 30F)
DJM Formula Ford 1600 Final	Jim Walsh (Royale RP21)
Forward Trust 1000 Special Saloons	Ginger Marshall (Mini Countryman)
Rochas Classic Cars	Richard Thwaites (Brabham BT8)

October 31 1976	
BARC Championship Finals meeting	
BP Formula 3	Geoff Lees (Chevron B34)
Modified Sports	John Cooper (Porsche 911)
Oceanair Clubmans Sports	Steve Farthing (Mallock MK16B)
Forward Trust Special Saloons	Gerry Marshall (Vauxhall Firenza)
Britax Production Saloons	Gerry Marshall (BMW CSL)
DJM Formula Ford 1600	Rod Bremner (Crossle 30F)

November 21 1976	
BARC meeting	
Mini Seven/Miglia	John Hazell (Mini Miglia)
MG Challenge	Keith Ashby (MG Midget)
Formula Ford	Kenny Gray (Royale RP24)
Special Saloons	Gerry Marshall (Vauxhall Firenza)
Clubmans Sports/ Formula 1300	Steve Farthing (Mallock MK16B)

Count down to drama. The Formula 3 field sets off on October 31st 1976. Photo: John Gaisford.

They shared the front row and the atmosphere was tense as the cars sat on the grid. But almost before the race had started, the matter was dramatically resolved when the title protagonists clashed at Allard, within yards of the start. Opinions about the incident varied, but both drivers were eliminated on the spot along with several others including Ian Flux, Stephen South and Patrick Bardinon. Keegan won the title amidst accusations that he had driven into Giacomelli. Some pundits suggested that Keegan knew full well that if they both crashed out, the title would be his. Whatever really happened, the fans were deprived of what should have been a nail-biting race. Almost un-noticed, Geoff Lees (Chevron B34) won the race as the recovery crews cleared up the tangled mess of cars from the barriers at Allard.

There was no televised meeting in 1976 as advertising wrangles continued to affect the sport. However, with a date allocated for November, the meeting went ahead and the non-championship races were dedicated to local villages, Fyfield, Kimpton, Thruxton and Quarley. Notable winners were South African Kenny Gray (Formula Ford) and Gerry Marshall (Special Saloons). A further winter meeting was mooted for the New Year Bank Holiday, January 3rd, but never came to fruition.

Moments later, cars litter the banking. Photo: John Gaisford.

Although he is out of the race, Rupert Keegan is champion. Photo: John Gaisford.

The damaged BAF Chevron is dragged back into the paddock. Photo: John Gaisford.

CHAPTER FIVE

Development continues as Formula 2 thrives

The 1977 season opened with controversy over the future of the racing school based at Thruxton. In February the school was being reformed but there was speculation as to exactly who had won the contract. The Winfield and SHARP operations both appeared to be in the running but, as the season approached, there was no confirmation from the BARC Council.

Of rather more concern to the senior officials of the BARC, however, was the prospect of another round of problems over the planned TV coverage of the Easter Formula 2 meeting. After considerable work, the Car Radio division of Phillips had been lined up as title sponsor, now so vital to the viability of the meeting which boasted a £35,000 purse for the Formula 2 race.

The BBC agreed to televise the meeting provided that the teams restricted advertising on cars to a maximum size of five inch lettering. The BBC was anxious not to have advertising at what they termed the centre of the action. In making this stipulation, the BBC had, in fact, climbed down slightly from their previous position about advertising on racing cars. However, when this revised plan was presented to the Formula 2 teams, most of the major outfits said that they would still not be prepared to race under these conditions. After a bout of lateral thinking, the remarkable compromise reached was that the BBC would only televise the support races and not the Formula 2 race!

Phillips Car Radio would still sponsor the meeting to the delight, and considerable relief of the BARC, and would gain the TV exposure that was central to the sponsorship deal. The support race teams from the Formula 3, Formula Ford and Thoroughbred Sports championships all readily agreed to carry smaller stickers and have their races televised.

But before the Easter weekend, there was the opening Formula 3 meeting of the 1977 season on March 13th. A youthful Ian Flux had a massive end-over-end shunt in his Ockley Racing Ralt during qualifying. The 21-year old broke his thumb and suffered minor burns on his leg when hot water spilt from the radiator. He was out of racing for six weeks while recovering. 'It was a damp morning, a typical March day at Thruxton,' recalls Flux. 'I was on pole by half a second and as I came past the pits, my board said 'P1 +0.5'. I thought, "There has got to be some more to come," but I went off on the exit of Goodwood. I'd been off there before and usually you could bounce down the grass, keep the car straight and then slowly creep it back onto the track.

'But the guy who ploughed the field must have ploughed another couple of furrows nearer the track. The car just fell into the first furrow and rolled five times. I hurt my hand and was out until Monaco in May. The plaster came off on the Tuesday and we tested at Brands on the Wednesday morning before we caught the boat. But I'd lost the rhythm of it all and I failed to qualify at Monaco by three-hundredths of a second. The year before, I'd finished eighth in the final... That's the only time I've damaged myself in a racing car,' says Flux. It was not Ian's first experience of Thruxton, however. As an eager youngster he had witnessed the 1968 Formula race from his father's shoulders! 'I distinctly remember Jochen Rindt winning,' he recalls.

March 13 1977	
Formula 3 meeting	
BP Formula 3	Stephen South (March 763)
Formula Ford 1600	David McClelland (Crossle 30F)
Formula Libre	John Bowtell (March 74B)
British Air Ferries Formula Ford 2000	Jeremy Rossiter (Reynard SF77)
Steel Tube Services Modified Sports	Jonathan Palmer (Marcos GT)
Oceanair Clubmans Sports	Dud Moseley (Mallock MK16BX)
Forward Trust Special Saloons	Tony Sugden (Ford Escort)

March 27 1977	
BARC meeting	
Special Saloons	Basil Dagge (Hillman Imp)
Formula Super Vee	Olly Hollamby (Crossle)
MG Challenge	Mike Donovan (Midget)
Formula Ford 1600	Frank Bayes (Image FF2B)
Britax Production Saloons	Derrick Brunt (BMW CSL)
AMHEC Formula Four/Formula Libre	Martin Murphy (Chevron B27)
Classic Saloons	Gerry Marshall (Jaguar)

In Flux's absence, the BP Formula 3 race was won in the rain by Stephen South. On the same day, Jonathan Palmer won the Modified Sportscar race in his Marcos. Palmer would go on to a successful single-seater career that included a spell in grand prix racing but South's potential was tragically cut short when he lost a leg in a dreadful Can-Am accident in Canada.

When the Formula 2 teams arrived in mid-April, lap times were dramatically reduced against those of 1976. Pole position was set at a stunning 1m8.87s by Alex Ribeiro (March 772P). That was almost certainly the first ever sub-1m10s lap and trimmed more than a second from the 1m10.1s that had taken Jacques Laffite to pole just 12 months earlier. Another landmark was reached in the race when the first official 120mph lap of the circuit was set by race winner Brian Henton who took the circuit record down to 1m10.67s, 120.02mph. The pace of the leading Formula 2 cars was all the more remarkable when you consider that, during qualifying on Saturday, snow showers swept across the circuit!

Henton went on to win the race in the Netherton & Worth Boxer PR276 of Brian Lewis, having driven a sensible race to conserve the tyres on the one-off but very successful design. Others to lead earlier in the race were Ribeiro, Eddie Cheever (Ralt) and Riccardo Patrese (Chevron B40). Derek Warwick came second in the Formula 3 race and Nigel Mansell came second in the Formula Ford race in the one-off Javelin in which the former kart racer really started his single-seater career.

The following month, Mansell was back at Thruxton to score his first major car win in a round of the Silverstone-based Brush Fusegear Formula Ford Championship. His determination to even get to the grid at Thruxton that day was indicative of the tenacity of a man who would climb to the very top of the sport by ability, determination and sheer perseverance. Mansell raced the Javelin at Oulton Park on Saturday, but retired with broken suspension. Nigel and his friends then drove to Gloucester and spent the night building up the spare four-year old Crossle 25F of Mike Taylor and fitting Mansell's spare engine into the car. They finished at 5am, loaded up and drove to Thruxton where he promptly won the race despite a night out of bed! Four weeks later, Mansell broke bones in his neck in a heavy shunt at Brands Hatch but was soon back racing again.

April 9/11 1977
Phillips Car Radio Formula 2 meeting

European Formula 2	Brian Henton (Boxer PR276)
Tricentrol Touring Cars	Vince Woodman (Ford Capri)
BP Formula 3	Eje Elgh (Chevron B38)
Formula Ford 1600	David Heale (Reynard 75/77FF)
Thoroughbred Sports Cars	David Preece (Jaguar XK120)
Ferraris/Porsches	Louis Lorenzini (Ferrari 312P)

May 8 1977
BARC meeting

Varley Monoposto	'The Streaker' (Lotus 35)
Leyland Cars Mini Seven	Tony Styles
Brush Fusegear Formula Ford 1600	Nigel Mansell (Crossle 25F)
Steel Tube Services Modified Sports	Bob Jarvis (Davrian MK7)
Atlas Formula 1300	John Law (Samantha U2 MK18B)
Production Saloons	Derrick Brunt (BMW CSL)
Leyland Cars Mini 1275GT	Steve Soper
Formula Ford 2000	Oscar Notz (Crossle 31F)
Esso Uniflo Special Saloons	Colin Hawker (DFVW)

June 6 1977
Shellsport Group 8 meeting

Shellsport Group 8	Tony Rouff (Ralt RT1)
Sodastream Sports 2000	Divina Galica (Lola T490)
Formula Ford 1600	David Heale (Reynard 75/77FF)
AFN Classic Sports	Chris Marsh (Marcos GT)
Formula Super Vee	Olly Hollamby (Crossle)

June 19 1977
Formula 3 meeting

BP Formula 3	Geoff Lees (Chevron B38)
Tricentrol Touring Cars	Chris Craft (Ford Capri)
Forward Trust Special Saloons up to 1000cc	John Homewood (Sunbeam Imp)
Steel Tube Services Modified Sports	Jonathan Palmer (Marcos GT)
Leyland Cars Mini Miglia	Paul Gaymer
RAC Formula Ford 1600	Trevor van Rooyen (Royale RP24)
Oceanair Clubmans Sports	Dud Moseley (Mallock MK18)
Special Saloons	Nick Whiting (Ford Escort)

June 1977.
Clubmans racers
Robert Glass and
Don Cressy come to grief.
Photo: Jeff Bloxham.

Formula Ford action from October 30th 1977. David McClelland leads David Leslie and Nigel Mansell.
Photo: John Gaisford.

Chris Craft and
Gordon Spice
battle in the 1977
Touring Car
Championship.
Photo:
Mark Owen.

In June 1977 Thruxton was touched by another tragedy. Phil Winter, who had marshalled regularly at the circuit before racing a Mini Special Saloon very successfully was killed in a road accident while on holiday to watch the TT motorbike races on the Isle of Man. Phil and his enthusiastic family came from West Moors near Poole in Dorset. With his well-developed Mini, Phil had won the 1975 Forward Trust Special Saloon title and BARC Presidents' Cup.

Jeremy Rossiter (Reynard SF77) heads Rad Dougall (Royale) into the Chicane in a 1977 Formula Ford 2000 race. Photo: Roger Standish.

After several months of speculation and negotiation, details of the new Thruxton racing school were finally announced in June. The Scorpion School started operating on July 20th with silenced single-seaters and saloons. The school was to use Royale Formula Ford 1600 and Formula Ford 2000 cars and Ford Escort and Renault 5TS saloons. Instructors included Kenny Gray, Derek Daly and Trevor van Rooyen who worked under school boss Michael Eastick. While the new school opened its doors to hopeful pupils, August 1977 marked two special

events in the history of the venue. Early in the month the paddock and spectator areas were used for the Thruxton War Day with military vehicles, battle re-enactments, and nostalgia from the second World War.

Then, three weeks later on August Bank Holiday Monday, the circuit celebrated its 25th anniversary as a car race circuit. Winners that day included Steve Soper (Mini 1275GT) and David Leslie (Formula Ford) during the early stages of careers that would later bring stardom in Touring Cars and GT racing. The first ever car race meeting had been held on August Bank Holiday Monday, 1952. At the same time, rumours started doing the rounds once more concerning a possible non-championship F1 race being planned for Thruxton in 1978! It never came to fruition, but it kept the motorsport press busy for a couple of weeks.

The Championship Finals meeting of 1977 once more marked the end of the British Formula 3 Championship after another hard-fought season. Rising Irish star Derek Daly clinched the BP Formula 3 title in the Derek McMahon-entered Chevron B38 despite major pressure from Geoff Brabham. It was a fitting final in which the best man on the day won the crown and went some way to dispelling memories of the Keegan/Giacomelli saga of the previous season. Winner of the Formula Ford race was Nigel Mansell, now equipped with a slightly later Crossle 32F and, like Daly, Mansell was back for another win in the TV meeting a fortnight later when the racing was backed by a fairly obscure film about car theft called 'Gone in 60 Seconds'.

Having finished her weekend duties for the season, a week later popular BARC Marshals' Secretary Del Evans married marshal Martin Slade in Andover.

Championship Finals Day, 1977. Derek Daly leads the Formula 3 grid away.

August 29 1977
BARC meeting

Atlas Formula 1300	John Law (Samantha U2 MK18B)
Formula Ford 1600	David Leslie (Royale RP24)
Leyland Cars Mini 1275GT	Steve Soper
AMHEC Formula 4	Alex Lowe (Chevron B20)
Steel Tube Services Modified Sports	Mike Franey (Porsche 911)
British Air Ferries Formula Ford 2000	Philip Bullman (Hawke DL16)
Forward Trust Special Saloons	Rob Mason (Bevan Stiletto)
Varley Monoposto	Peter Gillett (Genie Mk13)
Thoroughbred Sports	Dave Preece (Jaguar XK120)

September 11 1977
Shellsport Group 8 meeting

Shellsport Group 8	Guy Edwards (March 751)
Tricentrol Touring Cars	Tony Dron (Triumph Dolomite Sprint)
Townsend Thoresen Formula Ford 1600	David Leslie (Royale RP24)
Sodastream Sports 2000	John Cooper (Lola T490)
AFN Classic Sports	David Dawson (Lotus 23)
SKF Clubmans Sports	Creighton Brown (Mallock MK18B)

October 30 1977
BARC Championship Finals meeting

BP Formula 3	Derek Daly (Chevron B38)
British Air Ferries Formula Ford 2000	Jeremy Rossiter (Reynard 77SF)
Oceanair Clubmans Sports	Andrew Nielson (Mallock MK18BW)
Formula Ford 1600	Nigel Mansell (Crossle 32F)
Forward Trust Special Saloons	Gerry Marshall (Vauxhall Firenza)
Britax Production Saloons	John Brindley (BMW CSL)

November 13 1977
Gone in 60 Seconds raceday

Formula 3	Derek Daly (Chevron B38)
Formula Ford 1600	Nigel Mansell (Crossle 32F)
Production Saloons	Derrick Brunt (BMW)
Modified Sports	Alec Poole (Datsun 290ZG)
Formula Ford 2000	Richard Wills (Delta T77)

Appropriately, they used the BARC Volvo estate rescue unit for wedding transport! A few days earlier, Del and her colleagues had finally been installed in new purpose-built offices beneath the Club grandstand. This was part of the £120,000 improvement plan at the circuit and replaced the temporary buildings that the BARC staff had occupied for four years since moving from central London.

The new offices were opened by the Mayor of Test Valley, Councillor Parke, who cut the ribbon at noon on November 16th. To complete a good day, and indeed a good season, for Thruxton and the BARC it was announced on the same day that Phillips would again support the Formula 2 meeting over Easter 1978.

Work at the circuit over that winter included painting white lines on both sides of the track for the full length of the lap for the very first time. Doubtless, some of the drivers who found themselves short of reference points around the back of the circuit would at least now have some warning that they were about to go off! The grid was re-painted and new kerbs were installed at the Chicane and Allard. Lucas provided a new start gantry and backing from Shell allowed the timekeepers box to be doubled in size and the old press box over the pits replaced by a new one at the Chicane. Other improvements included a new trackside telephone system, a new paddock office next to the scrutineering bay and general repair and renewal of fences.

March 12 1978
Formula 3 meeting

BP Formula 3	Derek Warwick (Ralt RT1)
Britax Production Saloons	Gerry Marshall (Triumph Dolomite Sprint)
Phillips Formula Ford 1600	David McClelland (Van Diemen RF78)
Sodastream Sports 2000	Frank Sytner (Lola T492)
STP Modified Sports	Jon Fletcher (Lotus Elan)
Wendy Wools Special Saloons	Tony Sugden (Volvo)
Oceanair Clubmans Sports	Mike Barnby (Spectrum)

At the November 1977 TV meeting Nigel Mansell graduated to Formula 3 with the Alan McKechnie Lola. Photo: Jeff Bloxham.

Gerry Marshall powers 'Baby Bertha' out of the Chicane, October 1977. Photo: John Gaisford.

Ray Cunningham of Shell presents Sidney Offord with the keys to the new press box in 1978.

The 1978 season opened with a Formula 3 race on March 12th. That meeting also marked the 10th anniversary of the circuit as a permanent venue. Derek Warwick won the BP Formula 3 race, adding to his Silverstone win of a week earlier. Brazilian hotshot Nelson Piquet was fourth in another of Ron Tauranac's classic Ralt RT1 designs.

Later that month, Michael Eastick announced ambitious plans for the Scorpion school and his associated race hire business. The bold plans included running a total of 13 Formula Ford 1600 and Formula Ford 2000 hire cars, including a car for 18 year-old New Zealand prospect Mike Thackwell. Scorpion would also support school instructor James Weaver in the latest works Hawke DL20 Formula Ford 1600 car. The plan was that Eastick would run the race hire business while Richard Tyzack would be his assistant team manager and run the school. Ian Taylor was now chief instructor with Kenny Gray, Rob Wilson and Weaver as principal instructors. The school was using six Royale single-seater chassis and would soon take delivery of three Triumph TR7s to replace the Escort Mexicos. The school had been obliged to find new premises in Amesbury to accommodate all the cars and the eight mechanics needed to keep them all running.

March 25/27 1978	
Phillips Car Radio Formula 2 meeting	
European Formula 2	Bruno Giacomelli (March 782)
BP Formula 3	Derek Warwick (Ralt RT1)
Tricentrol Touring Cars	Gordon Spice (Ford Capri)
Historic Cars	Sid Hoole (Cooper Monaco)
Phillips Formula Ford 1600	David McClelland (Van Diemen RF78)
Thoroughbred Sports	David Preece (Jaguar XK120)

The Phillips Formula 2 meeting was particularly early due to the Easter date and the March 27th race was won by Bruno Giacomelli (March 782) in front of 12 million TV viewers. South African Rad Dougall drove a superb Formula 2 debut race to finish third behind Marc Surer as the top five positions were dominated by the March 782, arguably the best-ever Formula 2 design from the Bicester manufacturer. The lap record was left untouched with no one approaching Henton's record from the '77 race. Easter also marked the tenth Formula 2 race at Thruxton, with only the 1974 race missed due to the lack of a title sponsor for the meeting. That weekend, motorbike world champion Giacomo Agostini made his car racing debut but did not impress in a Chevron B42, while Derek Warwick again won the Formula 3 race in his Warwick Trailers-backed Ralt RT1.

Although the Formula 2 cars were adrift of the circuit record, it was a different matter at the May Bank Holiday Monday meeting which was headlined by a round of the Aurora AFX British Formula 1 Championship. Geoff Lees (March 781) set a new outright record at 1m10.41s (120.46mph) before retiring with a collapsed rear wing. The race was the first Formula 1 race at Thruxton and was won by Tony Trimmer in a McLaren M23.

Eddie Cheever (March 782) during the 1978 Formula 2 race. Photo: Fred Taylor.

Ian Flux was another of the early instructors. 'The most important memory of Thruxton is Ian Taylor and the racing school. The first time I ever taught at the school was in 1978 with Ian, Mike Thackwell, Rob Wilson and Kenny Gray. In those days I was often given the Complex to go and sit at with Mike Thackwell. If it was a nice sunny day we used to lie behind the bank and pop our heads over once or twice! The first time I ever saw Ian really lose his temper was the day that Kenny Gray was coming back from Church and managed to roll one of the Escorts coming into the Chicane,' remembers Flux.

On August Bank Holiday Monday, the first Brooklands meeting was held to commemorate the BARC heritage with a meeting focused on classic and historic cars. Three weeks later, the sky above Thruxton played host to the King's Cup Air Race which had been held over Brooklands previously.

April 9 1978
BARC meeting

Abdex Clubmans Sports	Alan Webb (Mallock MK20)
Shellsport Production Saloons	Jock Robertson (Opel Commodore GSE)
Leyland Cars Mini Seven	Chris Tyrrell
Esso Formula Ford 1600	Jim Walsh (Royale RP24)
Formula Ford 1600 Consolation race	Willie Moore (Van Diemen RF78)
Rivet Supply Special Saloons	Nick Whiting (Ford Escort)
Classic Saloons	Mike Bennion (Ford Zephyr)
Leyland Cars Mini Miglia	John Hazell

May 1 1978
BARC meeting

Oceanair Clubmans	Mike Barnby (Spectrum)
Phillips Formula Ford 1600	David McClelland (Van Diemen RF78)
Classic Sports Cars	Jeffray Johnstone (Lotus 23B)
STP Modified Sports	Bob Jarvis (Davrian MK6)
British Air Ferries Formula Ford 2000	Kenny Gray (Reynard SF78)
Thoroughbred Sports	John Chatham (Austin Healey 100/6)

May 29 1978
Radio 210 Raceday

Aurora AFX Formula 1	Tony Trimmer (McLaren M23)
BP Formula 3	Nelson Piquet (Ralt RT1)
Britax Production Saloons	Tony Lanfranchi (Opel Commodore)
Super Saloons	Nick Whiting (Ford Escort)

June 18 1978
BARC meeting

Classic Saloons	Bill Pinckney (Jaguar)
Formula Ford 1600 Qualification race	David Mercer (Van Diemen RF78)
Townsend Thoresen Formula Ford 1600	David McClelland (Van Diemen RF78)
Oceanair Clubmans Sports	Graham Kay (Mallock MK18CW)
Monoposto/ Formula Super Vee	Bruce Venn (Lola T326/8)
Sports 2000	Ian Taylor (Lola T492)
STP Modified Sports	Bob Jarvis (Davrian MK6)
AMHEC Formula 4	Ian Briggs (Delta 784)

Derek Warwick winning the Formula 3 race at Easter 1978 in his Warwick Trailers-backed Ralt RT1. Photo: Jeff Bloxham.

August 28 1978
Brooklands Memorial meeting

Leyland Cars Mini 1275GT	Jerry Hampshire
AMHEC Formula 4	Ian Briggs (Delta 784)
Britax Production Saloons	Tony Lanfranchi (Opel Commodore)
SodaStream Sports 2000	Nick Adams (Lola T492)
Brooklands Memorial Handicap	Alan Nye (Austin 7)
Phillips Formula Ford 1600	Kenny Acheson (Royale RP24)
Wendy Wools Special Saloons	Tony Dickinson (Skoda S110R)

September 10 1978
Aurora AFX British Formula 1 meeting

Aurora British Formula 1	Guy Edwards (March 781)
Porsche 924	Tony Dron
RAC Formula Ford 1600	Roberto Guerrero (Van Diemen RF78)
DB Motors Production Sports	Charles Morgan (Morgan +8)
Classic Sports Cars	Jeffray Johnstone (Lotus 23B)

October 29 1978
BARC Championship Finals meeting

BP Formula 3	Chico Serra (March 783)
Phillips Formula Ford 1600	Michael Roe (Van Diemen RF78)
Oceanair Clubmans Sports	Charlie Kirby (Mallock MK16E)
Britax Production Saloons	Derrick Brunt (BMW CSL)
Wendy Wools Special Saloons	Tony Dickinson (Skoda S110R)
British Air Ferries Formula Ford 2000	Adrian Reynard (Reynard SF78)

November 11 1978
Plastic Padding Raceday

Formula 3	Derek Warwick (Ralt RT1)
Formula Ford 1600	Peter Morgan (Lola T540)
Formula Ford 1600 Consolation race	David Jacklin (Crossle 25F)
Leyland Cars Mini Seven	Stephen Hall
Porsche 924	Tony Dron
Formula Ford 2000	Mike Blanchet (Lola T580)

The 1978 Formula 2 podium party with winner Bruno Giacomelli (centre) flanked by third-placed Rad Dougall (left) and Marc Surer who finished second.
Photo: Jeff Bloxham.

A landmark lap record fell during the Championship Finals meeting on October 29th when the six-year old Formula Ford 1600 record set by John Stevens (Merlyn MK11) back in 1972 was finally broken. Stevens' remarkable record stood for over six years before being topped by Irish duo Kenny Acheson (Royale RP26) and Michael Roe (Van Diemen RF78) in 1m25.3s. Although the Stevens' mark was finally bettered in October 1978, it had previously been matched by both Derek Warwick and Kenny Gray at the tail end of the '76 season.

Plastic Padding was a great supporter of Thruxton. This 1978 group comprises Lars Bernston (MD of the company), Formula 3 racer Eje Elgh and BARC trio Sidney Offord, John Wickham and Press Officer Mark Cole.

The November TV meeting was sponsored by Plastic Padding, and it proved to be a rather emotional day. At the meeting, a cheque for more than £1000 was presented to the Gunnar Nilsson Cancer Treatment Campaign. It was presented by Miss World 1977, Mary Stavin of Sweden, to David Mason, the campaign chairman. Half of the amount was donated by Plastic Padding and rest was contributed by drivers, officials and spectators at the meeting. Plastic Padding had come to prominence by sponsoring the other Swedish Grand Prix driver, Ronnie Peterson, in his early career. Tragically, Nilsson died from cancer at a cruelly young age, just as his grand prix career was gathering momentum. Then, the sport was dealt another awful blow when Peterson died as a result of injuries sustained in the Italian Grand Prix at Monza in September.

At that TV meeting, Derek Warwick won the final Formula 3 race of the season while young Scot Bryce Wilson made an impressive Formula 3 debut by finishing fourth in another Ralt. Nearly twenty years later he would be back winning again at Thruxton as his career enjoyed a renaissance. The year closed with the good news that Phillips had already confirmed their support for the 1979 Easter Formula 2 meeting.

As the '79 season opened up, the Scorpion school was doing brisk business and announced the Unipart Racing Scholarship. Backed by the Swindon-based motor parts organisation, this significant new scholarship would award a very worthwhile prize to a star pupil. Throughout the year, the best pupils would be given the chance to compete in a Formula Ford race and at the end of the year, the best newcomer would win a fully-sponsored drive in the 1980 Star of Tomorrow Formula Ford Championship. As one of the earliest scholarships of this kind, it generated enormous interest and, of course, increased business for the school! 'I had no money, so I thought this was my way into motorsport. So I paid my £300 or whatever it was, and off I went. I did the four-day course and set the quickest time of the month on one of the courses and won a free race,' remembers Bill Coombs.

As usual, the Mini Sevens use all of the track and the Chicane kerbs. This 1979 trio is Chris Tyrrell, Steve Taylor (34) and Gary Hall. Photo: Tony Lambden.

'On my first visit to the school in the Scorpion days, my instructor was Rob Wilson. We had a Fiat in those days and Rob went straight up to the Complex at 80mph. He didn't brake at all and we went straight across the dirt to Segrave. He just looked across and said, 'This is the saloon line!' Things have changed a lot since then and the standard of instructing has got a bit more professional,' admits Bill.

By this process, Bill made his car debut at Thruxton at the end of 1979 in a Townsend Thoresen race against drivers like Tommy Byrne and Jonathan Palmer. As a result of his performance, Bill won the Unipart Racing Scholarship for 1980. 'I can remember Ian Taylor, who was Chief Instructor at the school, ringing me up around Christmas to tell me I'd won the scholarship. It was a dream come true. I was working for Leyland in those days as a technical apprentice and I was earning £18 pounds a week take-home,' he recalls.

Once he started the scholarship, Mike Eastick suggested to Bill that he should start instructing at the school at a rate of £25 per day! 'All you had to do to instruct in those days was to win a race! In my first race, predictably, I crashed, in my second I won,' says Bill. His rivals in the Star of Tomorrow Formula Ford championship that year included Tim Lee-Davey, Andy Wallace and Andrew Gilbert-Scott.

March 11 1979
Formula 3 meeting

Vandervell Formula 3	Andrea de Cesaris (March 793)
Classic Saloons	Bill Pinckney (Jaguar MK1)
Formula Ford 2000	David Leslie (Reynard SF79)
Demon Tweeks Production Saloons	Tony Lanfranchi (Opel Commodore)
Mini Seven	Patrick Watts
Clubmans Sports	Phil Martin-Dye (Mallock MK18CW)

April 1 1979
BARC meeting

AMHEC Formula 4	Ian Briggs (Delta 784)
MCD Sports Racing 1700	Charlie Kirby (Mallock MK20B)
Shellsport Formula Ford 2000	Simon Kirkby (Reynard SF79)
Production Sports	Rob Wells (Morgan Plus 8)
Esso Formula Ford 1600	Jim Walsh (Royale RP26)
Formula Ford 1600 Consolation Race	Rick Morris (PRS RH01)
Hitachi Formula Atlantic	Ray Mallock (Ralt RT1)
Mini Miglia	Paul Gaymer

Having run so impressively in the 1978 Formula 2 race, Rad Dougall went even better in the '79 race and won convincingly in a March 782. Although the car was dubbed a 79B as it had '79 spec side-pods including the sliding skirts that proliferated at the time, it was in fact largely a year-old car. Dougall's new Toleman Group Ralt RT2 was not ready and so he ran the same car that he had taken to third a year earlier. The works team was running the latest 792s which, at this stage of the season, could not match the pace of the proven 782. Dougall dominated the race from Derek Daly (792). Daly was lucky to even start the race, however, after destroying a car in a massive testing accident on Thursday when Derek Warwick moved over inadvertently on the way up Woodham Hill. The 792 that Keke Rosberg had just won with at Hockenheim was wrecked but the Project Four team built up a new 792 in time for qualifying on Saturday.

Dougall set pole with the fastest ever lap of Thruxton, 1m08.43s. Sadly, much of the potential of the race was lost in a five-cap pile up at Allard on the first lap that eliminated Warwick (March 792), Brian Henton (Ralt RT2) and Stephen South (March 792). A new outright circuit record went to Marc Surer (March 792) in 1m9.11s, (122.73mph).

Easter '79 had been an expensive weekend for many teams with no less than 14 cars shunted and two more suffering fires. The biggest accident of all

Rad Dougall beat all the 1979 cars to win the Formula 2 race in his year-old March 782. Photo: Jeff Bloxham.

Brian Henton and Ron Tauranac discuss tactics before the 1979 Formula 2 race. Photo: Fred Taylor.

Derek Warwick, Grand Prix entrant Teddy Yip (centre) and Richard Speakman (left) chat in the assembly area before the 1979 Formula 2 race. Photo: Fred Taylor.

The 1979 Formula 2 field charges into Allard with trouble developing to the left. Photo: Fred Taylor.

befell little-known Argentinean Ariel Bakst, who was unlucky enough to have the front suspension of his Everest March collapse at Village. The car plunged into the undergrowth and flipped end-over-end with Bakst a helpless passenger. On his return to the paddock, the uninjured Bakst explained to waiting team members that, 'I had a little up and down in the country.' Then the sorry remains of his car arrived dangling from the back of a wrecker!

April 14/16 1979	
Phillips Car Radio Raceday	
European Formula 2	Rad Dougall (March 782)
Vandervell Formula 3	Andrea de Cesaris (March 793)
Tricentrol Touring Cars	Gordon Spice (Ford Capri)
P&O Formula Ford 1600	David Sears (Royale RP26)

May 7 1979	
Brooklands Raceday	
Thoroughbred Sports	Reg Woodock (Triumph TR3A)
Classic Sportscars	Jeffray Johnstone (Lotus 23B)
Rivet Supply Special Saloons	Tony Dickinson (Skoda S110R)
RAC British Formula Ford 1600	David Sears (Royale RP26)
Historic Special GT	Richard Bond (Lola T70)
Esso Historic Racing Cars	Bruce Halford (Lotus 16)

May 28 1979	
Aurora AFX British Formula 1 meeting	
Aurora AFX British Formula 1	Emilio de Villota (Lotus 78)
Mini Seven	Russell Grady
Chequered Flag Sports 2000	Ian Taylor (Tiga SC79)
STP Modified Sports	John Pugsley (Davrian Mk6)

Later in April, while testing for the Aurora AFX British Formula 1 race to be held on May 28, David Kennedy lapped in 1m8.4s in his Theodore Wolf Formula 1 car. But that race was run on a wet track, so Surer's lap record was never challenged as Spaniard Emilio de Villota guided his Lotus 78 to victory.

In testing for the September 1979 Aurora race, Villota took the unofficial best lap even lower by lapping in 1m7.7s in his ex-Gunnar Nilsson car. In the race, he crashed out at Segrave after tangling with David Kennedy (Wolf WR6). The race was won by Rupert Keegan in an Arrows FA1 in front of a 10,000 crowd after heavy promotion on Radio Victory. Keegan's team mate Ricardo Zunino set pole in 1m07.14s as the speeds increased ever more. But Villota's fastest lap in the race was only 1m09.43s. However, these times were put firmly into the shade in November when the Brabham team brought its latest grand prix car to the circuit for Nelson Piquet to test, prior to being raced in Canada. Knowing the circuit well from his Formula 3 days, Piquet scorched round in 1m5.5s, close to 130mph and set the fastest lap so far recorded at Thruxton.

The Championship Finals meeting was followed a week later by an STP-supported TV meeting as the curtain fell on the decade. The circuit had come a long way in the 1970s, with significant investment to improve the facilities. Despite the severe planning restrictions, the BARC had kept the track viable and had been able to plough any profits back into the venue. Further, the commitment of the Club to Formula 2 had endured through a decade that had been hit by a world-wide oil crisis and ensuing recession. Only once had Easter Monday at Thruxton not played host to the finest young racing drivers of the era. With further investment planned, there was every expectation that the

Starters Bob Lentell and Sidney Offord bravely turn their backs on the 1979 Easter Formula 3 grid. Photo: Fred Taylor.

1980s would continue the Thruxton success story.

Before the start of the 1980 season, a Shell filling station was created in the paddock to supply four star fuel. The five star brew preferred by some of the teams would not be available as it was being phased out. New tyre walls were installed in front of the free-standing marshals' posts and, at the same time, John Wickham left the BARC to become Formula 2 Team Manager at March.

'I left at the end of 1978 to go to March Engineering after five years with the Club. I met Max Mosley and Robin Herd, who were then directors of March, and they offered me the job of Formula 2 Team Manager,' says Wickham. Later, he spent four years as Team Manager with the Footwork Formula 1 team.

He was replaced at the BARC by Denis Southwood. Two months later, having served as Chief Flag Marshal before joining the BARC Council, Michael Groves would succeed Maurice Gorringe as Club Chairman.

August 27 1979
Radio 210 Raceday

Monoposto/ Formula 4	Tony Broster (Lyncar F2)
Wendy Wools Special Saloons	Tony Dickinson (Skoda 130RS)
P&O Ferries Formula Ford 1600	David Sears (Royale RP26)
Formula Ford 1600 Trophy	David Sears (Royale RP26)
Thoroughbred Sports	John Chatham (Austin Healey 3000)
Shellsport Production Saloons	Andy Rouse (Opel Commodore GSE)
Donington GT	Mick Hill (Skoda S130RS)
Mini 1275GT	Steve Harris

September 9 1979
Radio Victory meeting

Aurora AFX British Formula 1	Rupert Keegan (Arrows FA1)
Tricentrol British Touring Cars	Gordon Spice (Ford Capri)
Chequered Flag Sports 2000	James Weaver (Tiga SC79)
BMW County Championship	Derek Bell

September 30 1979
Walshe Builders Merchants Raceday

Vandervell Formula 3	Andrea de Cesaris (March 793)
P&O Ferries Formula Ford 1600	David Sears (Royale RP26)
Classic Saloons	Terry Heley (Ford Zodiac)
Oceanair Clubmans Sports	Phil Martin-Dye (Mallock MK18CW)
MGCC BCV8	Terry Osbourne (MGB)
Demon Tweeks Production Saloons	Andy Rouse (Opel Commodore GSE)
Computacar Formula Ford 2000	Mike White (Delta T79)
STP Modified Sports	Jon Fletcher (Lotus Elan)

October 28 1979
BARC Championship Finals meeting

Vandervell Formula 3	Mike Thackwell (March 793)
Oceanair Clubmans Sports	Phil Martin-Dye (Mallock MK18CW)
Demon Tweeks Production Saloons	Tony Lanfranchi (Opel Commodore GSE)
Wendy Wools Special Saloons	Tony Dickinson (Skoda 130RS)
Computacar Formula Ford 2000	Nick Foy (Reynard SF79)
P&O Ferries Formula Ford 1600	David McClelland (Van Diemen RF79)

November 3 1979
STP Television meeting

Formula 3	Kenny Acheson (March 793)
STP Modified Sports	John Pugsley (Davrian MK6)
Faberge Fiesta Ladies Championship	Guenda Eadie
Formula Ford 1600	James Weaver (Tiga FF79)
Graham Hill Memorial Minis	Roy Kwei
Formula Ford 2000	Mike White (Delta T79)

Emilio de Villota (Lotus 78) winning the Aurora AFX Formula 1 race in May 1979. Photo: Tony Lambden.

Rupert Keegan crashes out of the British Formula 1 race, May 28th 1979. Photo: Tony Lambden.

Gerry Marshall flat-out through Church in the Triumph Dolomite Sprint, September 1979. Photo: Jeff Bloxham.

CHAPTER SIX

Ayrton Senna makes his mark

Eighteen years after the Goodwood accident that ended his Grand Prix career and came close to claiming his life, Stirling Moss made a comeback to race a works-backed Audi 80 in the 1980 British Touring Car Championship. Of course, Stirling had never raced at Thruxton and so in the build-up to the season he was seen testing with a map of the circuit taped to the dashboard as he learnt his way around!

In March, it was announced that P&O Ferries would be backing the Easter Formula 2 meeting, and that agreement had been reached for the BBC to televise the Formula 2, Formula 3 and Formula Ford races. There was no sign of the advertising disputes that had dogged the negotiations in previous years. The Easter meeting, held on April 5th and 7th, was dominated by the new Toleman TG280s of Brian Henton and Derek Warwick. Reputed to have cost around £27,000 each to build, the new cars were the class of the field and crossed the line together for a formation finish in BP colours as Henton led Warwick home to score his second Thruxton Formula 2 victory.

March 9 1980	
Formula 3 meeting	
Vandervell British Formula 3	Roberto Guerrero (Argo JM6)
P&O Ferries Formula Ford 1600	Jonathan Palmer (Royale RP26)
Wendy Wools Special Saloons	Tony Dickinson (Skoda 130RS)
Derwent Sports 2000	Ian Taylor (Tiga SC80)
Austin Morris Mini Seven	Russell Grady
Imperial Leather Formula Ford 2000	Simon Kirkby (Royale RP27)
Oceanair Clubmans Sports	Phil Brown (Mallock MK18CW)

April 5/7 1980	
P&O European Ferries European Formula 2 meeting	
European Formula 2	Brian Henton (Toleman TG280)
Tricentrol British Touring Cars	Gordon Spice (Ford Capri)
Vandervell British Formula 3	Kenny Acheson (March 803)
P&O Ferries Formula Ford 1600	Tommy Byrne (Van Diemen RF80)
Captain C Gull Formula Ford 1600 Race	Rick Morris (Royale RP26)

The first race of the 1980s. The Formula Ford 1600 pack heads off with Roberto Moreno leading from Donald McLoed (number 3) and Tommy Byrne (40). Photo: Peter Tempest.

The 1980 Formula 2 field in the assembly area. The line up is Manfred Winkelhock (March 802), Teo Fabi (March 802), Mike Thackwell (March 802), Huub Rothengatter (March 802) and Miguel Angel Guerra (Minardi GM75). Photo: Fred Taylor.

Easter 1980. Brian Henton and Derek Warwick pull up after finishing one-two in the Formula 2 race for the Toleman team. Photo: Peter Tempest.

Eje Elgh retires his Maurer from the 1980 Formula 2 after a puncture did extensive damage. Photo: Fred Taylor.

Warwick had taken pole on Saturday with a best lap of 1m7.60s. But it took all of Derek's undoubted bravery and ability to extract the time. 'I can take it flat all the way round the back, but honestly I'd rather not. I've had some pretty big moments over that bump and I'm not sure my heart can take it,' he said after qualifying. The March runners were decimated by tyre problems and only 10 cars finished a race of attrition. Young Italian Andrea de Cesaris was third from Brazilian Chico Serra. Henton set fastest lap in the race at 1m9.04s (122.85mph) which was a new outright record, just 0.07s better than the previous standard.

Easter Monday 1980. Formula Ford winner Tommy Byrne hides behind Captain C Gull from P&O Ferries. Photo: Fred Taylor.

failed to gain any real degree of support and was quickly dropped.

At the end of May, the Aurora AFX British Formula 1 Championship switched to Thruxton for its third race of the season. It was a weekend that nearly cost Ray Mallock his life when he suffered a mighty accident at Goodwood. Mallock was racing a Surtees TS20 and the car was sufficiently improved from the opening two races to be quickest in the first qualifying session. Suddenly, the championship favourites like Guy Edwards and Eliseo Salazar took an interest in the small team. In the second session, a rear tyre burst and damaged the suspension sufficiently to force the team back to base overnight to repair the damage.

The only fresh tyre they had was one that had been around for some time and it was to cost Mallock dear. At the very fast Goodwood corner, on the first lap at full racing speed, the tyre failed and the Surtees plunged backwards into the banking with massive force. The engine and transmission were embedded in the bank as the tub skated down the track on fire with Ray still in it. 'I'd established myself then as a leading single-seater driver and it could have worked at that point but the accident really set us back. I broke my collar bone and had some small burns and I was in hospital overnight,' says Ray.

Ironically, he had turned down an alternative offer for that ill-fated

Although the circuit was unchanged, the Chicane had a different look for the 1980 season as the barriers that had lined the left-handed middle element of the corner had been removed, and replaced by kerbs and catch-fencing. The racing line was no different, but it made a psychological difference as drivers were no longer looking at a wall of steel as they turned through the corner!

A small piece of motorsport history was made during the April 27th club meeting when Simon Hamilton-Smith raced his MG Midget in the Modified Sportscar race under LPG power. The car was sponsored by Landi Hartog who manufactured systems to convert cars to run on propane gas. He finished 16th overall and 5th in class from 22 starters, but the experiment never really caught on. Around the same time, the Brands Hatch promoters created the methanol-powered Formula Talbot single-seater class but that also

Tony Mann (Anglia) was one of the many to get the Chicane wrong! Photo: John Gaisford.

weekend. Mallock had been doing some testing work for Ron Tauranac with the prototype Honda-engined Formula 2 Ralt and had been asked to do some more work over that weekend. With the race at Thruxton, he turned down the offer. 'I did the race, ended up in hospital, and Nigel Mansell was given the job of doing the testing. He went on to race the car. That was another turning point in my career.'

Some heroic marshalling saved his life as the fire was considerable. Thankfully, Ray made a full recovery and later went on to establish a very successful career as a team manager. In September, at the second Aurora race of 1980 at Thruxton, Ray presented each of the marshals from post N with an inscribed silver salver in thanks for their efforts. Earl Howe was at the presentation to represent the BARC.

April 27 1980
BARC meeting

Monroe Production Saloons	Gerry Marshall (Ford Capri)
Clubmans Sports	Mike Dixon (Mallock MK18)
DB Motors Production Sports	Colin Blower (TVR)
Derwent Sports 2000	Ian Taylor (Tiga SC80)
Mini Miglia	Roly Nix
Esso Formula Ford 1600	Jim Walsh (Royale RP26)
Wendy Wools Special Saloons	Tony Dickinson (Skoda 130RS)
STP Modified Sports	Mike Chittenden (Ginetta G4)
Classic Saloons	Bob Meacham (Jaguar)

May 5 1980
Brooklands Raceday

Vandervell British Formula 3	Roberto Guerrero (Argo JM6)
Thoroughbred Sports	Reg Woodcock (Triumph TR3)
Varley Formula Junior	Mike Harrison (Brabham BT2)
STP Modified Sports	Nicky Ellis (Lotus Elan)
Classic Sports	Mike Harrison (Elva MK7S)
Post Historic Road Sports	Alex Boswell (AC Cobra)
Historic Special GT	Malcolm Clube (McLaren M1B)
RAC Formula Ford 1600	Tommy Byrne (Van Diemen RF80)
Brooklands Memorial Handicap	David Taylor (Aston Martin Le Mans)

May 26 1980
Aurora AFX British Formula 1 meeting

Aurora AFX British Formula 1	Eliseo Salazar (Williams FW07)
Pre '74 Formula Ford 1600 qualification race	Cyril Levy (Titan MK6)
Pre '74 Formula Ford 1600	Chris Woodcock (Dulon MP15)
Wendy Wools Special Saloons	Tony Dickinson (Skoda 130RS)
Austin Morris Mini 850	Jonathan Lewis
Thoroughbred Sports	Reg Woodcock (Triumph TR3)

August 25 1980
BARC meeting

Muraspec Formula 4	Ian Briggs (Delta 804)
MGCC BCV8 Championship	Martin Harvey (MGB)
Formula 1300	Chris Kite (ERM U2 MK20B)
Oceanair Clubmans Sports	Nigel Corry (Mallock MK21)
STP Modified Sports	Mike Chittenden (Ginetta G4)
Varley Batteries Monoposto	Alex Lowe (Chevron B20)
P&O Ferries Formula Ford 1600	Rob Tennant (Royale RP26)

September 7 1980
Aurora AFX British Formula 1 meeting

Aurora AFX Formula 1	Eliseo Salazar (Williams FW07B)
Tricentrol British Touring Cars	Gordon Spice (Ford Capri)
Shell Super Sunbeams	Barrie Williams
Willhire Historic GT	Malcolm Clube (McLaren M1C)
Classic Sports	John Corfield (Diva GT)
Motorcraft Formula Ford 2000	Tim Davies (Royale RP27)
BMW County Championship	Andy Rouse

September 28 1980	
BARC meeting	
Mini Miglia	Rick Cutting
Varley Batteries Formula Junior	John Narcisi (Lotus 20)
Derwent Sports 2000	Mike Blanchet (Lola T590)
Wendy Wools Special Saloons	Tony Dickinson (Skoda 130RS)
Hitachi Formula Atlantic	David Leslie (Ralt RT4)
STP Modified Sports	Rob Cox (Caterham 7)
Motorcraft Formula Ford 2000	Mike Taylor (Royale RP27)
Classic Saloons	Terry Heley (Ford Zodiac)

A month later, the Championship Finals meeting heralded the climax of the Vandervell British Formula 3 championship. This would be the 20th race in a demanding season and three drivers arrived at Thruxton with a chance of sealing the title. Kenny Acheson, Roberto Guerrero and Stefan Johansson were the contenders, and all three would later reach grand prix racing with varying degrees of success.

October 26 1980	
Championship Finals meeting	
Vandervell British Formula 3	Stefan Johansson (Ralt RT3)
Monroe Production Saloons	Gerry Marshall (Ford Capri)
Oceanair Clubmans Sports	Malcolm Jackson (Mallock MK20)
Wendy Wools Special Saloons	Tony Dickinson (Skoda 130RS)
STP Modified Sports	Rob Cox (Caterham 7)
P&O Ferries Formula Ford 1600	David McClelland (Van Diemen RF80)

However, Johansson had seemed beaten with four races to go and needed to win all of them and take fastest lap to steal the title. Remarkably, under the management of Ron Dennis in the Project Four team, he did just that and won the title. This would be a springboard into Formula 2 for 1981, then on to Formula 1 and later Indycars and ultimately team management. Stefan won the Thruxton race by beating off the determined challenge of Guerrero. Acheson lost his chances by spinning after a clash with Rob Wilson under braking for Club.

At the November TV meeting, Peter Baldwin was confirmed as Wendy Wools Special Saloon champion from Tony Dickinson. Both were regular winners at Thruxton and crowd favourites during the golden era for the championship. The 1000cc section was tied between Brian Cutting (Sunbeam Stiletto) and the late Barry Reece (Mini), with Reece taking the title on a tie-break.

November 8 1980	
BARC Television meeting	
Wendy Wools Formula 3	Rob Wilson (Ralt RT3)
Formula Ford 1600	Tommy Byrne (Van Diemen RF80)
Wendy Wools Special Saloons	Tony Dickinson (Skoda 130RS)
Minis	John Simpson
Formula Ford 2000	Mike Taylor (Royale RP27)
Production Saloons	Gerry Marshall (Ford Capri)

It was for his giant-killing exploits in his screaming BDA-engined Mini Special Saloon that Baldwin is best remembered at Thruxton. Over a 13-year period, he scored countless wins in the car, notably during the years of the Wendy Wools Special Saloon Championship and frequently beat far more powerful cars.

'One memorable race was with Gerry Marshall with 'Baby Bertha', the Chevvy-engined Vauxhall Firenza. It was when all the bumps were there and Gerry used to brake for the big bump at Church. I used to go over it flat, take off and the car would jump about six feet sideways and the momentum took me under his wing to go up to the Chicane. The Mini was pulling over 11,000rpm up there and on the last lap, I was just tucked under his wing. When Gerry went to brake, I went up the inside of him and beat him to the line. Poor old Gerry, he couldn't believe that a Mini had beaten 'Baby Bertha'! Normally, you'd change up at about 10,200rpm but this huge thing was just drafting the Mini along in this big vacuum,' recalls Baldwin.

'Later on, Ginger Marshall was there with his Reliant Kitten and I did a 1m20-something lap, which was the first time the 1300cc Special Saloons had lapped at more than 100mph. That was very quick! You were flat out all the way round the back, but the car used to be really on the ragged edge through Village. Usually in the wet, the Mini was really good against the big cars, like Tony Dickinson's 2-litre Skoda and the Capris of Mick Hill and Tony Strawson earlier on,' says Baldwin.

Like Baldwin, Dickinson raced at Thruxton over more than two decades and was another crowd-favourite. 'I grew up in karting, racing with Roger Williamson and we both went into Special Saloons. In the late 1960s I raced in the Hepolite Glacier series in an 850cc Mini against Roger and one day in the soaking rain at Thruxton I finished fourth overall! The car was awash inside,' recalls Dickinson.

Mike Blanchet has a
hairy moment after
going straight
through the Chicane
in his Formula 3 Lola
in May 1980.
Photo: Simon Hare.

September 1980.
Ray Mallock makes
a presentation to the
marshals who
helped him after his
major accident in
May. Photo: Tony
Lambden.

Having destroyed his
Surtees in the accident
at Goodwood in May,
Ray Mallock returned in
September with a Wolf
for the Aurora Formula 1
race in September.
Photo: Trevor Collins.

David Sears narrowly heads Eddie Jordan in a Formula 3 battle at Easter 1980.

Peter Baldwin and Tony Dickinson lead the Special Saloon pack in 1980. Photo: Tony Lambden.

Jeff Allam flies the Chicane kerbs in the mighty Rover SD1 during the 1980 season. Photo: Fred Taylor.

'I enjoyed every minute of it. Treated with respect, Thruxton is a good, fast and safe circuit. It's got smoother over the years but that hasn't changed the character. Peter Griffin at Wendy Wools was very good to us for many seasons. The Thruxton finals meeting at the end of the season was always make or break for the championship,' says Dickinson.

Later, when racing an Escort RS2000 in the British Touring Car Championship, Tony had a major scare when the fire extinguisher broke loose during a Thruxton race and discharged itself inside the car. To add insult to injury, the car was then disqualified after the race for being underweight!

After the ambitious plans announced in 1978, there was a major change at the Thruxton-based racing school in March 1981 with the news that Ian Taylor, Chief Instructor at the Scorpion school, had taken over the running of the school with assistance from James Weaver. The school re-opened in May with three Tiga Formula Ford 1600s and a pair of Sports 2000 chassis.

March 22 1981	
BARC meeting	
Wendy Wools Special Saloons	Alan Humberstone (Sunbeam Stiletto)
Oceanair Clubmans Sports	Malcolm Jackson (Mallock MK20B)
STP Modified Sports	Pat Thomas (Lotus Elan)
Esso Formula Ford 1600	Howard Groos (Pacer FF81)
Staw Renault 5	Brian Farminer
Monroe Production Saloons	Gerry Marshall (Ford Capri)

The drama of Easter 1981 happened even before qualifying started when, during pre-race testing on Thursday, Mike Thackwell had a massive accident in the works Ralt-Honda RH6. The car bottomed badly on only his third lap and turned sharp left into the barriers at Kimpton. It took 45 minutes to release Thackwell from the wreckage with a broken heel and toe. After a meteoric rise through the junior racing classes Thackwell was likely to be out of racing for eight weeks as a result. Nevertheless, the pace in qualifying was faster than ever before and Belgian Thierry Boutsen set the pole time in a blistering 1m06.38s with his March 812. This was the first ever sub-1m07s lap of Thruxton, while in the race, Marc Surer (March 812) set a new outright record of 1m8.00s (124.73mph). However, the Marches may have had the edge in terms of single laps, but it was the German-backed Maurers that won a race in which tyres played a typically important part.

'In 1981 we decided to put Thierry Boutsen on Bridgestone tyres. He and I went to a race in Japan and saw what we thought was a very good product. We flew the tyres back as hand luggage on Aeroflot through Moscow! We were on pole and led the race until the front tyre failed,' recalls John Wickham, March Formula 2 Team Manager at the time.

The race ended with a one-two for the Maurers of Roberto Guerrero and Eje Elgh but there were post-race protests over the bodywork of the Gustav Brunner-designed cars. Initially Elgh was disqualified from second over the size of rear wing end plates, but

Kenny Acheson (March 812) at speed in the 1981 Formula 2 race. Photo: Chris Davies

March 8 1981	
Formula 3 meeting	
Marlboro British Formula 3	Jonathan Palmer (Ralt RT3)
CAV Production Sports	Tony Lanfranchi (Porsche 911SC)
Townsend Thoresen Formula Ford 1600	Rick Morris (Royale RP29)
Oceanair Clubmans Sports	Richard Mallock (Mallock MK21B)
Monroe Production Saloons	Gerry Marshall (Ford Capri)
Pace British Formula Ford 2000	Ian Briggs (Lola T580)
Mini Miglia	Rick Cutting

Guerrero remained the winner. Eventually, after several hearings and appeals, Elgh was reinstated in the results at an FIA Court of Appeal in late September. Instead, the team was fined 3000 francs.

At a club meeting on June 14th, a new medical centre was opened thanks to a generous donation by the Phil Winter Memorial Fund. At that meeting Tommy Byrne, another in a string of gifted Irish racers that proliferated at the time, won the Pace Petroleum British Formula Ford 2000 race for Van Diemen and then jumped into a Shell Sunbeam for a Celebrity race and won that as well. As was now becoming the norm at Thruxton, the June meeting was followed by a lengthy summer break before racing resumed with the August Bank Holiday Monday meeting.

The Autosport headline for that meeting read 'Da Silva again'. Young Brazilian Ayrton Senna da Silva dominated the Townsend Thoresen Formula Ford 1600 race on his way to adding that title to the RAC title he had already clinched. Observers undoubtedly noted a fine talent emerging, but few people present that day would have predicted that Ayrton would go on to become one of the greatest drivers the world has even seen.

Closing the season was the traditional TV meeting in November which, unusually, included the final rounds of several season-long championships. Remarkably, the winners of the Star of Tomorrow Formula Ford 1600 and Formula Ford 2000 races both came from the small mid-Wales town of Lampeter! Karl Jones (FF1600) and Tim Davies (FF2000) had both chosen racing rather than the rallying that dominated their home region. Dave Scott romped to victory in the non-championship Formula 3 race with, as ever, backing from the family owned Swift Caravans concern.

Whilst still racing for fun, Ian Taylor was ploughing his energy into developing the racing school

Geoff Lees (Ralt-Honda) takes his place on the grid for the 1981 Easter Monday Formula 2 race. Photo: Trevor Collins

Easter 1981. Stefan Johansson and Eje Elgh share a joke before the Formula 2 race. Photo: Fred Taylor.

1981 Formula 2 winner Roberto Guerrero is flanked by second-placed Eje Elgh (right) and Ricardo Paletti (third). Photo: Fed Taylor.

April 18/20 1981
P&O European Formula 2 meeting

European Formula 2	Roberto Guerrero (Maurer MM81)
Tricentrol British Touring Cars	Vince Woodman (Ford Capri)
Marlboro British Formula 3	Thierry Tassin (Ralt RT3/81)
P&O Ferries Formula 1600	Alfonso Toledano (Van Diemen RF81)
European Formula Super Vee	John Nielsen (Ralt RT5)

May 4 1981
Brooklands Raceday

Marlboro Formula 3	Mike White (March 813)
Willhire Historic GT	Malcolm Clube (McLaren M1C)
Varley Batteries Formula Junior	Roy Drew (Lola MK2)
Thoroughbred Sports	Reg Woodcock (Triumph TR3)
Post Historic Road Sports	Roger Mac (Jaguar E-Type)
Seldon Classic Sports	John Brindley (Lotus 23)
Bentley and Brooklands Handicap	Ian Bentall (Bentley MK6)

June 14 1981
BARC meeting

Pre '74 Formula Ford 1600 qualification race	Peter Hancock (Merlyn MK20A)
Pre '74 Formula Ford 1600	Steve Bradley (Van Diemen RF73)
Shell Sunbeam Celebrity race	Tommy Byrne
BARC/MGOC	Dr Spike Milligan (MGA)
Pace British Formula Ford 2000	Tommy Byrne (Van Diemen RF81)
Wendy Wools Special Saloons	Pat Mannion (Sunbeam Stiletto)
Wilcomatic Production Saloons	Gerry Marshall (Ford Capri)

August 31 1981
BARC meeting

Formula 1300	Chris Kite (ERM U2 MK20B)
Varley Batteries Monoposto	Tony Broster (Lyncar FA001)
MGCC BCV8	David Franklin (MGB V8)
Pre '57 Saloons	Roger Andreason (Jaguar MK1)
STP Modified Sports	Rob Cox (Caterham 7)
Muraspec Formula 4	Brian Turner (BTC 004)
Townsend Thoresen Formula Ford 1600	Ayrton da Silva (Van Diemen RF81)
Pace British Formula Ford 2000	Tim Davies (Royale RP30)

Roberto Guerrero guides the Maurer to victory in 1981. Photo: Chris Davies.

September 20 1981	
British Touring Car meeting	
Tricentrol British Touring Cars	Jeff Allam (Rover V8)
Formula Atlantic	Ray Mallock (Ralt RT4)
Derwent Sports 2000	John Sheldon (Tiga SC81)
Mini Sevens	Nigel Gaymer
Ford Fiesta Challenge	Rob Hall
Unipart Metro Challenge	Paul Taft
RAC British Formula Ford 1600	Andrew Gilbert-Scott (Van Diemen RF81)
Protectol Clubmans Sports	Richard Mallock (Mallock MK23)

October 25 1981	
BARC Championship Finals meeting	
Marlboro British Formula 3	Thierry Tassin (Ralt RT3/81)
STP Modified Sports	Steve Soper (Fiat X1/9)
Oceanair Clubmans Sports	Malcolm Jackson (Mallock MK20B)
Wendy Wools Special Saloons	Brian Cutting (Sunbeam Stiletto)
Monroe Production Saloons	Gerry Marshall (Ford Capri)
P&O Ferries Formula Ford 1600	Enrique Mansilla (Van Diemen RF81)

and in April 1982, the school, now called the Ian Taylor Racing Drivers' School, added three brand new Lancia Beta Coupes to their fleet. With a strong business sense, Taylor started to develop corporate business alongside race tuition and the school's popular open days.

In the early 1980s, the school was fairly quiet but then started to build into the mid-80s as Taylor moved the emphasis into the corporate market and the circuit experience type days for the public. 'Then, in 1985 we first started to do manufacturer track days. The following year, we did 50 track days all over the UK for Rover and that was really the fore-runner of the track day programme,' says Bill Coombs, an instructor at the time.

At the end of 1982, the managers at Leyland had sat Bill down and made him decide about his future. Was he going to take the security of a career with the company or was he going to go off and go racing? 'They looked at me as though I was insane when I said I was going to carry on racing. I was trying to be a professional racing driver until about 1987. Then I finally decided that my future was more with the school than as a driver. And I could earn more money out of the school!'

It was not only Coombs who found the school changing his life. Ian Flux was similarly influenced by working with Ian Taylor. 'Through Ian and the school it changed a lot of our lives. All of a sudden we could have a sort of a full-time job without having a proper job. When the corporate days arrived they transformed our lives as suddenly we were on £80 a day. It still gave us the time to go and sort out deals because you only really needed £150 to get through the week,' says Flux.

Eje Elgh (left) and grand prix racer Keke Rosberg in the paddock.
Photo: Chris Davies.

November 7 1981
BARC Television meeting

Canon Copiers Formula 3	Dave Scott (Ralt RT3/81)
Star of Tomorrow Formula Ford 1600	Karl Jones (Royale RP29)
Pace British Formula Ford 2000	Tim Davies (Royale RP30)
Wendy Wools Special Saloons	Tony Dickinson (Skoda 130RS)
Mini Challenge	Stewart Fowler
Protectol Clubmans Sports	Chris Hodgetts (Mallock MK23B)

March 14 1982
Formula 3 meeting

Marlboro Formula 3	Tommy Byrne (Ralt RT3C/81)
Oceanair Clubmans Sports	Malcolm Jackson (Mallock MK20B)
Wendy Wools Special Saloons	Peter Baldwin (Mini)
Sports 2000	Richard Eyre (Tiga SC81)
Monroe Production Saloons	Graham Scarborough (Ford Capri)
Townsend Thoresen Formula Ford 1600	Andrew Gilbert-Scott (Reynard FF82)
Mini Miglia	Mike Fry

April 10/12 1982
P&O European Formula 2 meeting

European Formula 2	Johnny Cecotto (March 822)
Trientrol British Touring Cars	Vince Woodman (Ford Capri)
Marlboro Formula 3	Tommy Byrne (Ralt RT3C/81)
P&O Ferries Formula Ford 1600	Gianfranco Cane (Van Diemen RF82)

Although an inherently safe track, the high speeds attained at Thruxton did sometimes have disastrous consequences when things went wrong. And it certainly went wrong for impecunious Formula 3 racer Tony Trevor on Easter Monday 1982 during the Formula 2 meeting sponsored by P&O European Ferries. Trevor had a huge accident at Church when he lost control of his Ralt RT3. The car cartwheeled to destruction across the field on the outside of the corner and virtually reached the hedge at the circuit perimeter. Trevor was lucky to escape with injuries that included a broken arm and ankle. A BARC marshal, Mark Richards, cracked a bone in his leg when he slipped down a rabbit hole while running to the accident! Trevor spent a couple of weeks in hospital recovering from his injuries but later made a full recovery after a frightening accident.

Former world motorbike champion Johnny Cecotto won the Formula 2 feature in a works March 822 despite having to make a pit stop to change a tyre. He took the lead with just four of the 55 laps to go. Stefan Johansson led for 26 laps from pole before he too had a tyre explode. Johansson pitted and then fought back to second behind Cecotto when his Spirit Honda shed a wheel nut and pitched him into the bank on the exit of Segrave. In the closing laps, Cecotto and Johansson had to catch and pass Thierry Boutsen and Kenny Acheson who were struggling with tyre problems. In fact, tyres were the big talking point of the weekend. In a dramatic race, Corrado Fabi (March 822) also led before a stone hit a chunk out of his distributor and put him out. A big shunt at Allard on the first lap eliminated Thierry Tassin and Roberto del Castello.

Johansson had taken pole with a stunning lap in 1m05.33s, while Fabi and Cecotto both qualified under the 1m06s mark. In the race, Cecotto set a new outright record in 1m07.37s (125.90mph), the first time that the record had broken through the 125mph barrier. It would be seven years before the record was broken again.

Although circuit time for racing cars remained severely restricted, road car use of the circuit was permitted during week days and Thruxton was a popular venue for motor manufacturers to show off their models to prospective customers. On one such day in May 1982, cricket star Ian Botham managed to crash two Saab 900s, both at Church!

May 3 1982
Brooklands Raceday

Post Historic Road Sports	John Atkins (AC Cobra)
Gates Varley Formula Junior	John Brindley (Lotus 22)
Thoroughbred Sports	Reg Woodcock (Triumph TR3)
Pre '65 Single Seaters	Mike Littlewood (Brabham BT2)
Atlantic Computers Historic GT	Ray Mallock (Lola T70MK3B)
Brooklands Handicap	Robert Campbell (Austin)
Seldon Classic Sports	John Brindley (Lotus 23)
Reliant 750 Formula	Gary Randall (Hague 767)

May 29/31 1982
British Touring Car meeting

Tricentrol British Touring Cars	Vince Woodman (Ford Capri)
British Formula 1	Jim Crawford (Ensign N180B)
P&O Ferries Formula Ford 1600	Gianfranco Cane (Van Diemen RF82)
Ford Fiesta Challenge	Charles Tippett
Staw Renault 5	Brian Farminer
Muraspec Formula 4	Brian Turner (BTC 004)

August 30 1982
BARC meeting

Formula 1300	Martyn Lane (Mallock MK16)
Gates Varley Monoposto	Terry Mills (March 743)
MG Midgets	Tim Cairns
Muraspec Formula 4	Max Samuel-Camps (Ralt RT1)
Classic Saloons	Dave Burrows (Jaguar MK1)
Pace British Formula Ford 2000	Ayrton da Silva (Van Diemen RF82)
MGCC BCV8	Mike Chalk
P&O Ferries Formula Ford 1600	Mauricio Gugelmin (Van Diemen RF82)

September 19 1982
BARC meeting

Shell Sunbeams	Steve Soper
Mini Sevens	Nigel Gaymer
RAC British Formula Ford 1600	Julian Bailey (Lola T640)
Lucas CAV Production Sports	Steve Cole (Morgan +8)
Pre '74 Formula Ford 1600	Peter Rogers (Merlyn MK20A)
Unipart Metro Challenge	Patrick Watts
BARC/MGOC Championship	John Hewitt (MGB)
Esso Formula Ford 1600	Rick Morris (Royale RP31M)

When racing resumed at the end of August, there was tragedy in the MG Midget race when Manchester racer Tony Williams suffered a heart attack while leading the race in his modified Midget. He then crashed at Allard where the rescue crews worked hard but were unable to revive him.

Having won at Thruxton in Formula Ford and Formula Ford 2000, it was fitting that Tommy Byrne clinched the Marlboro British Formula 3 title by finishing second to Martin Brundle on Championship Finals day. Byrne needed to finish ahead of rival Enrique Mansilla to clinch the title and that was just what he did in a controlled drive as Mansilla finished third on a wet track. A few days later, many of the Formula 3 teams were back at Thruxton testing in readiness for the TV meeting on November 13th. The sensation of that test was Ayrton Senna da Silva who not only shattered the existing Formula 3 lap record, but lapped consistently beneath the record in the West Surrey Racing Ralt RT3. Team manager Dick Bennetts was impressed with Ayrton's aptitude and his cool approach to his Formula 3 debut.

October 24 1982
BARC Championship Finals meeting

Marlboro Formula 3	Martin Brundle (Ralt RT3D/82)
STP Modified Sports	Richard Gamble (Marcos GT)
Wendy Wools Special Saloons	Peter Baldwin (Marshall Mini)
Oceanair Clubmans Sports	Peter Richings (Mallock MK21M)
Monroe Production Saloons	Gerry Marshall (Ford Capri)
BP Junior Formula Ford 1600	Mark Newby (Royale RP31M)

November 13 1982
City Business Machines Television meeting

Formula 3	Ayrton Senna da Silva (Ralt RT3D/82)
Special GT	Jeff Wilson (BMW M1)
Formula Ford 2000	Tim Davies (Van Diemen RF82)
Formula Ford 1600 Qualification race	David Mears (Van Diemen RF81)
Formula Ford 1600	Rick Morris (Royale RP33M)
Sports 2000	Mike Taylor (Royale S2000M)

After winning both the Formula Ford 2000 titles in 1982, Ayrton went home to Brazil for some sunshine and talked to his sponsors about contesting the City Business Machines Thruxton Formula 3 race, his first in the

Rad Dougall explores the limits of a Group 1 Rover through the Chicane in May 1982.
Photo: Trevor Collins.

A dejected Corrado Fabi (March 822) surrenders the lead of the 1982 Formula 2 race.
Photo: Trevor Collins.

With several photographers unaware of the impending danger, Thierry Tassin shunts heavily off the grid at the start of the 1982 Formula 2 race.
Photo: Trevor Collins

category. He duly returned to England in time to test before the race which went out live on BBC TV. After winning his first Formula 3 race, Ayrton was invited to meet Ron Dennis at McLaren to discuss his future! 'Obviously the TV race was very important to me and I hope it will help me find the budget for next season,' he said after the race. He won convincingly by 13 seconds from a 26-car field. Second was Bengt Tragardh and fourth was Henri Toivonen, who was warming up for the Lombard RAC Rally that started from Bath a week later!

At the same meeting, there was carnage with three separate accidents in the GT race. Costas Los ended up on top of the bank in his Fiat X1/9 after a first corner multi-car accident in which anaesthetist David Enderby broke an ankle when his new VW Karmann Ghia-clone was hit by John Salisbury's AMC Spirit. Then, to complete the drama, Dale Minton rolled his Escort RS2000 heavily at Kimpton, fortunately without injury.

At the end of the season, Mark Poynton was appointed Competitions' Director of the BARC to succeed Rick Gorne who had left to become General Manager at Reynard Racing cars after a two-year term. Poynton had formerly been with the Thames Estuary Automobile Club, the organisation that pioneered rallycross events in Britain.

More good news for the development of the circuit came when it was announced that the BARC had obtained planning permission to build 15 hospitality suites over the winter as part of the programme of continuing improvements. Up to ten of the units would be ready for the Easter '83 Formula 2 meeting and would be available at £3500 for a two-year lease.

The big occasion of the 1983 season enjoyed backing once more from P&O Ferries. Qualifying times were slightly down on '82, with Mike Thackwell (Ralt-Honda RH6) taking pole on 1m05.78s. The fastest race lap also went to Thackwell in 1m7.70s. The young New Zealander had bravely returned to the track for the first time since his massive accident there two years earlier.

Beppe Gabbiani drove a perfect race to score his second Formula 2 win in two races in an Onyx-run March-BMW 832. The Italian went the distance without tyre problems while his rivals faltered. Coached by engineer Peter Gethin, Gabbiani took it easy in the opening laps having started eighth on the grid, and nursed his tyres as he moved up to second after 17 laps. By lap 25, leader Thackwell had his tyres going off and struggled home second, losing the lead to Gabbiani into the Chicane at the end of lap 37. Gabbiani went on to win by seven seconds after a well-planned drive.

On the same day, Martin Brundle again chased Ayrton Senna, as he was now known, home in the Formula 3 race. 'Why doesn't he make any mistakes?' asked a frustrated Brundle after the race. When they returned in early May for round seven, the result was just the same. To his great credit, Brundle never stopped chasing his rival and was the only driver to match the Brazilian's pace. Indeed, he was the only driver to beat

March 13 1983
Formula 3 meeting

Marlboro British Formula 3	Ayrton Senna da Silva (Ralt RT3E/83)
Esso Formula Ford 1600	Andrew Gilbert-Scott (Lola T642E)
Townsend Thoresen Formula Ford 1600	Andrew Gilbert-Scott (Lola T642E)
Wendy Wools Special Saloons	Peter Baldwin (Mini BDA)
GPI Sports 2000	Ian Taylor (Tiga SC83)
Monroe Production Saloons	Gerry Marshall (Ford Capri)
Jaguars	Roger Wilkinson (MK10)

April 2/4 1983
P&O Ferries Formula 2 meeting

European Formula 2	Beppe Gabbiani (March 832)
Marlboro British Formula 3	Ayrton Senna da Silva (Ralt RT3E/83)
Trimoco RAC British Touring Cars	Peter Lovett (Rover Vitesse)
Ford Credit Fiestas	Dave Loudoun
P&O Ferries Formula Ford 1600	Peter Hardman (Van Diemen RF83)
STP Modified Sports	Rob Cox (Caterham Super 7)

May 2 1983
Brooklands Raceday

Marlboro British Formula 3	Ayrton Senna da Silva (Ralt RT3E/83)
Atlantic Computers Historic GT	John Foulston (McLaren M8C/D)
Post Historic Road Sports	John Atkins (AC Cobra)
Thoroughbred Sports	Mike Salmon (Aston Martin DB4)
Classic Sports	Mike Pendlebury (Lotus 23B)
Brooklands Handicap	Keith Fantom (Humber)
Pre '60 Sports Cars	Chris Smith (Lotus 17)
Pre '65 Single Seaters	John Brindley (Lotus 22)

Senna in a straight fight in Formula 3 that summer and their respective levels of success in Grand Prix racing in subsequent seasons never really did justice to Brundle's ability.

In August 1983, it was announced that a new pits complex was being planned for the circuit, to replace the rather temporary structure that had served for 15 years since the opening of the track. Sidney Offord, Executive Director of the BARC, said that it was now a priority to press ahead with 28 pit garages, a new timekeeping building and a tarmac paddock area behind. Planning permission was still being sought for the project.

In September, Martin Brundle triumphed in the British Formula 3 round during his epic season against Senna and their season-long battle went down to the wire at the final back at Thruxton on October 23rd. Brundle started the final race one point ahead but Senna and the West Surrey Racing team were the class of the field that day and dominated the race to clinch the title. Brundle's Eddie Jordan-entered car was stricken by oversteer and could only finish third behind American Davy Jones.

May 30 1983	
British Touring Car meeting	
Trimoco RAC British Touring Car	Peter Lovett (Rover Vitesse)
Ford Credit Fiestas	Dave Loudoun
P&O Ferries Formula Ford 1600	Andrew Gilbert-Scott (Lola T642E)
Formula 4	Mike Whatley (March 773)
Pre '57 Saloons	Terry Heley (Ford Zephyr)

July 24 1983	
Thundersports meeting	
Thundersports	Eddie Arundel/ James Weaver (Chevron B36)
BARC/MGOC	Grahame Davis (MGB GT V8)
STP Modified Sports	Robert Speak (Lotus Elan)
P&O Ferries Formula Ford 1600	Peter Hardman (Van Diemen RF83)
MG Midgets	Steve Everitt

1983 was the classic year of Ayrton Senna (left) and Martin Brundle in Formula 3. At the final round of the season, they share the applause. Photo: Duncan Hands.

August 29 1983
BARC meeting

Gates Varley Monoposto	Godfrey Hall (Lynx GH2)
Racing Displays British Formula Ford 2000	Tim Davies (Reynard SF83)
Wendy Wools Special Saloons	Pat Mannion (Sunbeam Stiletto)
P&O Ferries Formula Ford 1600	Peter Hardman (Van Diemen RF83)
Formula 1300	Paul Overton (WEV 2B)
STP Modified Sports	Rob Cox (Caterham 7)
Jaguars	Roger Wilkinson (MK1)
750 Formula	Mick Harris (Darvi MK4/5C)

September 18 1983
Formula 3 meeting

Marlboro British Formula 3	Martin Brundle (Ralt RT3E/83)
BARC/MGOC	John Hewitt (MGB)
MG Metros	David Carvell
ASCAR Challenge	Ray Taft (Aston Martin DBS V8)
BP Junior Formula Ford 1600	Graham de Zille (Lola T642E)
Formula 4	Mike Whatley (March 773)
STP Modified Sports	Rob Cox (Caterham Black Brick 3)
MGCC BCV8	John Lodge

October 23 1983
Championship Finals meeting

Marlboro Formula 3	Ayrton Senna da Silva (Ralt RT3)
Racing Displays British Formula Ford 2000	Tim Davies (Reynard 83SF)
Oceanair Clubmans Sports	Dave Orchard (Centaur 14X)
Wendy Wools Special Saloons	Peter Baldwin (Marshall Mini)
Monroe Production Saloons	Gerry Marshall (Ford Capri)
BP Junior Formula Ford 1600	Peter Rose (Lola T640E)

November 12 1983
City Business Machines Television meeting

Formula 3	Davy Jones (Ralt RT3E/83)
BBC Grandstand Trophy Formula Ford 2000	Tim Davies (Reynard 83SF)
Formula Ford 1600 qualification race	Maurice Crockett (Royale RP29)
Formula Ford 1600	David Harper (Van Diemen RF82)
Special Saloons	Peter Baldwin (Marshall Mini)
Mini Seven/Miglia	Chris Lewis (Mini Miglia)

CHAPTER SEVEN

The end of the road for Formula 2

The planning permission for the new pits was granted in February 1984 and work started soon afterwards. Remarkably, while the racing season kicked-off, work continued apace with a target of July for completion. The season opened on March 11th with a Formula 3 race that featured an impressive debut for 21-year old New Zealander Paul Radisich. The Kiwi took pole despite only seeing the circuit for the first time when he walked round it on the Saturday! In the race, he clashed with Canadian Allen Berg at the complex but recovered to finish sixth. Johnny Dumfries won the race, his second Formula 3 win of the season, after a victory at Silverstone a week earlier.

The Formula 2 meeting, the 16th in Thruxton's history, was again backed by P&O Ferries but a disappointing field of only 17 cars arrived. This time, Thackwell got the win he had missed in '83 and drove to a comfortable 22-second victory. Emanuele Pirro finished fourth but his bumpy ride aggravated a shoulder injury sustained in a Formula 3 accident. He left the circuit with his left arm in a sling, unable to take his overalls off! Thackwell took pole in 1m5.68s and set fastest lap in 1m7.38s, one-hundredth of a second outside Johnny Cecotto's lap record. Christian Danner (March 842) was second and Phillipe Streiff (AGS) third. At the same meeting, Salisbury racer Alan Curnow went head-on into the barriers at the Chicane during the Touring Car race in his Datapost Escort and was later diagnosed as having broken his foot. He aimed to be fit for the next Thruxton round at the end of May, however.

Though the Easter meeting was blessed with good weather, it seemed that the notoriously bumpy surface and limited facilities at Thruxton were starting to become a problem with some of the teams and drivers. Was the writing on the wall for the fixture? Sadly, it seemed that it was and Thruxton's severely limited number of track days meant that it simply could not generate the amount of profit needed to compete with venues that had Formula 1 races to bank-roll other activities and investment.

Easter Monday 1984. Canadian Allen Berg gets the Chicane wrong as Johnny Dumfries takes the conventional route. Photo: Duncan Hands.

March 11 1984	
Formula 3 meeting	
Marlboro British Formula 3	Johnny Dumfries (Ralt RT3E/83)
Racing Displays British Formula Ford 2000	Andy Wallace (Reynard SF84)
Townsend Thoresen Formula Ford 1600	Dave Coyne (Van Diemen RF84)
Monroe Production Saloons	Colin Blower (Colt Starion Turbo)
P&O Ferries Formula Ford 1600	Dave Coyne (Van Diemen RF84)
GPI British Sports 2000	Mike O'Brien (Aquila RO83S)
Jaguars	Paul Stephens (MK2)

April 21/23 1984	
P&O Ferries Formula 2 meeting	
European Formula 2	Mike Thackwell (Ralt-Honda RH6/84)
Trimoco RAC British Touring Cars	Andy Rouse (Rover Vitesse)
Marlboro British Formula 3	Johnny Dumfries (Ralt RT3E/83)
Ford Credit Fiestas	Ian Briggs
Wendy Wools Special Saloons	Bob Trotter (Escort Rover)
P&O Ferries Formula Ford 1600	Charles Tilley (Van Diemen RF82)

May 7 1984	
Brooklands Raceday	
Marlboro British Formula 3	Johnny Dumfries (Ralt RT3/83)
Pre '70 Single Seaters	John Foulston (McLaren M19A)
Thoroughbred Sports	Mike Wilds (Aston Martin DB4)
Atlantic Computers Historic GT	John Foulston (McLaren M8)
Post Historic Road Sports	Roger Connel (TVR Griffith)
Pre '65 Single Seaters	John Foulston (Lotus 24)
Pre '60 Sports Cars	Don Shead (Lister Chevrolet)
Classic Sports	Roger Ealand (Marcos GT)

May 28 1984	
British Touring Car meeting	
Trimoco RAC British Touring Cars	Steve Soper (Rover Vitesse)
Mini Seven	Chris Gould
Jaguar Saloons	John Young
Wendy Wools Special Saloons	Terry Nicholls (Ford Capri)
RAC British Formula Ford 1600	Dave Coyne (Van Diemen RF84)
Mini Miglia	Jim McDougall
Pre '57 Saloons	Terry Heley (Ford Zephyr)
ASCAR Challenge	Brian Rice (Chevrolet Camaro)

July 8 1984	
Thundersports meeting	
Thundersports	Ray Bellm/Mike Wilds (Chevron B36)
Sabre Pre '80 Formula Ford 2000	David Jacklin (Lola T580)
BARC/MGOC	Richard Horn (MGB)
Townsend Thoresen Formula Ford 1600	John Pratt (Reynard 84FF)
Donington GT	Jeff Wilson (BMW M1)

The new pits complex was opened at the Thundersports meeting on July 8th 1984. A run of 28 concrete garages and new timekeepers and race control buildings were constructed by local builder A J Dunning

Ltd. The pit road had been widened and a transporter park behind the pits was soon to be completed. Ironically, competitors at the meeting were grateful for the garages as they offered shelter from blazing sunshine! The race was won by Ray Bellm and Mike Wilds in the former's Chevron B36, which had undergone an engine change in the pit garage after qualifying.

At just such a Thundersports meeting, Bill Coombs had one of the more embarrassing moments of his racing career. 'I was doing a Thundersports race in a Royale Sports 2000 with Mark Goddard and I was on my last lap before pitting to hand over when a rear wheel centre pulled out as I turned into Church flat out!' The car speared off into the field, bounced but thankfully stayed the right way up and finally came to a halt near the hedge. The first marshal on the scene was Fred Reeves, part of the team at the racing school. 'I took a lot of stick for that...' recalls Coombs.

Also on the programme for that July Thundersports meeting was a round of the popular Donington-based GT Championship. It was a race that ended in dramatic style for Tony Sugden racing the AET Engineering Lotus Esprit Turbo. 'Going up into the Chicane, the engine blew in a big way and sprayed oil all over the turbocharger. Instantly, the back of the car was a ball of flame. I managed to keep it going the right way and by blipping the throttle a couple of times it sucked most of the fire out, but the photographs were pretty spectacular!' Sugden guided the car to a halt after the Chicane where the marshals doused him and the car in extinguishant.

At the very last Formula 2 race, held at Brands Hatch in September 1984, Sidney Offord announced that the BARC was going to eradicate the notorious bump at Church before the start of the 1985 season. 'It's going to cost us £20,000 but we will do it,' he said. However, Ron Tauranac and Mike Thackwell are reported to have told him that the challenge of getting over the bump was the best reason for racing at Thruxton.

August 27 1984	
BARC meeting	
Racing Displays British Formula Ford 2000	Tim Davies (Reynard SF84)
Monoposto Class A	George Whitehead (WRA 82M)
Monoposto Class B	Simon Davey (Van Diemen RF78)
Formula 1300	Martin Walford (WEV 2B)
Pre '74 Formula Ford 1600	Jesse Crosse (Merlyn MK17)
Formula 4	Mike Whatley (Delta T81/4)
Road-Going MG Midgets	Peter Hiley
Reliant 750 Formula	Simon Fry (Nimrod MK2A)

Alan Curnow charges the Chicane barriers aboard the Datapost Escort in 1984. Photos: Frank Cowburn.

September 30 1984
Formula 3 meeting

Marlboro British Formula 3	Johnny Dumfries (Ralt RT3/83/4)
Racing Displays British Formula Ford 2000	Mauricio Gugelmin (Reynard 84SF)
Esso Formula Ford 1600	John Pratt (Reynard 84FF)
Wendy Wools Special Saloons	Alan Humberstone (Skoda S130RS)
MG Metro Challenge	David Carvell
74-78 Formula Ford 1600	Christian Radage (Merlyn MK31)
Special GT	Rob Cox (Lotus Elan)

October 21 1984
Championship Finals meeting

Racing Displays British Formula Ford 2000	Andy Wallace (Reynard 84SF)
BP Junior Formula Ford 1600	Ross Hockenhull (Reynard 84FF)
Wendy Wools Special Saloons	Ginger Marshall (Reliant Kitten)
Oceanair Clubmans Sports	Mike Sanders (Mallock MK24B)
P&O Ferries Formula Ford 1600	Jonathan Bancroft (Reynard 84FF)
Monroe Production Saloons	Andy McLennan (Colt Starion Turbo)
Special GT	Rob Cox (Lotus Elan)

At the 1984 Championship Finals meeting in October, Ross Hockenhull won the final round of the BP Superfind Junior Formula Ford 1600 Championship. In his wake, youngsters Mark Blundell and Damon Hill battled for second and their tussle was only settled when Hill spun at Club on the final lap and dropped to fourth. Hockenhull went on to race in Formula 3 before quitting the sport, but the men he beat that day did rather better!

November 17 1984
City Business Machines meeting

BBC Grandstand Trophy Formula Ford 2000	Martin Donnelly (Reynard 84SF)
Formula Ford 1600	John Booth (Reynard 84FF)
MGs	Tim Cairns (Midget)
Clubmans Sports	Paul Gibson (Vision V85A)
Porsches	Barry Robinson (Carrera)

March 10 1985
Formula 3 meeting

Marlboro British Formula 3	Russell Spence (Reynard 853)
Racing Displays British Formula Ford 2000	Dave Coyne (Van Diemen RF85)
Monroe Production Saloons	Andy McLennan (Colt Starion Turbo)
Powerscreen Sports 1600	Dave Orchard (Centaur 14X)
MGA/TR Challenge	Nick Parrott (MGA)
B&Q British Sports 2000	Ian Flux (Aquila RO83S)
Pre '68 Jaguars	Rob Newall (MK2)

The traditional end of year meeting was a little different in 1984. Absent were the Formula 3 cars and TV cameras, but City Business Machines provided backing for a third year. Despite the lack of cameras, the feature race was a round of the Brands Hatch-based BBC Grandstand Trophy Championship for Formula Ford 2000 cars, which was won by rising Irish star Martin Donnelly.

The 1985 season kicked off with testing in late February and with the switch from Formula 2 to Formula 3000 for the new season, several teams tested in readiness for the Easter meeting. However, with a vast range of cars from road-going MGs upwards, clear laps were few and far between. Mike Thackwell was quickest in the latest Ralt and managed a 1m7.95s on a cold day. The bump at Church had been removed, as Sidney Offord had promised the previous autumn.

The 1985 Easter meeting was sponsored by Townsend Thoresen, who took over from long-time backers P&O Ferries. However, it was still in the family as P&O had recently been taken over

Mike Thackwell and team boss Ron Tauranac before the 1985 Formula 3000 race. Photo: Fred Taylor.

February 1985. Mike Thackwell avoids the snow to test the new Formula 3000 Ralt. Photo: John Gaisford.

by Townsend Thoresen. In the first meeting of the season, Bradford racer Russell Spence won the Formula 3 race at what had always been a bogey track for him. Some extensive tuition from Ian Taylor at the school had sorted out his lines and put him right on the pace. He beat Tim Davies, a Thruxton ace in Formula Ford 2000, and Brazilian Mauricio Gugelmin to win the race.

The Easter meeting was the second round of the new European Formula 3000 Championship, which had started at Silverstone two weeks earlier. It was a dramatic race with a shower of rain, while the cars were on the grid, throwing tyre choice into confusion. Emanuele Pirro started his Marlboro Onyx March 85B on slicks and took the lead on lap nine. Mike Thackwell

April 6/8 1985	
Townsend Thoresen Formula 3000 meeting	
European Formula 3000	Emanuele Pirro (March 85B)
Marlboro British Formula 3	Russell Spence (Reynard 853)
Trimoco RAC British Touring Cars	Dave Brodie (Colt Starion Turbo)
Racing Displays British Formula Ford 2000	John Pratt (Van Diemen RF85)
Ford Credit Fiestas	Graham Hathaway

The start of the only European Formula 3000 race at Thruxton, Easter 1985. Photo: Fred Taylor.

(Ralt RT20) started from pole having lapped in 1m6.33s, but had to stop early to replace a nosecone damaged in early battling. Once back on the circuit he chased hard after Pirro and started the final lap less than a second behind the leader. However, Pirro had kept just a little in reserve, and was able to hold on for a superbly-judged victory. In fifth place was young Italian newcomer Gabriele Tarquini, paying his first ever visit to the circuit. He would return to Thruxton nearly 10 years later to win Touring Car races. Christian Danner set the fastest race lap at 1m9.40s. In the supporting Formula 3 race, the new Ralt RT30 nearly scored its first win over the previously dominant Reynard 853s. However, Mauricio Gugelmin spun at Church on the final lap and handed victory to Russell Spence.

May Bank Holiday Monday produced a dramatic meeting headlined by Formula 3 and Touring Cars. Reports of the Touring Car race made the national daily papers after Barry Sheene's Toyota Supra was involved in a destructive eight-car accident at Allard on the first lap. Sheene's car was nudged into a spin and was T-boned in the driver's door by Chris Hodgetts (Escort) who was driving almost blind in the spray. Patrick Watts (Escort) was also eliminated. Early reports that Sheene was trapped in the wreckage were unfounded and he was able to drive himself home before a broken bone in his foot was diagnosed. The impact pushed the drivers door in as far as the seat but Sheene saw the Escort coming and squeezed out of the way. Since then, door bars have improved the safety of drivers involved in similar incidents.

In the Formula 3 race, Russell Spence lost his championship lead after sliding off at Allard. Out of the Chicane, he challenged second-placed Tim Davies on the right and was squeezed into the pit lane exit road as neither was prepared to give way. Although there was no contact, Spence then slid off at Allard and ended his race against the barriers. Davies was later fined £50

while Andy Wallace won the race and ultimately the title. That meeting witnessed the first British race for Renault 5 Turbos which was won by grand prix racer Jonathan Palmer in the celebrity car. The Townsend Thoresen Formula Ford 1600 race at the same meeting had a top four comprising Bertrand Gachot, Damon Hill, Mark Blundell and Johnny Herbert!

May 6 1985	
Formula 3 meeting	
Marlboro British Formula 3	Gary Evans (Ralt RT30)
Thundersports	John Brindley/John Foulston (Lola T530)
Mini Miglia	David Carvell
Wendy Wools Special Saloons	Brian Chatfield (BMW 320)
Mini Seven	Michael Jackson

May 27 1985	
British Touring Car meeting	
Marlboro British Formula 3	Andy Wallace (Reynard 853)
Trimoco RAC British Touring Cars	Andy Rouse (Ford Sierra Turbo)
Ford Credit Fiestas	Matt Johnson
Renault 5 Turbos	Jonathan Palmer
MG Metro	Paul Taft
RAC/Townsend Thoresen Formula Ford 1600	Bertrand Gachot (Van Diemen RF85)

July 7 1985
Brooklands meeting

Failsafe Historic GT	John Foulston (McLaren M8C)
Classic Sports	Steve Hitchins (Lotus 23B)
Pre '70 Single Seaters	John Foulston (McLaren M19A)
Post Historic Road Sports	John Atkins (AC Cobra)
Thoroughbred Sports	Reg Woodcock (Triumph TR3)
Formula Junior/ Historic Formula 3	Keith Norman (Brabham BT28)
Pre '60 Sports Cars	Mike Freeman (Lister Jaguar)

August 26 1985
BARC meeting

Townsend Thoresen Junior Formula Ford 1600	Adrian Willmott (Van Diemen RF85)
BARC/MGOC	Grahame Davis (MGB GTV8)
74-78 Formula Ford 1600	Jeff Gresswell (Hawke DL19)
Pre '80 Formula Ford 2000/Monoposto A	Peter Boutwood (Lola T580)
Wendy Wools Special Saloons	Brian Chatfield (BMW 320)
Failsafe Historic GT	John Foulston (McLaren M8C)
Pre '65 Saloons	Phil Wight (Lotus Cortina)
TUK Monoposto B	Simon Davey (Kinell 85MB)

September 15 1985
BARC meeting

B&Q British Sports 2000	Ian Flux (Royale RP38)
Renault 5 Turbos	David Kay
Esso Formula Ford 1600	Paulo Carcasci (Van Diemen RF85)
Shell Oils Thundersaloons	Vince Woodman/ Jonathan Buncombe (Ford Capri)
Donington Formula Ford 2000	Ross Hockenhull (Reynard 84SF)
Road Saloons	David Shead (Ford Capri)

Hill was back in the news at the September meeting when he had a road accident on the way to the meeting. Damon and then-girlfriend Georgie were innocent parties when their Escort was hit by another car that was overtaking. Damon was unhurt but Georgie suffered whiplash and needed hospital treatment before they both travelled on to the circuit in a borrowed car. Hill missed the qualifying session for the Esso Formula Ford 1600 race and had to start from the back of the grid with a 10-second penalty, from where he fought up to sixth place before heading off to try and find another car to replace the written off Escort!

October 20 1985
Championship Finals meeting

Racing Displays British Formula Ford 2000	John Pratt (Van Diemen RF85)
RAC/Townsend Thoresen Formula Ford 1600	Bertrand Gachot (Van Diemen RF85)
Powerscreen Sports 1600	Dave Orchard (Centaur 14X)
Wendy Wools Special Saloons	Rod Birley (Ford Sierra)
Monroe Production Saloons	Colin Blower (Colt Starion Turbo)
Townsend Thoresen Junior Formula Ford 1600	Jason Elliott (Van Diemen RF85)
BARC/MGOC	John Simpson (Midget)

The 1985 Championship Finals meeting had no Formula 3 race. Instead, the feature race was the 20th and final round of the British Formula Ford 2000 Championship. However, Canadian Bertrand Fabi had secured the title two weeks earlier at Oulton Park at the expense of Martin Donnelly, and neither of them were in the thin 11-car field. The mercurial John Pratt won the race during a career that never took him as far as his obvious talents deserved. Tragically, Fabi lost his life a few months later when testing a Formula 3 car at Goodwood in readiness for the 1986 season. The Townsend Thoresen Formula Ford title went down to the wire, however, as Bertrand Gachot won the race and the championship after fending off impressive junior Formula Ford racer Jason Elliott. Mark Blundell was a title contender going into the race but crashed out almost immediately along with Damon Hill.

The news that many had been expecting for several seasons finally came in December 1985, when the BARC announced that it had withdrawn Thruxton from the 1986 Formula 3000 calendar. It was a simple question of economics. The FOCA regulations for Formula 3000 in '86 required a prize fund of around £100,000 and the Club decided that the potential loss on such an outlay

The wreck of Barry Sheene's Toyota Supra is dragged away after a first-corner accident on Whit Monday, 1985. Photo: National Motor Museum.

focal point of the Thruxton season over the next 17 years. Its loss was a terrible blow for everyone involved in the Thruxton story and for the many fans who made Easter Monday at Thruxton a permanent fixture on their spectating calendar. The BARC was determined to continue with a prestigious Easter race meeting, but international motorsport offered few sensible alternatives. Eventually, in place of the Formula 3000 race, the BARC organised a round of the Interserie Coupe d'Europe as the feature event, to be run in two 20-lap heats. The Interserie sports car class had last been at Thruxton in 1971, while the programme also included the third round of the British Formula 3 Championship.

was too big a risk to take. The Club pointed out that it had lost £35,000 on the 1985 race on a promotion of £85,000 and with Easter 1986 falling early on March 31st, the problem of attracting spectators would exacerbate the probability of losing money.

A statement read: 'While mindful of the purpose of the Club's existence, to promote motor racing, the Council of the Club felt it would be inappropriate to spend Club funds in this way. We are now in competition in some instances with foreign governments and certainly with town councils adjacent to the circuits, who are prepared to fund races out of the public exchequer or some other means. It seems likely that Birmingham may be competing with established motor racing organisers.'

The BARC ran the first European Formula 2 event to be held in Britain and the annual Easter fixture was the

Sadly only 15 cars finally arrived for the Interserie races and they offered little in entertainment. Though the series offered potential, the lack-lustre racing simply amplified the sense of loss that everyone felt at the demise of the single-seater feature event. One of the Interserie heats was won by Austrian Jo Gartner and, tragically, this was to be his last race win as he lost his life at Le Mans in June that year.

In February 1986, the traditional pre-season test days had to be postponed due to snow and ice on the circuit. Even the re-scheduled days were not free of winter as the Thursday session started late due to ice on the edge of the track and Friday's running had to be curtailed when fresh snow arrived.

When the season opened on March 9th with the first round of the British Formula 3 Championship, conditions

Championship Finals Day, 1985. Jason Elliott steers around the abandoned Formula Fords of Steve Robertson and Gary Ayles. Photo: Duncan Hands.

Formula 3
Easter 1986.
Bill Coombs
gets the Anson
out of shape.
Photo: Fred
Taylor.

Quick set-up changes are
made to Dave Coyne's Van
Diemen RF86 Formula Ford
2000 during qualifying on
Easter Monday. Van Diemen
boss Ralph Firman (back
right) keeps an eye on the
opposition.
Photo: Fred Taylor.

The Interserie races at
Easter 1986 were not a
success. Jo Gartner (Porsche
962) won one of the races.
Photo: Colin Taylor.

were not much better. The opening Silverstone race planned for the previous weekend had been lost to snow but the Thruxton meeting went ahead in very wet weather. Maurizio Sandro Sala slithered away from a strong field to beat Andy Wallace and Martin Donnelly. At the same meeting, Paul Warwick, younger brother of Derek had his second ever race. The first one had been at a Silverstone club meeting the day before and Paul duly won both Formula Ford races on his debut weekend. The 17-year old was overseen by Derek as he won the opening round of the Townsend Thoresen Junior Formula Ford 1600 series at Thruxton in very wet conditions.

March 9 1986
Formula 3 meeting

British Formula 3	Maurizio Sandro Sala (Ralt RT30)
Racing Displays British Formula Ford 2000	Dave Coyne (Swift DB3)
Townsend Thoresen Junior Formula Ford 1600	Paul Warwick (Van Diemen RF86)
Wendy Wools Special Saloons	Brian Chatfield (BMW 320)
Sports 1600	Nick Bridge (Mallock MK27S)
Monroe Production Saloons	Colin Blower (Colt Starion Turbo)
74-78 Formula Ford 1600	Chris Whibley (Royale RP21)

March 29/31 1986
Townsend Thoresen Interserie meeting

Interserie race one	Jo Gartner (Porsche 962C)
Interserie race two	James Weaver (Porsche 956C)
British Formula 3	Maurizio Sandro Sala (Ralt RT30)
Racing Displays British Formula Ford 2000	Paulo Carcasci (Van Diemen RF86)
Wendy Wools Special Saloons	Terry Nicholls (Ford Capri)
Townsend Thoresen Junior Formula Ford 1600	Antonio Russo (Van Diemen RF86)
Renault 5 Turbos	Charles Tippett

April 20 1986
BARC meeting

Road-going Midgets	Peter Hiley
Saab Turbos	John Llewellyn
74-78 Formula Ford 1600	Douglas Lague (Van Diemen RF78)
B&Q British Sports 2000	Mike Taylor (Royale RP42)
Monroe Production Saloons	Graham Scarborough (Colt Starion Turbo)
Esso Formula Ford 1600	Jason Elliott (Van Diemen RF86)
MGA/TR race	Martin Shaw (MGA)

May 5 1986
Formula 3 meeting

Lucas British Formula 3	Gerrit van Kouwen (Ralt RT30)
Thundersports	Chester Wedgwood/ John Morrison (Tiga TS85)
MGOC Standard Class	Jeremy Lindley (Midget)
Slington & PHM Sports 1600	Dave Orchard (Centaur 14X)
MGOC Modified Class	Richard Horn (MGB)

May 26 1986
British Touring Car meeting

RAC British Touring Cars	Mike Newman (BMW 635)
RAC/Townsend Thoresen Formula Ford 1600	Phil Andrews (Van Diemen RF86)
Mini Seven	Gary Hall
Ford Credit Fiestas	Barrie Williams
Mini Miglia	Chris Lewis
Townsend Thoresen Junior Formula Ford 1600	Paul Spooner (Van Diemen RF86)
Pre '65 Saloons	Phil Wight (Lotus Cortina)

Generally, the 1986 season was a disappointing affair. The May Bank Holiday meeting was headlined by the British Touring Car Championship but even that series was weak at the time. Mike Newman won the race in his BMW 635CSi, but the championship was in the doldrums and was yet to undergo the transformation

Paulo Carcasci heads Bertrand Gachot and Mark Blundell in the Formula Ford 2000 class of 1986. Photo: Colin Taylor.

that, in the 1990s, would make it second in TV-viewer popularity to grand prix racing.

After a series of fairly low-key club meetings, the October Championship Finals meeting heralded the conclusion of two hard-fought championships and closed the season in the absence of a TV meeting. The RAC/Townsend Thoresen Formula Ford 1600 and Racing Displays British Formula Ford 2000 were both finely balanced going into the final race and promised traditional end of season fireworks. Bertrand Gachot and Mark Blundell had enacted a furious battle for the Formula Ford 2000 title and, while Dave Coyne won the race, Gachot just out-paced his rival to make sure of the title with fourth place at the end of a gruelling 20-race schedule. While Phil Andrews won the Formula Ford race, third place behind title rival Phillipe Favre was enough to secure a championship double for Jason Elliott who had already clinched the Esso title.

In November 1986, the resurfacing of the complete circuit was started at a projected cost of £160,000. Traditionally, the existing surface had been considered abrasive and increasingly bumpy for the fastest single-seaters. Other work going on included raising spectator banking so that much of the circuit could be seen from the approach to the Complex.

The airfield also received a new tarmac runway measuring 800m long by 23m wide. This would eliminate the problems caused by water-logging of the previous grass runway. This latest development work, added to the new pit complex and the refurbishment of the Eagle Star grandstand at the Chicane brought the total invested in the circuit in two years to around £300,000.

In December 1986, it was confirmed that the Easter fixture would again be headlined by the Interserie Cup. The BARC was committed to maintaining international racing at Thruxton and there were high hopes that the Easter 1987 meeting would be a considerable improvement over the '86 event. Sadly, those hopes were never realised for, a month before the meeting, the Interserie race was cancelled and so the Easter meeting would now be a one-day National event topped by a Formula 3 race.

June 29 1986	
Brooklands Raceday	
Pre '60 Sports/ Pre '65 GP Cars	John Brindley (Brabham BT10)
Pre '71 Single Seaters	John Foulston (McLaren M19)
Atlantic Computers 2-litre Historic GT	Simon Hadfield (Chevron B6)
Post Historic Road Sports	Paul Weldon (TVR Tuscan)
Atlantic Computers Historic GT	John Foulston (McLaren M8D)
Classic/ Thoroughbred Sports	Mike Harrison (Elva 7S)
Formula Junior/ Historic Formula 3	John Skinner (Lotus 59)

August 25 1986
BARC meeting

Racing Displays British Formula Ford 2000	Bobby Carville (Reynard 86SF)
Shell 74-78 Formula Ford 1600	Douglas Lague (Van Diemen RF78)
Alfa Romeo Class A	Ian Johnson (Alfasud)
Monoposto Kent	Jim Blockley (Reynard SF78)
Wendy Wools Special Saloons	Bob Jarvis (Sunbeam Stiletto)
Alfa Romeo Classes B-E	Roberto Giordanelli (Alfa Zagato)
Monoposto	Brian Turner (Chevron B47)

September 21 1986
Renault Raceday

Mini Miglia	Jonathan Lewis
Ferraris	Nick Harvey (308GTB)
Phoenix Pre '81 Formula Ford 2000	Peter Boutwood (Lola T580)
BARC/MGOC	Richard Horn (MGB)
Renault 5 Turbo	Chris Maries
Mini Seven	Gary Hall
Saab Turbo	Tiff Needell
Formula 4/ Formula 1300	Rob Moores (Chevron B38)

October 19 1986
Championship Finals meeting

Racing Displays British Formula Ford 2000	Dave Coyne (Swift FB3)
RAC Townsend Thoresen Formula Ford 1600	Phil Andrews (Van Diemen RF86)
Wendy Wools Special Saloons	Brian Chatfield (BMW 320)
BARC/MGOC Standard Class	Nigel Petch (MGB)
BARC/MGOC Modified Class	Richard Horn (MGA)
Saab Turbos	Maurizio Sandro Sala
Townsend Thoresen Junior Formula Ford 1600	Paul Warwick (Van Diemen RF86)

March 15 1987
Formula 3 meeting

Lucas British Formula 3	Johnny Herbert (Reynard 873)
Mobil 1 British Formula Ford 2000	Jyrki Jarvilehto (Reynard 87SF)
URS Pre '82 Formula Ford 2000	Rod Townsend (Royale RP27)
Wendy Wools Special Saloons	Terry Nicholls (Ford Capri)
Townsend Thoresen Junior Formula Ford 1600	Derek Higgins (Ray 87F)
Monroe Production Saloons	Mike Smith (Ford Sierra Cosworth)
Jaguar Saloons	Tony Williams (MK2)

March 29 1987
BARC meeting

Road-going MG Midgets	Peter Coates
Shell Oils 74-78 Formula Ford 1600	John Wardle (Van Diemen RF78)
Slington & PHM Sports 1600	Guy Woodward (Vision V86)
Esso Formula Ford 1600	Alain Menu (Van Diemen RF87)
Sports 2000	Mike Taylor (Royale RP42)
Monoposto/ Monoposto Kent	Jon Bradshaw (Raffo MK9B)
MGA/TR Challenge	Martin Shaw (MGA)

Before that, the season kicked-off with a meeting that included the opening Formula 3 race of the season. Just as in '86, the opening round at Silverstone was lost to snow. In the Thruxton race, Johnny Herbert was dominant as he started what would be a successful title bid in a Reynard run by Eddie Jordan's team. A first lap shunt at the Complex accounted for Damon Hill, Ross Hockenhull, Craig Simmiss and Grahame de Zille.

Over the early meetings of 1987, lap records fell regularly as the new surface proved notably quicker than the original surface. At the end of March, Steve Robertson trimmed a massive two seconds from John Pratt's three year old Formula Ford mark during a round of the Esso championship. That race ended in controversy as the top four finishers were excluded from the results for failing to respond to yellow flags. Mark Hazell had crashed heavily and racing continued unabated as rescue crews tended to Hazell. Eddie Irvine, Antonio Simoes, Steve Robertson and Pedro Chaves were excluded, fined £120 and had their licences endorsed, leaving victory to fifth-placed Alain Menu!

The Formula 3 teams were back on Easter Monday when tyre problems dominated the meeting. While Herbert romped to his third win in four races, Damon Hill was among those in rubber trouble when a tyre delaminated after just 10 laps of the race. With the next Formula 3 race scheduled for May Bank Holiday, there was concern among the

Easter 1987 Formula 3. Ross Hockenhull and Giles Butterfield tangle at the Chicane with Damon Hill right behind. Photo: Andrew Priest.

teams about further problems on the new surface. Qualifying on Easter Monday had been wet and the new surface had proved very tricky for the drivers and teams were worried about the likely outcome if the Whitsun race ran in wet conditions. Conversely, the tyre failures experienced on the dry track at Easter was another concern should the race be dry! However, Avon worked on the tyre specification and the dry race ran without any hitches.

By the time of the Championship Finals meeting in October, Herbert had already sewn up the British Formula 3 title. However, he then turned in one of his best drives of the season to stage a stunning recovery after tangling with Thomas Danielsson at the Complex on the first lap. Herbert rejoined in 23rd and last place and proceeded to storm through to third at the end of 20 laps with a performance that had the crowd on their feet. At the chequered flag, he was a mere six seconds behind winner Bertrand Gachot. At the same meeting, young Finnish racer Jyrki Jarvilehto crashed out of the Formula Ford 2000 final but had already clinched the title. He was watched that day by rally ace and fellow Finn Markku Alen and would soon shorten his name to JJ Lehto.

The August Bank Holiday meeting in 1987 was headlined by a Thundersports race, won by the March 847 of Tiff Needell and Richard Piper. 'I had my closest ever finish in that race with the Can-Am car,' says Ian Flux. 'Piper had a bit of a lead, but Mike Wilds had driven our first shift and we put new tyres on at our pit stop. It took a bit longer but gave me an advantage and I caught Richard coming out of Church on the last lap. We ran side by side but he had the inside line coming up to the Chicane. We went single file through the Chicane and then sprinted to the line. To this day, I'm still convinced I was an inch in front of him...'

'The first race I actually won at Thruxton was in Sports 2000 in 1985 against Sean Walker. So it took a long time to win. It always makes for good racing

April 20 1987	
British Touring Car meeting	
Dunlop British Touring Cars	Dennis Leech (Rover Vitesse)
Lucas British Formula 3	Johnny Herbert (Reynard 873)
Pirelli Porsche - Class A	Tony Dron (Carrera RSL)
Pirelli Porsche - Classes B, C and D	Paul Edwards (911S)
Renault 5 Elf Turbo UK Cup	David Cox
Saab Turbo Mobil Challenge	Tiff Needell

May 4 1987	
Brooklands Raceday	
Pre '65 Single Seaters	Chris Smith (Chevron B17)
2-litre GTs	Michael Schryver (Chevron B6)
Classic Sports	Mike Littlewood (Lotus 23)
Atlantic Computers Historic GT	John Foulston (McLaren M8B)
Post-Historic Road Sports	Paul Weldon (TVR Tuscan)
Pre '71 Single Seaters	John Foulston (McLaren M19A)
HSCC Novices	Tim Wright (Lotus Elan)

May 25 1987
Formula 3 meeting

Lucas British Formula 3	Thomas Danielsson (Reynard 873)
Owen Brown RAC Formula Ford 1600	Eddie Irvine (Van Diemen RF87)
Ford Credit Fiestas	Graham Churchill
Renault 5 Elf Turbo UK Cup	Bill McGovern
Slington & PHM Sports 1600	Martin Wood (Mallock MK23)

June 21 1987
BARC meeting

Mini Miglia	Russell Grady
Dutton Forshaw MGCC BCV8	Tim Ransom
Alfa Romeo Challenge	Peter Hilleard (GTV6)
DAF Trucks Pre '74 Formula Ford 1600	David Porter (Elden MK10)
Mini Seven	Peter Bonas
MGA/TR Challenge	Roy McCarthy (MGA)
Formula 4	David Sheppard (Van Diemen RF82)

August 31 1987
Thundersports meeting

Thundersports	Tiff Needell/Richard Piper (March 847)
Mobil 1 British Formula Ford 2000	Jonathan Bancroft (Reynard 87SF)
Wendy Wools Special Saloons	David Enderby (VW Karmann Ghia)
Saab Turbo Mobil Challenge	John Llewellyn
Jaguar XJ Challenge	Paul Craymer (XJ6)

because you can overtake anywhere at Thruxton. Along with the Brands Grand Prix track, the corners are the most challenging in the country. From a driver's point of view, Goodwood is one of the hardest places to turn into, because you've got to go through there flat-out,' says Flux.

Ian has other reasons to recall the '87 season at Thruxton, however. He and his girlfriend Jane got married in February 1987 and came back from honeymoon in Madeira a week early so that Ian could test at Thruxton. However, when they arrived at the circuit it was covered in snow and the testing was cancelled.

Bertrand Gachot fends off Johnny Herbert in a 1987 Formula 3 battle. Photo: Peter Tempest.

September 20 1987
BARC meeting

Shell Oils 74-78 Formula Ford 1600	Mike Gardiner (Van Diemen RF78)
Pre '65 Saloons	Alan Mills (Ford Mustang)
MG Owners Club	Grahame Davis (Midget)
Townsend Thoresen Junior Formula Ford 1600	Cal Foster (Van Diemen RF87)
Monroe Production Saloons	Robb Gravett (Ford Sierra Cosworth)
Kit Cars	Mark Walkett (Ginetta G27)
Pre '57 Saloons	Terry Heley (Ford Zephyr)

October 18 1987
Championship Finals meeting

Lucas British Formula 3	Bertrand Gachot (Ralt RT31)
Townsend Thoresen Junior Formula Ford 1600	Derek Higgins (Van Diemen RF87)
Wendy Wools Special Saloons	Ginger Marshall (Reliant Kitten)
Slington & PHM Sports 1600	Martin Wood (Mallock MK23)
Owen Brown RAC Formula Ford 1600	Eddie Irvine (Van Diemen RF87)
Mobil 1 British Formula Ford 2000	Jason Elliott (Reynard 87SF)

CHAPTER EIGHT

Heading into the recession

Before the 1988 racing season opened, there were a couple of notable changes at Thruxton. In February, Mark Poynton left the BARC and was replaced by Dennis Carter, a former executive with Imperial Tobacco and club racer.

'I first came to Thruxton as a marshal and driver of a breakdown vehicle! I drove the breakdown truck at Formula 2 meetings as I lived in Southampton. Then I came back to race in Clubmans and an MGA, but I never did very well at Thruxton as a driver,' says Carter. Then, he joined the BARC as Competition Manager and that move effectively brought his own racing career to a conclusion.

'During the Formula 2 days, Thruxton was very much part of the international calendar. When Formula 2 ceased to exist and became Formula 3000, Thruxton ran one FIA Formula 3000 race which wasn't successful. At that point, along with a lot of other circuits, it lost its international status because there was nothing for it to run,' continues Carter. 'Everybody knew Thruxton Easter Monday and that was very much what it was famous for. From that, the circuit went to running major national meetings and a lot of club racing.'

Alex Postan vacates his Renault 5GT Turbo on Easter Monday, 1988.
Photo: National Motor Museum.

March 13 1988	
Formula 3 meeting	
Lucas British Formula 3	JJ Lehto (Reynard 883)
MG Maestro Challenge	Jenny Nadin
Wendy Wools Special Saloons	Brian Fisher (Skoda Rapide)
Monroe Production Saloons	Sean Brown (Ford Sierra Cosworth)
P&O Junior Formula Ford 1600	Andy Charsley (Ray 87F)
Mobil 1 British Formula Ford 2000	Stephen Robertson (Reynard 88SF)

At the same time as Carter joined the team, Kimpton corner was re-named Noble in honour of British World Land Speed Record holder Richard Noble. His efforts in following after the legends of Campbell, Cobb and Segrave had not gone unnoticed.

In time for the start of the new season, a complete new set of marshals' huts supplied by Shell were installed. Every one of the previous wooden huts had been completely destroyed by the gales that swept southern England in October '87. Damage was also done to other circuit buildings, including the pit garages, during more gales early in 1988 and the circuit staff had to work flat-out to have everything repaired in time for the first meeting.

The racing season opened with the first round of the Lucas Formula 3 Championship. A remarkable top four comprised JJ Lehto, Martin Donnelly, Damon Hill and Eddie Irvine. The high quality entry also included Alain Menu, Paul Warwick and Roland Ratzenberger. Lehto was in the wars when the Formula 3 cars returned for the Easter meeting. On the third lap of the race, the Finn was battling with Martin Donnelly and ran wide on the approach to the Chicane before plunging into the barriers. He was carefully removed from the car in some pain and spent the night in Salisbury hospital before being sent home. It was a bad day for the Pacific Racing team headed by Keith Wiggins as Evan Demoulas had gone off backwards at the same place in qualifying. The damage to the pair of wrecked Reynards was estimated at around £40,000! Donnelly went on to win the race. At the same meeting, the first Vauxhall Lotus Challenge race was held and a good grid of 21 of the new single-seaters gathered. Allan McNish won from Mika Hakkinen and Phillipe Adams. When the series returned in June, Adams was fortunate to escape with only a broken ankle after a heavy accident while battling with Eugene O'Brien under braking for the Chicane.

April 4 1988	
Formula 3 meeting	
Lucas British Formula 3	Martin Donnelly (Ralt RT32)
Vauxhall Lotus Challenge	Allan McNish
P&O Junior Formula Ford 1600	Kurt Luby (Van Diemen RF88)
Wendy Wools Special Saloons	Brian Chatfield (BMW 320)
Renault 5 Elf Turbo Cup	Niki Phillips
Saab Turbo Mobil Challenge	John Llewellyn

May 2 1988	
British Touring Car meeting	
Dunlop RAC British Touring Cars	Steve Soper (Ford Sierra Cosworth)
Mini Seven	Steve Cooper
BARC/MGOC	Nigel Petch (MG Maestro)
Ford Credit Fiestas	Brian Farminer
Mini Miglias	Russell Grady
Modified Porsches	John Greasley (935)
Pre '65 Saloons	Stephen Phillips (Lotus Cortina)

May 30 1988	
Formula 3 meeting	
Lucas British Formula 3	Damon Hill (Ralt RT32)
RAC British Formula Ford 1600	Derek Higgins (Van Diemen RF88)
Slington & PHM Sports 1600	Tony Bridge (Mallock MK27/9)
Saab Turbo Mobil Challenge	Andy Dawson
Renault 5 Elf Turbo UK Cup	Niki Phillips

June 12 1988	
BARC meeting	
Vauxhall Lotus Challenge	Peter Hardman
Cox & Buckles TR Challenge	Stephen Hall (TR4)
DAF Trucks Pre '74 Formula Ford 1600	Peter Hancock (Merlyn MK20/25)
Road-Going Midgets	Colin Mowle
Brands Hatch Travel Sports 2000	Nick Baird (Shrike P15)
ESSO Formula Ford 1600	Jose Cordova (Reynard 88FF)
Jaguars	Geoff Burraway (XJ12)

Lehto's Thruxton jinx continued at the end of May for the eighth Formula 3 race of the season when he slid off early in a soaking wet race. Damon Hill won the race convincingly, while Paul Warwick scored an excellent fourth place. The fourth and final Thruxton Formula 3 race of the season was the penultimate round of the championship in late September. By now, Lehto had secured the title but was beaten in the race by Gary Brabham. His brother David won Class B to make it a good day for the sons of Sir Jack.

In May '88, planning permission was granted for a new restaurant complex to replace the existing Goodwood bar and restaurant. In a swift piece of construction work, the old building

Formula Vauxhall Lotus was born in 1988. Mika Hakkinen was one of the early stars. Photo: Colin Taylor.

Talent abounded in the Formula 3 field of 1988. The March 13th Thruxton race was won by JJ Lehto (centre) who was joined by Damon Hill (left) and Martin Donnelly on the podium. Photo: Gary Kimber.

was pulled down the day after the motorbike meeting on April 18th and the new one was completed in time for the May 30th meeting. Other changes that year included a new name on the pedestrian bridge when it was repainted in the colours of P&O European Ferries. The main circuit access road also gained a large scale Dunlop tyre in the style of the famous Le Mans landmark.

The September 25th meeting was dedicated to the McLaren-Honda Grand Prix team in recognition of their sweeping victory in the Formula One Constructors title. During the meeting, John Watson returned to a Formula 1 car to demonstrate a 1987 McLaren-Honda MP4 during the Honda-supported race meeting. Winner of a frenetic Honda CRX race was Patrick Watts in a race that also included David Leslie and the late Ian Taylor. The day closed with the very first Formula First race at Thruxton which was won by the unknown Darren Dalwood. Among his rivals in the newly-conceived single-seater class were Scott Lakin, Bobby Verdon-Roe and Thomas Erdos, who all went on to go further in the sport than Dalwood.

August 29 1988	
BARC meeting	
Mobil 1 British Formula Ford 2000	Cal Foster (Swift DB88)
BMW Challenge	Nigel Corry (535)
URS Pre '83 Formula Ford 2000	Dave Nichols (Van Diemen RF82)
BARC/MGOC	Darryl Davies (Maestro)
Monroe Production Saloons	Sean Brown (Ford Sierra Cosworth)
Trueseal Modified Production Saloons	Jon Woodward (Talbot Sunbeam Lotus)
LMF/Motoring News Formula E	Roger Eccleston (Crossle 25F)

September 11 1988	
Brooklands Raceday	
Post Historic Road Sports	Roger Connel (TVR Griffith)
Pre '65 Racing Cars	Mike Littlewood (Merlyn MK5/7)
Classic Sports	Tony Thompson (Lotus Elan)
Historic Formula 1	John Fenning (Wolf WR1)
2-Litre GT Cars	Richard Dodkins (Chevron B6)
Pre '71 Single Seaters	Richard Peacock (Surtees TS9B)
Novices	Bodo Linhoff (Lotus Elan)

September 25 1988	
British Formula 3 meeting	
Lucas British Formula 3	Gary Brabham (Ralt RT32)
Intercon 74-78 Formula Ford 1600	Simon Davey (Van Diemen RF78)
Honda CRX Challenge	Patrick Watts
Slington & PHM Sports 1600	Tony Bridge (Mallock MK27SG)
Wendy Wools Special Saloons	Bob Jarvis (Ray Stiletto)
URS Pre '83 Formula Ford 2000	Dave Nichols (Van Diemen RF82)
Cellnet Formula First	Darren Dalwood

At the championship finals meeting in mid-October, Adrian Cottrell scored a memorable victory in the final race of 1988 when he was drafted into the Saab Turbo race at the last minute to handle the second Abbott Racing entry. In an epic battle, the local ace out-dragged John Llewellyn out of the Chicane on the last lap to win by a coat of paint! At the same meeting, Bob Jarvis took the Wendy Wools Special Saloon honours in his Ray Stiletto and in the process finally broke the 12 year-old lap record set by Gerry Marshall in 'Baby Bertha'. During the lunch-break at that meeting, Saab racer Charles Tippett organised a charity run around the circuit in aid of Leukaemia Research. A total of 98 runners took part and they all finished the lap, eventually! Winner was Special Saloon racer Ben Bowlby and a superb total of £3000 was raised. But that wasn't the only charity event going on at Thruxton as 1988 drew to a close. In December, the 4th Salisbury Farnham Scouts pulled Richard Morgan's March 803 Toyota Formula 3 car around the track for four laps to raise money for the BBC's Children in Need appeal.

October 16 1988
Championship Finals meeting

RAC British Formula Ford 1600	Jose Cordova (Reynard 88FF)
Vauxhall Lotus Challenge	Mika Hakkinen
Mobil 1 British Formula Ford 2000	Steven Robertson (Reynard 88SF)
P&O Junior Formula Ford 1600	Nick Hart (Van Diemen RF88)
Wendy Wools Special Saloons	Bob Jarvis (Ray Stiletto)
Saab Turbo Mobil Challenge	Adrian Cottrell

The 1989 season was, as usual, preceded by several test days in February and at the first of these, a promising young Scot caught the attention of Autosport's Marcus Pye. On his first sight of Thruxton, 18-year old David Coulthard lapped a Van Diemen RF87 within 1.5s of the lap record! The former karter had signed with the David Leslie team to contest the junior Formula Ford 1600 championships and was to go all the way to the top of the sport. A week later, Niko Palhares became the first Formula Ford 1600 driver to break the 1m20s barrier when he lapped in 1m19.7s, while testing the latest works Van Diemen RF89.

March 12 1989
BARC meeting

Firestone Production Saloons	Jerry Mahony (Ford Sierra Cosworth)
Modified Production Saloons qualification	Mike Price (Rover SD1)
Modified Production Saloons	Jim Edwards Jnr (Ford Fiesta)
74-79 Formula Ford 1600	John Wardle (Van Diemen RF78)
Special Saloons	Bob Jarvis (Ray Stiletto)
P&O Junior Formula Ford 1600	David Coulthard (Van Diemen RF89)
Pre '74 Formula Ford 1600	Billy Burke (Merlyn MK20A)

March 27 1989
Formula 3 meeting

Lucas British Formula 3	Rickard Rydell (Reynard 893)
British Formula 3000	Gary Brabham (Reynard 88D)
Renault 5 Elf Turbo Cup	Niki Phillips
P&O Junior Formula Ford 1600	David Coulthard (Van Diemen RF89)
Special Saloons	Bob Jarvis (Ray Stiletto)

As the Thruxton season opened in dreadful weather conditions a few weeks later, Coulthard won his first ever car race in the opening round of the P&O Junior Formula Ford 1600 Championship. His biggest challenge that day, as it would all season, came from Kelvin Burt. Ironically, two weeks later on Easter Monday, the opening Formula 3 race of the season was won by Rickard Rydell, who, seven years later would be teamed with Burt in the Volvo Touring Car team.

March 1989. David Coulthard (Van Diemen RF89) romps to victory in his first ever car race in the P&O Junior Formula Ford season opener. Photo: Duncan Hands.

Easter Monday 1989 also saw the outright circuit record smashed after standing for seven seasons to Johnny Cecotto. Though the International Formula 3000 Championship was far from economically accessible to the BARC, Easter 1989 at Thruxton still echoed to the sound of Cosworth racing engines as a round of the British Formula 3000 Championship joined the Formula 3 race on the programme. The second round of the championship only brought 10 cars to Thruxton, but the pace was hot as Roland Ratzenberger lopped a massive three seconds off the record to leave it at 1m04.44s, over the 130mph average for the first time. Andrew Gilbert-Scott had taken pole with a best of 1m04.54s, but the race was won in style by Gary Brabham who was dumped to last at Campbell on the first lap after a nudge from Marco Greco spun his Reynard 88D. Brabham fought back to take the lead after 16 of the 40 laps.

On the same day, Lord Brabazon of Tara, the Minister for Aviation and Shipping, officially opened the new Thruxton suite, which offered seating for up to 80 people and would be available for functions and events at any time of the year. A new medical centre and administration block were also ready for that meeting.

May 1 1989
British Touring Car meeting

Esso RAC British Touring Cars	Tim Harvey (Ford Sierra RS500)
Ford Credit Fiestas	Brian Farminer
Formula Ford 2000	Jose Cordova (Reynard 89SF)
Thundersports	Jim McGaughay/ Duncan Bain (Tiga TS85)
Formula Renault	Neil Riddiford (Van Diemen FR89)
Agip/MGOC	Nigel Petch (MGC)

May 29 1989
British Touring Car meeting

Esso RAC British Touring Cars	Andy Rouse (Ford Sierra RS500)
Lucas British Formula 3	Allan McNish (Ralt RT33)
Renault 5 Elf Turbo Cup	Niki Phillips
Formula Forward	Tony Hancock
Vauxhall Finance Sports	Vernon Davies (Mallock MK28)
LuK RAC British Formula Ford 1600	Dave Coyne (Swift FB89)

Having christened Vauxhall Lotus a year earlier, Thruxton hosted the very first Formula Renault race on May 1st 1989. Only five cars started that race, which

was won by Neil Riddiford. However, the class would go from strength to strength in subsequent seasons. At the same meeting, Thundersports racer Robin Smith had a lucky escape when a rear tyre blew on his March 827 Can-Am car when he was pulling more than 150mph round the back of the circuit! Thankfully, the car spun harmlessly into the infield.

At the end of May Bank Holiday meeting, a good crowd witnessed a Formula 3 and Touring Car double-header. In the BTCC race, Robb Gravett made a spectacular exit, captured by the TV cameras, at Segrave after tangling with the Toyota Corolla of Phil Dowsett. Andy Rouse and Tim Harvey duly claimed a one-two in their Ford Sierra RS500s.

June 11 1989
BARC meeting

Formula Vauxhall Lotus	Eugene O'Brien
Esso Formula Ford 1600	Dave Coyne (Swift FB89)
Mini Miglia/ Mini Seven	Myk Cable (Mini Miglia)
Vauxhall Finance Sports	Mike Swinnerton (Mallock MK20)
Pre '65 Classic Saloons	Les Nash (Lotus Cortina)
Monoposto/ Monoposto Kent	David Dudley (Anson SA4)
BMWs	John Costelloe (320i)

August 28 1989
BARC meeting

Cellnet Formula Firsts	James Rhodes
Road-Going Midgets	Peter Hiley
Formula Renault	Gino Ussi (Swift FR89)
Firestone Production Saloons	Keith Odor (Ford Sierra Cosworth)
URS Pre '83 Formula Ford 2000	Jeff Gresswell (Van Diemen RF82)
Wurth Multisports	Shaun Hollamby

During May, Dennis Carter, who had been Competitions Director since February 1988, announced that he was leaving to return to industry. However, his decision was later reversed when he successfully applied for the post of Chief Executive when Sidney Offord retired in October. The new Competitions Manager, Dale Wells, would join the Club in February 1990. Before then, the Club would take on a 50-year lease to operate the new Pembrey circuit in South Wales.

Offord had been an enormous influence on the development of both the BARC and Thruxton circuit. Frequently outspoken and intransigent, he had ruffled many feathers during his 17 years as Chief Executive. However, he was also a warm-hearted man who loved the sport dearly. During his leadership of the Club, he achieved a great deal and was responsible for putting the whole operation onto a sound financial footing. 'Sidney Offord was largely responsible for our turn round in fortunes, both the BARC and Thruxton circuit,' says BARC Chairman Michael Groves.

Sadly, after just three years of a well-earned retirement, he passed away in November 1992 after a short illness. Just three days before his death, Sidney had celebrated the 80th anniversary of the BARC at Goodwood.

The 1989 season closed with the traditional Championship Finals meeting and marked the racing debut of former Welsh Guardsman Simon Weston who had been so badly burnt during the 1982 Falklands conflict. His race, in a Firestone Production Saloon Sapphire Cosworth, was part of a fund-raising venture for his Weston Spirit Charity.

For the start of the new decade, Thruxton had a new look thanks to a revised pit wall built to the latest international standards. However, there were a couple of snags with the new brickwork. The first time it was built a gale blew it over before the cement had set and then the timekeepers had a job to see the car numbers over the top of it! Other improvements for the 1990 season included a new interior security fence so that spectators could park and then pay for admission rather than queue up in their cars. Soon to be granted was planning permission for a new scrutineering bay which would open on July 28th.

The 1990 Easter meeting again featured a Formula 3 and British Formula 3000 double-bill. In the Formula 3 race, Mika Hakkinen beat off fellow Finn Mika Salo to take the early championship lead, while Pedro Chaves was top of the 13 Formula 3000s. He also trimmed just 0.01s from Ratzenberger's year old lap record, though Chaves had qualified in a stunning 1m03.01s.

September 10 1989	
BARC meeting	
Dimsdale Formula 4	Bob Davis (Davis T6)
Formula Ford 2000	Jose Cordova (Reynard 89SF)
Forwell Group K Sports	Nigel James (Ultima)
Formula Renault	Adrian Cottrell (Reynard FR89)
Special Saloons	Alistair Fenwick (Skoda)
74-78 Formula Ford 1600	John Wardle (Van Diemen RF78)
Sports 1600	Glenn Eagling (Mallock MK20)
Minister Pre '85 Formula Ford 1600	Andrew Colson (Ray 84F)

September 24 1989	
BARC meeting	
BRDC Sportscars	Tim Harvey/ Laurence Bristow (Spice SE89)
Agip/MGOC	Darryl Davies (Maestro)
BF Goodrich Porsche Classes A & C	Barrie Williams (Carrera)
BF Goodrich Porsche Classes B & D	Steve Kevlin (944S)
MGCC BCV8/MGA	Tony Price (MGB)
Milbank Trucks Morgans	Rob Wells (+8)
Cox & Buckles TR	Stephen Hall (Triumph TR4)

October 8 1989	
BARC meeting	
Pre '65 Saloons	Les Nash (Lotus Cortina)
P&O Junior Formula Ford 1600	Kelvin Burt (Van Diemen RF89)
Mini Miglia	Myk Cable
Mini Seven	Michael Jackson
Formula Renault	Neil Riddiford (Van Diemen RF89)
Road-Going Midgets	Bill Lancashire
Monoposto	David Dudley (Anson SA4)
Monoposto Kent	Francis Phillips (Reynard 83FF)
Pre '57 Saloons	Richard Ward (Alfa Romeo Giulietta)

October 15 1989	
Championship Finals meeting	
Lucas British Formula 3	Allan McNish (Ralt RT33)
Vauxhall Finance Sports	Vernon Davies (Mallock MK28)
P&O Junior Formula Ford 1600	Kelvin Burt (Van Diemen RF89)
Firestone Production Saloons	Mark Hales (Ford Sierra Cosworth)
Agip/MGOC	Darryl Davies (Maestro)
URS Pre '83 Formula Ford 2000	Jeff Gresswell (Van Diemen RF82)

March 11 1990
BARC meeting

P&O Junior Formula Ford 1600	Jeremy Cotterill (Van Diemen RF90)
Robolift Sports 1600	Dave Facer (Mallock MK18B)
Modified Production Saloons Classes C & D	Terry Stone (Toyota Corolla)
Modified Production Saloons Classes A & B	Andrew MacKenzie (Ford Sierra XR4i)
Vauxhall Finance Sports	Nick Carr (Mallock MK28B)
QED Classic Formula 3	Winston Bunn (Ensign LNF3)
Pre '74 Saloons	Peter Brown (Triumph Dolomite Sprint)

March 25 1990
BARC meeting

Formula Renault	Dave Coyne (Swift FR90)
74-78 Formula Ford 1600	Barry Pomfret (Royale RP26)
BARC/MGOC	Rae Davis (Maestro)
Renault 5 Elf Turbo Cup	James Kaye
Cellnet Formula First	Phillip Bate
Special Saloons	Brian Fisher (Skoda Rapide)
Mini Miglia/ Mini Seven	Ian Gunn

April 16 1990
Formula 3 meeting

British Formula 3	Mika Hakkinen (Ralt RT34)
British Formula 3000	Pedro Chaves (Reynard 90D)
Formula Renault	Thomas Erdos (Swift FR90)
Firestone Production Saloons Classes C & D	Tony Lanfranchi (Vauxhall Astra GTE)
Firestone Production Saloons Classes A & B	Andy Middlehurst (Ford Sierra Cosworth)
P&O Junior Formula Ford 1600	Warren Hughes (Van Diemen RF90)

May 7 1990
BARC meeting

BARC/MGOC Class A	Noel Wincote (MGB)
BARC/MGOC Class B	Colin Crump (Maestro)
Firestone Production Saloons	Andy Middlehurst/ Mark Hales (Ford Sierra Cosworth)
BRDC Sportscars	Tony Trevor/ 'Pierre Chauvet' (ADA 02)
BMWs	Keith Morley (2002t)

May 28 1990
British Touring Car meeting

Esso British Touring Cars	Robb Gravett (Ford Sierra RS500)
British Formula 3	Mika Salo (Ralt RT34)
URS Pre '83 Formula Ford 2000	Jeff Gresswell (Van Diemen RF82)
Vauxhall Finance Sports	Tony Bridge (Mallock MK27)
Pre '65 Saloons	David Missions (Lotus Cortina)

June 17 1990
BARC meeting

Formula Vauxhall Lotus	Kurt Luby
Formula Forward	Mark Goddard
Mazda MX5 Cup	Patrick Watts
Vauxhall Finance Sports	Tony Bridge (Mallock MK27)
Chris Knott Insurance Alfa Romeos	Terry Stacey (33)
Chris Knott Insurance Alfa Romeos Class F	Paul Edwards (Alfasud)
Caterham 7s	Magnus Laird

When the Formula 3 circus returned at the end of May, Salo turned the tables on Hakkinen as their title battle continued to rage. However, Hakkinen's drive was remarkable as he had stalled on the parade lap and started dead last! By the time the teams returned to Thruxton in late September, Hakkinen had clinched the title but Salo claimed another win.

September 9 1990
BARC meeting

Robolift Sports 1600	Glenn Eagling (Mallock MK20)
Spheric Monoposto	David Dudley (Anson SA4)
Firestone Production Saloons	Andy Middlehurst (Ford Sierra Cosworth)
LMF Formula E	Austin Kinsella (Van Diemen RF78)
Motorola Codex Handicap	Alan Feaver (Ford Capri)
Delta Freight Monoposto	Kevin Pope (Reynard SF82)
Morgans	Rob Wells (+8)
Wurth Multisports	Wayne Bryant

September 23 1990
British Touring Car meeting

Esso British Touring Cars	Andy Rouse (Ford Sierra RS500)
British Formula 3	Mika Salo (Ralt RT34)
Ford Audio Fiestas	Ian Briggs
P&O Junior Formula Ford 1600	Simon Harrison (Van Diemen RF90)
Honda CRX	Patrick Watts
Classic Roadsports	John Goldsmith (Aston Martin DB4)

October 14 1990
Championship Finals meeting

Modified Production Saloons Classes C & D	Terry Stone (Toyota Corolla)
Modified Production Saloons Classes A & B	Andrew MacKenzie (Ford Sierra XR4i)
Vauxhall Finance Sports	Nick Carr (Mallock Mk28B)
HSCC Historic Formula 1	Mike Wilds (March 811)
Firestone Production Saloons	Andy Middlehurst (Ford Sierra Cosworth)
Classic Roadsports	Martin Shaw (MGA)
CK Tools Sports 2000	Mike Wright (Lola T90)

In October, kart racing returned to Thruxton after a long break with a round of the European Super Kart Challenge. On two-wheels, although the endurance race had switched to Brands Hatch in 1978, one or two meetings continued each season. In 1991, Truck racing arrived at Thruxton and, after necessary modifications to cope with the racing monsters, the diesel-dicers wowed the crowd with their antics.

March 17 1991
BARC meeting

Midtherm 74-80 Formula Ford 1600	Nigel Greensall (Royale RP26)
BARC/MGOC Class A	Andrew Storer (Midget)
Firestone Production Cars	Michael Woodcock (Ford Sierra Cosworth)
Vauxhall Finance Sports	Richard Mallock (Mallock MK29)
BARC/MGOC Class B	Lance Pickering (Maestro)

April 1 1991
Formula 3 meeting

British Formula 3	Rubens Barrichello (Ralt RT35)
Motorcraft Formula Ford 1600	Marc Goossens (Van Diemen RF91)
Modified Production Saloons Classes A & B	David Tetley (Rover SD1)
Modified Production Saloons Classes C & D	Ray West (Opel Ascona)
Honda Mobil CRX	Andy Ackerley
Dunlop Rover 216GTi	Tiff Needell
Bebecar Toyota Formula 3	Steve Maxted (Argo JM6)

Easter Monday 1991, April 1st, was headlined by the second round of the British Formula 3 Championship. Despite muffing the start for the second race in a row, Brazilian Rubens Barrichello stormed through the field to win from Jordi Gene and Rickard Rydell. Also in the field were David Coulthard and Pedro Diniz!

At the end of April, the BARC rescue unit was called into action when returning from Brands Hatch! The unit, crewed by Terry Williamson and Paul Golding, was flagged down to assist at a road accident on the A303 when a car had rolled and injured the occupants. The rescue unit crew helped stabilise the casualties until the normal emergency services arrived.

March 1991. Production Saloon racer Michael Edwards gives the marshals a scare on the approach to the Chicane.
Photo: Nick Rose.

May 6 1991	
BARC meeting	
Renault Clio Elf UK Cup	David Kay
Thundersaloons	Pete Stevens/Chris Millard (Vauxhall Carlton)
Firestone Production Cars	Michael Woodcock (Ford Sierra Cosworth)
HSCC Pre '75 Sportscars	Sean Walker (Toj SC205)
P&O Formula Renault	Jason Plato (Van Diemen FR91)

Jun 16 1991	
BARC meeting	
Formula Vauxhall	Warren Hughes
Formula Vauxhall Junior	Dario Franchitti
Pre '74 Formula Ford 1600	Stuart Kestenbaum (Rostron CT3)
Pre '65 Saloons	Nickie Torregiani (Ford Mustang)
Vauxhall Finance Sports	Tony Bridge (Mallock MK29V)
Formula First	Oliver Gavin

May 27 1991	
British Touring Car meeting	
Esso British Touring Cars	John Cleland (Vauxhall Cavalier)
British Formula 3	Stephen Robertson (Ralt RT35)
Ford Audio Fiestas	Brian Farminer
Porsche Supercup	Barrie Williams (Carrera)
Molyslip Sports 2001	Chris Gilbert (Lola T89/50)

August 11 1991	
British Formula 3000 meeting	
British Formula 3000	Dave Coyne (Reynard 90D)
Motorcraft Open Formula Ford 1600	Andrew McAuley (Swift FB91)
Sports 1600	Clive Woodward (Centaur 14X)
BARC/MGOC Classes B and C	Robert Oldershaw (Maestro)
BARC/MGOC Class A	Grahame Davis (MGB)

The outright circuit record took another step nearer the 60s barrier when the British Formula 3000 teams gathered for round seven of the series in August '91. An impressive 16-car field was headed throughout the meeting by Dave Coyne in a GJ Motorsport Reynard 90D who took the record down to 1m03.66s (133.23mph). However, a cloud had been cast over this meeting by the death of Paul Warwick in the previous round at Oulton Park a month earlier. Ironically, Paul still led the championship points table as the cars switched to his home track.

Two months earlier, Thruxton lost a key figure when Ian Taylor died in a Rover 216GTi at Spa. Having concluded his professional racing career several years before, Taylor was racing for fun but tragically lost his life in a violent accident at the Belgian circuit. Later, a children's play area would be constructed adjacent to the Goodwood restaurant and named in Taylor's memory.

By then, Bill Coombs was effectively managing the school as his racing took very much a back seat. The pair had become close friends during the years they had worked together and it was an awful time for everyone involved. 'Ian was a very close friend and we raced a lot of things together. His accident really hit me hard and then I had to go and replace him in the Rover,' remembers Ian Flux.

'I just continued working with the business in mind and straightaway got on the phone to all the major clients,' recalls Coombs. Throwing his energies into keeping the business running was one way of helping him over the grief of losing a close friend. Since then, Bill has become a director of the company along with Moya Taylor. Her son James would later work at the school as an instructor.

August 26 1991	
Truck Race meeting	
Firestone National 2CVs	David O'Keefe
Renault 5GT Turbos	Nigel Albon

September 8 1991	
BARC meeting	
Historic GT	Lawrence Rose (Osella PA3)
AMOC Intermarque	Jonathan Baker (Porsche 930B)
Historic Formula 1	Patrick Blakeney (March 811)
Classic Sports	Tony Thompson (Lotus Elan)
QED Classic Formula 3	Mike Wilds (Ensign LNF3)
Standard Road Sports	Nigel Reuben (TVR Griffith)
Improved Road Sports	Gery Wainwright (Lotus Elan)

September 22 1991	
British Touring Car meeting	
Esso British Touring Cars	Steve Soper (BMW M3)
Motorcraft Formula Ford 1600	Dino Morelli (Reynard 91FF)
Unipart Club Metro	Peter Baldwin
ARP Formula 3	Paul Quinn (Reynard 863)
Mazda MX5 Cup	Robin Parsons

In September there was high drama in the penultimate round of the British Touring Car Championship. With the title firmly in sight, Will Hoy arrived at Thruxton with a real chance of settling the

matter in his Omega-backed BMW M3 run by Vic Lee's team. While Steve Soper ran away at the head of the field in his works BMW, Hoy held second until a clash with Jonathan Palmer's BMW sent him spinning at Club.

Hoy's nightmare continued, however, as he resumed in seventh place immediately behind title rival John Cleland in the Vauxhall Cavalier. The tension in the situation showed as the title contenders clashed several times over the next couple of laps and Hoy was eventually forced to retire when damaged bodywork fouled a tyre. Cleland, with his tyres well past their best, struggled home eighth to keep the title open until the final round at Silverstone two weeks later. There, it all went right for Hoy as he made sure of the crown.

October 13 1991	
Championship Finals meeting	
British Formula 3	Steve Robertson (Ralt RT35)
P&O Formula Renault	Jason Plato (Van Diemen RF91)
Formula Vauxhall Junior	Dario Franchitti
Vauxhall Finance Sports	Tony Bridge (Mallock MK29V)
Renault Clio Elf Cup	Mike Mills
URS Pre '83 Formula Ford 2000	Steve Pontin-Warltier (Van Diemen RF82)

Three weeks later at Thruxton, the 1991 British Formula 3 title was settled on Championship Finals Day. David Coulthard started the day with a chance of grabbing the title from Rubens Barrichello but, while Steve Robertson won the race, Coulthard lost his chance when a very defensive Hideki Noda cut across his bows at the Complex. With a nose fin pointing skywards, Coulthard knew that his chances were gone and retired to the pits as Barrichello took a safe fifth to clinch the title. But it wasn't an entirely bad day for aspiring Scottish single-seater racers as 18-year old Dario Franchitti clinched the inaugural Formula Vauxhall Junior title. Dario pipped David Leslie Racing team-mate David Cuff to the title by winning the race while Cuff struggled home seventh as an electrical gremlin slowed his car. Significantly, Cuff soon disappeared from the sport while Franchitti went on to success in the International Touring Car series and then Indy Cars.

Another rising talent first made his mark on the British single-seater scene as the 1992 season opened. While the works cars of Andrew McAuley (Swift) and Jamie Spence (Van Diemen) clashed in the first round of the Rapid Fit Open Formula Ford 1600 Championship, 18-year old Jonny Kane picked his way through to victory. His privately-run ex-Warren Hughes car had only been collected the previous day, but the Ulsterman drove a fine race to put his name on the map.

Derek Warwick encourages brother Paul before the start of the March 1989 Formula 3 race. Photo: BRDC Archives.

Keith Odor (left) and Laurence Bristow battle in Touring Cars, May 1991. Photo: Duncan Hands.

Tim Maitland (number 14) is central to a Formula Vauxhall Junior drama going into Campbell in June 1991. Photo: John Gaisford.

March 15 1992	
BARC meeting	
Rapid Fit Open Formula Ford 1600	Jonny Kane (Van Diemen RF91)
Falken Modified Production Saloons B & D	John Hammersley (Vauxhall Astra GTE)
Falken Modified Production Saloons A & C	David Tetley (Rover SD1)
Sports 1600	Malcolm Jackson (Mallock MK20B)
Ford Fiestas	Trevor Reeves
Renault 5 Turbos	Craig Albon

April 5 1992	
BARC meeting	
BMWs	Steve Guglielmi (M3)
Molyslip Sports 2000	Glenn Dudley (Lola T87/90)
Classic Roadsports	Graham Warren (Aston Martin DB5)
Tandon ARP Formula 3	Paul Quinn (Reynard 863)
Pirelli Production Porsches	Chris Heeley (Carrera RS)
QED Classic Formula 3	Winston Bunn (Enslgin LNF3)

Qualifying for the Formula Ford race was marred by a frightening accident that befell New Zealander Andrew Neale. On his first flying lap, Neale was caught by a strong gust of wind at Goodwood that lifted the nose of his Reynard. With no steering, the car speared off the track and somersaulted as many as eight times before coming to rest upside down. Neale was removed carefully by the BARC rescue crews and transferred to Odstock Hospital in Salisbury with two crushed vertebrae and five broken toes. He subsequently made a full recovery but the cost of the accident effectively ruined his chances of furthering his career in England.

Easter was late in 1992 but, as usual, the meeting was headlined by a round of the British Formula 3 Championship. However, the race ended in tragedy as young Dutch racer Marcel Albers lost his life in a dreadful accident at the Chicane. His Ralt RT35 was battling with the similar car of team mate Elton Julian when they touched wheels under braking. Albers' car was pitched into the air and then flipped several times before clearing the tyre wall and hitting the debris fencing. The marshals were immediately on the scene but could not aid poor Albers who had sustained head and neck injuries. Although one or two spectators were slightly injured,

the debris fencing had done its job and halted the car. The delays while the fencing was repaired meant that the race was not re-started. Just short of his 25th birthday, Albers had previously won the opening round of the championship and was a popular member of the Formula 3 fraternity. The BARC rescue crews were tested again at the end of the day when Jake Benson rolled his Formula Ford after a clash of wheels with Paul Wighton at Allard. His Van Diemen landed upside down on the track and it took nearly 30 minutes to carefully extract him from the car. Fortunately, his injuries were restricted to concussion but the delay ran up to the 6.30pm curfew and the race was declared void after just three racing laps.

Just two weeks after the tragic Easter meeting, the Formula 3 teams were back for the fifth round of the championship on May Day Monday. Remarkably, 17-year old Julian claimed pole position and won the race under pressure from Gil de Ferran. After the tragedy of just two weeks earlier, it was an emotional win for Julian and the Alan Docking team. On the podium, Julian dedicated his victory to Marcel Albers, having raced with Albers' name across the top of his helmet in tribute to the Dutchman. At that meeting, the Reverend Williams

April 20 1992	
British Touring Car meeting	
Esso British Touring Cars	John Cleland (Vauxhall Cavalier)
British Formula 3	Gil de Ferran (Reynard 923)
P&O Formula Renault	Ivan Arias (Alpa FR92)
Renault Clio UK Cup	Matt Johnson
Rapid Fit Open Formula Ford 1600	Vincent Radermecker (Van Diemen RF92)

May 4 1992	
Formula 3 meeting	
British Formula 3	Elton Julian (Ralt RT35)
Historic Touring Cars	Garry Townsend (Lous Cortina)
Supersports Vauxhall	Peter Cocks (Mallock MK27/29)
Porsche Supercup	Robin Gray (Carrera RS)
TVR Tuscans	Gerry Marshall
Clearway Sports/ Saloons	Tony Sugden (Skoda Coupe)

American Elton Julian (May 1992) races with his helmet bearing tribute to former team-mate Marcel Albers. Photo: Words & Pictures.

of Chilbolton performed a blessing on the startline for newly-wed marshals Gary Cole and Kerry Sleeman from Southampton! The couple had become engaged in the pit lane the previous September.

In his report to the BARC Annual General Meeting at the end of 1992, Michael Groves reported that both circuit use and spectator attendances were down on previous years and that the profit for the circuit was lower than expected. The recession was undoubtedly biting.

May 25 1992
BARC meeting

Formula Vauxhall Lotus	Jeremy Cotterill
P&O Formula Renault	Ivan Arias (Alpa FR92)
Formula Vauxhall Junior	Guy Smith
Renault Clio UK Cup	Matt Johnson
Falken Modified Production Saloons B & D	John Hammersley (Vauxhall Astra)
Falken Modified Production Saloons A & C	Brian Cox (Peugeot 205GTi)

June 14 1992
British Formula 2 meeting

Halfords British Formula 2	Jason Elliott (Reynard 91D)
Formula Vauxhall Lotus	Piers Hunnisett
Formula Vauxhall Junior	Dan Liddle
Production Cars	Frank Cundell/John Wilson (BMW M3)
Supersports Vauxhall	Tony Bridge (Mallock MK29)

September 27 1992
Formula 3 meeting

British Formula 3	Gil de Ferran (Reynard 923)
P&O Formula Renault	Pedro de la Rosa (Alpa FR92)
Renault Clio UK Cup	Dave Cox
Prosport 3000/ Sports 2000	Peter Hardman (Prosport 3000)
Silhouette Specials	Robin Hooker (Ferrari 308)

August 31 1992
BARC meeting

MGOC Class A	Grahame Davis (MGB)
Cox & Buckles TR Register	Mike Richards (TR7 V8)
MGOC Classes B & C	Paul Willows (Maestro)
Westfields	Richard Smith
Historic Formula Racing Cars	Michael Schryver (Lotus 69)
Classic Roadsports	Alister Sinclair (Aston Martin DB4)
Morgans	Tony Dron (+8)
RJB Mining Group 6 Sports	Mike Wilds (Chevron B31/36)

Gil de Ferran (left) takes on fellow Brazilian Pedro Diniz on the Thruxton podium!
Photo: Words & Pictures.

September 13 1992	
BARC meeting	
Rapid Fit Open Formula Ford 1600	Andrew McAuley (Van Diemen RF92)
Post Historic Touring Cars	Ian Lawless (Mazda RX3)
Mobil Honda CRX	Warren Briggs
Production Cars	Lionel Abbott (Saab 9000CS)
Thundersaloons - race one	Nigel Mustill (Ford Sierra RS500)
Thundersaloons - race two	Pete Stevens (Vauxhall Carlton)

October 11 1992	
Championship Finals meeting	
Formula Vauxhall Junior	Guy Smith
URS Pre '83 Formula Ford 2000	Mike Whatley (Van Diemen RF81)
Production Cars	Lionel Abbott (Saab 9000CS)
Westfields	Stephen Kimber
Supersports Vauxhall	Martin White (Mallock MK28)
Sports Car Invitation	Guy Parry (Caterham 7)

CHAPTER NINE

The Silver Jubilee and beyond

March 21 1993	
BARC meeting	
Falken Modified Production Saloons B & D	John Hammersley (Vauxhall Astra)
Falken Modified Production Saloons A & C	Ray West (Opel Ascona)
Monoposto/ Monoposto Kent	Mark Storer (Reynard SF86)
Mini Seven	Stephen Woodrow
750MC Road Sports	Matthew Wurr (Morgan +8)
Mini Miglia	Bill Sollis

April 4 1993	
Formula 3 meeting	
British Formula 3	Marc Goossens (Reynard 933)
Post Historic Touring Cars	Brian Stevens (Jaguar XJ12)
Concept Supersports Vauxhall	Tony Bridge (Mallock MK29)
Maranello Ferrari Challenge	Rob Schirle (308GTB)
Pirelli Production Porsches	Bob Berridge (944 Turbo)
Production Cars	Lionel Abbott (Saab 9000CS)

May 3 1993	
Brooklands Raceday	
Classic Formula 3	Barrie Maskell (GRD 373)
RJB Mining Group 6 Sports	Mike Wilds (Chevron B31/36)
ARP Formula 3	Jeff Gresswell (Reynard 873)
Historic Formula 1	Geoff Farmer (Theodore N183)
Standard Road Sports	Guy Evans (Lotus Elan)
Historic Formula Ford 1600	Mike Whatley (Crossle 20F)

May 31 1993	
BARC meeting	
Moss Europe MGCC BCV8	Peter Hiley
MGOC Classes B & C Qualification race	Michael Weidner (Maestro)
MGOC Classes B & C	Paul Willows (Maestro)
MGOC Class A	Alan Springle (Midget)
Halfords MG Midgets - Modified	Steve Westwood
Halfords MG Midgets - Road Going	Terry Farman
Austin Healeys	Nigel Bance (Sprite)
Classic Sports	Ronnie Farmer (Aston Martin DB5)

Despite the gloomy economic situation, plans went ahead for the Silver Jubilee Meeting in June 1993. With support from The European newspaper, a very special meeting was organised to include a variety of action on two and four wheels along with a showground area, air displays and classic car cavalcades. For this special occasion, the Jochen Rindt Memorial Trophy was presented to Marc Surer, who dominated the Historic Formula 2 race in his beautifully-presented March 792. A race for Le Mans Sports Prototypes was won by Mike Knight in his rare Matra MS650 while other races catered for historic racing motorbikes and karts.

June 27 1993	
Silver Jubilee meeting	
Le Mans Sports Prototypes	Mike Knight (Matra MS650)
Jochen Rindt Memorial Trophy Historic Formula 2	Marc Surer (March 792)
National Saloon Car Cup	Charlie Cox (Ford Escort Cosworth)

July 25 1993	
Truck Race meeting	
Firestone Citroen 2CVs	Tim Grey
Castrol Honda CRX	Andy Ackerley

However, the star performer of the Silver Jubilee meeting on June 27th was due to be Damon Hill in the latest Williams-Renault FW15C. With a large crowd gathered around, disaster struck when the engine refused to start. It was undoubtedly a major disappointment for the crowd but Frank Williams generously offered to return to Thruxton for the October 10th Finals meeting to give the car a run. Then, with the car running cleanly, Damon stunned the crowd with a 15-lap demonstration that produced the fastest ever laps of the circuit. Damon's best was an incredible 57.6s, a speed of 147.25mph. It was an awesome performance that left the crowd open-mouthed.

Handling a current grand prix car around Thruxton left Damon open-mouthed! Photo: John Gaisford.

August 27/29 1993	
British Touring Car meeting	
Auto Trader British Touring Cars	David Leslie (Vauxhall Cavalier)
Formula Vauxhall Junior	Ralph Firman Jnr
P&O Formula Renault	Tim Stafford (Orion FR91)
Ford Credit Fiestas	Trevor Reeves
Elf Oil Renault Clio Cup	Dave Cox
Formula Vauxhall Lotus	Martin O'Connell
Open Formula Ford 1600	Russell Ingall (Van Diemen RF93)

For the only time in the circuit's history, there was no Easter meeting at Thruxton in 1993 as the European Grand Prix was being held at Donington that weekend. Headline meeting of the season, aside from the Silver Jubilee, was the British Touring Car Championship meeting over the August Bank Holiday which drew a 14,000 crowd. They witnessed David Leslie score a memorable victory in the Ray Mallock-run Ecurie Ecosse Vauxhall Cavalier.

September 26 1993	
BARC meeting	
Caterham Vauxhall	Robert Nearn
Dunlop Rover GTi	Russell Grady
British Formula 2	Phillipe Adams (Reynard 91D)
VW Polo G40 Cup	Stephen Day
BMWs	Colin Wells (M3)

Though a relatively quiet affair, the September 1993 meeting brought another new outright circuit record as a small British Formula 2 grid did battle. The race was dominated by Belgian Phillippe Adams who trimmed

the record to 1m02.75s en route to victory. The '93 racing season closed with the final Formula 3 meeting of the season. Having already clinched the title, Kelvin Burt took his ninth win from 15 races to underline his superiority as Oliver Gavin and Jan Magnussen led the chase.

October 10 1993	
Championship Finals meeting	
British Formula 3	Kelvin Burt (Dallara F393)
Concept Supersports Vauxhall	Guy Woodward (Mallock MK27SG)
Production Cars	Lionel Abbott (Saab 9000CS)
Sports 1600	Clive Woodward (Centaur 14X)
URS Pre '83 Formula Ford 2000	Steve Nichols (Van Diemen RF82)
Westfields	Steve Newey

At the end of the 1993 season, the Thruxton company had enjoyed a better year and made a profit. However, the report to the AGM pointed out that the profit was not enough to support major re-investment on the type of improvements needed to keep up with other major British circuits. Even so, the entire paddock would be re-surfaced in time for the following season.

Easter 1994 brought the British Touring Car Championship package of races to Thruxton and a huge crowd swamped the traffic arrangements as queues backed up onto the A303. Spectators complained of long delays to get in, and some never did, being forced to abandon their visit as racing started while they were still in the queue. When the Touring Cars returned in

Marc Surer's March 792
was a star of the Silver
Jubilee meeting in
June 1993.
Photo: David Dickson.

May 1995, the lesson of '94 had been learnt and greatly improved traffic arrangements were in place.

The 16,000 spectators who did get into the circuit witnessed Gabriele Tarquini draw first blood for Alfa Romeo with its 155TS. At the start of his successful title campaign, Tarquini fended off John Cleland's Vauxhall Cavalier in a nail-biting finish. The meeting also marked a piece of history as three sixteen year-olds contested the opening round of the Formula Vauxhall Junior Championship. Changes to the race licensing requirements now permitted 16-year olds with suitable karting backgrounds to race cars before they could legally drive on the road. Marc Hynes, Chris Buchan and Stuart Moseley were the history-makers and it was Buchan who finished the best of three in 10th place.

The Whitsun Bank Holiday meeting featured British Formula 3 and marked another victory for rising Danish star Jan Magnussen who was to be the dominant force of the Formula 3 season. On the same programme was a rare Thruxton race for the mighty TVR Tuscans which allowed the evergreen Ian Flux yet another victory. Through the summer months, a series of relatively low-key meetings brought a mix of classic and historic cars to the circuit, before a second Formula 3 meeting in mid-September.

Magnussen duly claimed yet another Formula 3 victory as he fended off Vincent Radermecker and Ricardo Rosset. Already secure as champion, Magnussen had his sights set on another record as he started the race. His hero, Ayrton Senna, had won 12 races in his British Formula 3 campaign, and Magnussen wanted to beat that statistic. Sure enough, his 13th win from 17 races followed. 'I like to think I'm a good driver, but I always thought he was the best,' said Jan after the race. Four months earlier, of course, Senna had lost his life at Imola and that news had shaken Magnussen to the core as he stood in the Silverstone paddock on that fateful first day of May.

Highlight of the October Championship Finals meeting was a nail-biting climax to the Supersports Vauxhall Championship. Three drivers started the day almost level on points and, in beautiful autumnal sunshine, enacted their battle in a tremendous atmosphere of sporting rivalry. Mike Evans and Mike Swinnerton, neighbours and friends, represented the Mallock marque while BARC legal adviser Guy Woodward carried the Phantom hopes. In a commendably clean yet hard-fought race, Evans held his nerve to win under immense pressure from his rivals and clinched a hugely popular title.

October 10th 1993.
Damon Hill stunned the
crowd with some
demonstration laps in
the Williams FW15C.
Photo: John Gaisford.

March 20 1994
BARC meeting

Classic Saloons	Allen Lloyd (Jaguar MK1)
MGOC Class A	Nigel Woolcott (Midget)
MGOC Classes B & C	Robert Oldershaw (Maestro)
Harlow Renault 5 Turbos	Steve Alderton
URS Pre '83 Formula Ford 2000	Nick Owen (Van Diemen RF82)
Historic Touring Cars	Les Nash (Lotus Cortina)
Post Historic Touring Cars	Brian Stevens (Jaguar XJ12)

April 2/4 1994
British Touring Car meeting

Auto Trader British Touring Cars	Gabriele Tarquini (Alfa Romeo 155TS)
Formula Ford 1600	Jonny Kane (Swift SC94F)
Formula Vauxhall	Jamie Davies
Elf Renault Clio UK Cup	David Shaw
Ultrafilter Formula Renault	James Matthews (Van Diemen RF94)
Ford Credit Fiestas	Matt Johnson
Formula Vauxhall Junior	Henry Stanton
ICS Historic Racing Saloons	Dennis Clark (Chevrolet Camaro)

May 2 1994
BARC meeting

Pro Sport 3000	Peter Hardman
Caterham Challenge	Chris Johnson
Thoroughbred Sports	David Heynes (Aston Martin DB4)
Honda CRX	Tim Hood
Slick 50 Road Saloons	Paul Rose (VW Golf GTi)

May 30 1994
Formula 3 meeting

British Formula 3	Jan Magnussen (Dallara F394)
TVR Tuscans	Ian Flux
Foxboro Production Cars	Lionel Abbott (Saab 9000CS)
Dunlop Rover GTi	Warren Briggs
Caterham Vauxhall	Keith Farrance
BRC Formula Ford 1600	Nigel Greensall (Van Diemen RF86)

June 26 1994
BARC meeting

Morgans	Matthew Wurr (+8)
Production Porsches Classes A & B	Hugh Price (911 Carrera)
Production Porsches Classes C & D	Peter Chambers (911SC)
Thoroughbred Sports	Peter Foster (Aston Martin DB4)
Maranello Ferrari Challenge	Mike Millard (512BB)
Historic Replicas	Cheng Lim (RAM SC)
AMOC Intermarque	Gerry Marshall (Aston Martin DBS V8)

July 24 1994
Haynes Historic Superprix

RJB Mining Historic Sports	Willie Green (Chevron B31/36)
Oregon Classic Formula 3	David Proctor (Brabham BT38)
Jochen Rindt Trophy Historic Formula 2	Martin Stretton (March 712)
Thoroughbred Grand Prix Cars	John Wilson (Williams FW08C)
BARC 2-Litre Formula 2	Steve Jewell (Chevron B48)
Classic Formula Ford 1600	Stuart Tilley (Dulon MP15)

September 1994. Rover Turbo racers Rob Mears and Brian Heerey come to grief. Photo: S Cranston.

August 29 1994	
Brooklands Raceday	
Classic Sports	Roy Eaton (Marcos GT)
Historic Formula Ford 1600	Keith Norman (Merlyn MK11)
Sports Racing Cars	Ryan Hodges (Flintstone)
Historic Single Seaters	Simon Hadfield (Lotus 78)
Improved Road Sports	Nick Randall (Jaguar E-Type)
Standard Road Sports	John Henderson (Lotus Seven)
Road Sports	Andrew Stafford (Datsun 240Z)

September 11 1994	
Formula 3 meeting	
British Formula 3	Jan Magnussen (Dallara F394)
Dunlop Rover Turbo Cup	Nick Carr
National Saloon Car Cup	Charlie Cox (Ford Escort Cosworth)
BRDC GT	Chris Hodgetts (Marcos LM500)
Foxboro Production Cars	George Agyeton (Ford Escort Cosworth)

At the close of the 1994 season, Fred Reeves finally stood down as Chief Marshal at Thruxton, after 20 years in the role. In the 30 years of Thruxton as a permanent circuit, Fred marshalled at most meetings and probably missed less than 10 meetings in 30 seasons. 'I took the job for a year and kept it for 20,' he admits. During that time he became a respected and popular face with the marshals during his customary circuit walkabouts. In his report on the 1994 season, BARC Chairman Michael Groves reported that an increase in racing school days had helped the viability of the track. Improvements for 1995 centred on an extension to the spectator banking out from the Complex towards Noble and a newly-constructed press box at the Chicane.

October 9 1994	
Championship Finals meeting	
Westfields	Anthony Brown
Modified Production Saloons Classes B & D	John Hammersley (Vauxhall Astra)
Modified Production Saloons Classes A & C	Craig Davies (Ford Sapphire)
Formula Renault	David Henderson (Swift FR94)
Supersports Vauxhall	Mike Evans (Mallock MK31)
URS Pre '83 Formula Ford 2000	Nicholas Pearce (Van Diemen RF82)

After a season-opening club meeting in late March, the Easter Monday meeting featured a pair of races for the Formula 3 Championship. Oliver Gavin returned to Formula 3 for '95 after being pipped to the '93 title by Kelvin Burt and ultimately won both races but only after Warren Hughes and James Matthews had clashed in the first race. With two Formula 3 races planned for the one-day meeting, each race was a frantic 10-lap sprint.

The first race was run on a damp track and as Hughes and Matthews battled up towards the Chicane, a wayward backmarker inadvertently got in their way. Hughes suddenly lost his advantage and into the

Chicane for the last time, Matthews saw a chance for his first Formula 3 victory. However, the challenge didn't quite work and the cars inter-locked wheels and spun off, leaving Gavin to motor through to victory.

March 26 1995	
BARC meeting	
Sports/Saloons	Tony Sugden (Skoda 130RS)
Chris Knott Alfa Romeos Classes A-E	Chris Snowdon (GTV6)
Chris Knott Alfa Romeos Class F	Mark Ticehurst (33)
BARC/MGOC Class A	Alan Yeomans (MGB)
BARC/MGOC Class B	Richard Hollebon (Maestro)
Modified Production Saloons Classes A&C	Andrew Mackenzie (Opel Monza)
Modified Production Saloons Classes B&D	Derek Wileman (Vauxhall Cavalier)
Monoposto/ Monoposto Kent	Jim Blockley (Ralt RT3)

April 17 1995	
Easter Formula 3 meeting	
British Formula 3 - race one	Oliver Gavin (Dallara F395)
British Formula 3 - race two	Oliver Gavin (Dallara F395)
Maranello Ferrari Challenge	Ian Khan (F355)
Dunlop Rover Turbo Cup	Alastair Lyall
Pirelli Porsche Cup	David Jones (928GTS)
Classic Grand Prix Cars	John Fenning (Williams FW07)
Morgans	Peter Garland (+8)

The second race was held on a fully wet track and Ralph Firman led going into the final lap. However, when he got to an increasingly-wet Complex, his car snapped into a spin and for the second time in one afternoon, Gavin gratefully accepted the lead on the final lap. Ironically, the same meeting would produce further drama in both 1996 and '97.

On the same programme, Stockbridge veteran John Fenning scored a local win in the Classic Grand Prix Car race by steering his Williams FW07 to victory, while an action-packed Dunlop Rover Turbo Cup race will be

remembered for the massive accident that befell Russell Grady on the exit of Segrave. After a clash of cars, his Rover Turbo rolled several times but Grady was thankfully unhurt.

May 6/8 1995	
British Touring Car meeting	
British Touring Cars	Alain Menu (Renault Laguna)
British Touring Cars	James Thompson (Vauxhall Cavalier)
Formula Renault Sport	Guy Smith (Van Diemen RF95)
Slick 50 Formula Ford	Mario Haberfeld (Van Diemen RF95)
Formula Vauxhall	Martin O'Connell
Formula Vauxhall Junior	Marc Hynes
Elf Renault Clio Cup	David Shaw
Historic Racing Saloons	Roly Nix (Chevrolet Camaro)
Ford Credit Fiestas	Colin Stancombe

In early May 1995, James Thompson made a piece of history by becoming the youngest ever winner of a British Touring Car Championship race when he steered his Vauxhall Cavalier to victory in the second race of the day. The Yorkshireman had celebrated his 21st birthday just 12 days earlier. In the first Touring Car race of the day, the Williams Touring Car Engineering team had scored its first ever win with the Renault Laguna of Alain Menu. The grand prix squad had taken over the works Renaults from the start of the '95 season, running them from a separate set-up under team-manager Ian Harrison.

But that May Bank Holiday Monday meeting will also be remembered for a terrifying accident that befell Total Cup privateer Charlie Cox. The popular Aussie was lucky to escape major injury when his Ford Mondeo speared off the track on the approach to the Chicane at around 135mph. The car then launched into a sickening series of rolls before coming to rest against a bank. The marshals were quickly on hand and Cox was released with great care from an accident he was fortunate to survive. He will never forget that meeting...

'I always, always loved Thruxton and for whatever reason I'd always done really well there. It's one of those circuits where you need a lot of balls, or stupidity! The first time I raced there was in a Porsche when I was learning the British circuits in 1992. I was in fifth gear everywhere! I thought 'What is going on?' I'd never been on a circuit that flowed like this, I couldn't believe how fast it was. It wasn't like anything at home in Australia. It was so fast that everything seemed to be in slow motion. When you have a moment there, it takes 10 or 15 seconds. It all happens so slowly,' explains Cox.

'I did well there in the Escort Cosworth and the people were very helpful. But it is so different, there are British circuits and then there is Thruxton. A set-up for Thruxton is useless anywhere else and vice versa. The first time we raced there in the Escort, we won, set the lap record and it had been so hard on the springs that when we finished, the suspension had punched through the top of the coil tower and split the inner wing. And that was in a 10-lap screamer!`

'So we went there in the Touring Car and I thought "This is a piece of cake, I know Thruxton, this'll be no problem at all.' In the race before at Brands we'd had one of the highest finishes that a privateer ever had and I arrived at Thruxton with my tail up. I started the first race off the back of the grid with a 10-second penalty after a weight infringement in qualifying. But I passed a lot of people in the race and finished second or third in the privateers,' recalls Charlie.

'In the second race, we went around on the first lap and I locked up going into the Complex because we had a problem with the brakes. I should have stopped then but I thought the tyres were cold and told myself not to think about it. All the way round the back of the circuit you don't use the brakes... I didn't even open my eyes for most if it!

'When you hit the brakes going up the hill to the Chicane you are doing 140mph and you are going to drop down to 50mph. I hit the brakes and it was like pulling the handbrake on. One rear wheel locked up, but the front tyres didn't even get flat-spotted because they had no brakes at all. It turned the car sideways, if it had spun a few times I'd have lost some energy. As bad luck would have it, the car went off at 90 degrees parallel with a track off the side of the circuit,' he says.

'At 130mph and going sideways, both wheels on the driver's side dropped into the dirt. That drop stopped the car dead, lifted it into the air where it pirouetted about three times then tumbled and tumbled and tumbled. It rolled 11 times, we counted later, and eventually landed on the service road. I needed a pass to get back into the circuit! My first thought was that I'd landed in the grandstand. The impact had split my helmet open. On the first impact, my head hit the roll cage and that knocked me out.

'The door came off and my arms were flailing around. The roof rolled on my arm at one point and as a result of that, the international Touring Car regulations were changed. Now, the window nets have to be attached to the roll cage and not to the door. It was only because I had a mechanical failure that the car darted off to the left. You wouldn't naturally go off there. I was actually hurt more than was said at the time. I had a fractured skull, fluid on the brain and a partially detached retina. I was in hospital for a couple of weeks and off work for a couple of months,' remembers Cox.

'But for all that, Thruxton has always been my favourite circuit and I've still gone well there since. Old habits die hard, I haven't learnt yet. I was unlucky to have the accident and lucky to survive it. There was a big post mortem and it turned out before we got the car, someone had washed the master cylinder out with some sort of solvent. That reacted badly with brand new brake fluid and before the race we had changed the fluid completely,' he explains.

'There was plenty of pedal but it had distorted the seals within the master cylinder and when I hit the brakes, the seals were so swollen that no fluid got to the front. Enough fluid got to the rear to lock them on

1995 Ford Fiesta Challenge. Champion John Bintcliffe, during his rapid rise to Touring Car fame, kerb-hops the Halfords Racing Fiesta. Photo: Action 35.

and it couldn't move back. They reconstructed the remains of the braking system on the bench and that it was they found.

'Also, I wouldn't be here if I hadn't been wearing my neck brace. At the end of '94 I hurt my neck in a big shunt at Oulton Park and I got a neck brace. Professor Watkins, who looked after me in hospital, said if I hadn't been wearing the brace I'd have broken my neck. I still wear it, it's my lucky neck-brace!'

The BRDC GT Championship was back on August 6th 1995 when Dorset veteran Win Percy guided the Harrier LR9C to victory and later in the month Gerry Marshall showed that he had lost none of his flair by bagging a brace of wins in two different Aston Martins during the August Bank Holiday meeting. Another Aston Martin victory that day went to Ian Taylor Racing School instructor Pat Blakeney who showed his versatility in a car from the Goldsmith and Young stable.

Just two meetings in 1995 featured Formula 3 but the championship showdown headlined the October Finals meeting. While Warren Hughes won the race, a measured drive to fourth secured the title for Oliver Gavin after a season-long battle with Ralph Firman. That day, Firman could only struggle home seventh as Gavin bagged the title by eight points. The Championship Finals meeting also marked a piece of history when Mike Evans scored the first win for a rear-engined Mallock as he steered the latest works MK32 to victory in the final round of the Supersports Vauxhall Championship.

The first major event of 1996 was a Formula 3 meeting in mid-April. After an aborted start when Mark Shaw stalled on the grid, the race start procedure

May 29 1995	
Brooklands Race Day	
Retro Sports GT	Trevor Taylor (GTD40)
Classic Formula Ford 1600	Mark Harrison (Lola T540E)
Classic Saloons	Reg Palmer (Ford Zodiac)
Historic Touring Cars	Allen Lloyd (Jaguar MK2)
Thoroughbred Sports	Gerry Marshall (Aston Martin DB4)
Post Historic Touring Cars	Allen Lloyd (Jaguar VJ12)
Moss Europe MGCC BCV8	Steve Williams (MGB)
Pre '83 Formula Ford 2000	Tony Hancock (Van Diemen RF82)
Group 1 Touring Cars	Steve Hirst (Ford Escort RS2000)

June 18 1995	
BARC meeting	
BRC Formula Ford 1600	Gavin Wills (Swift SC92F)
ARP/Toyota Formula 3	Simon Tate (Reynard 863)
Kumho Tyres BMW Challenge	Peter Challis (M5)
Prosport 3000	William Hewland
Dunlp Rover GTi	Alfonso Emanuele
Formula Renault 1700	David Henderson (Swift SC94R)
Pre '85 Formula Ford 1600	Bruce Evans (Reynard FF84)

August 6 1995	
BARC meeting	
Production Cars	Andy Britnell (Ford Escort Cosworth)
Unipart Mini Miglia	Bill Sollis
Caterham Vauxhalls	David Walton
BRDC GT Championship	Win Percy (Harrier LR9C)
Unipart Mini Seven	Steve Bell
Caterham K Series	Dan Eaves
Saloon 2000	Andy Middlehurst (Nissan Skyline)

August 28 1995	
BARC meeting	
ERF Inter-Marque	Gerry Marshall (Aston Martin V8)
Thoroughbred Sports	Gerry Marshall (Aston Martin DB4)
Pirelli Porsche Classics	Chris Heeley (911)
Post-War Aston Martins	Pat Blakeney (DB4)
Pirelli Porsche Cup	Phil Hindley (944T)
One-Hour Endurance Race	David Heynes/ Gerry Marshall (Aston Martin DB4)
Allcomers Race	Bob Watson (Porsche Carrera RSR)

September 17 1995	
Festival of Motorsport	
Big Boys Toys VW Beetles	Shaun Hollamby
Renault 5GT Turbos	Steve Alderton

October 15 1995	
Championship Finals meeting	
British Formula 3	Warren Hughes (Dallara F395)
Supersports Vauxhall	Mike Evans (Mallock MK32)
Lucas VW Ventos	Dave Brodie
Formula Renault 1700	Simon Graves (Swift SC94R)
BARC Renault Clio	Glenn Board
Production Cars	Andy Britnell (Ford Escort Cosworth)

March 24 1996	
BARC meeting	
Classic & Historic Saloons	Alec Hammond (Jaguar MK2)
BARC/MGOC - Class A	Matthew Read (Midget)
BARC/MGOC - Class B	Adrian Olsson (Maestro)
Boiling Point ARP Formula 3	Gareth Burnett (Dallara F388)
Post Historic Touring Cars	Nigel Garrett (Triumph Dolomite Sprint)
Supersports Vauxhall	Richard Andrew (Phantom P94)
Group 1 Touring Cars	Nigel Garrett (Triumph Dolomite Sprint)

recommended as dark clouds gathered over the circuit. Before the race could be started, it rained for about five minutes. Virtually the whole field opted to change to wet tyres, with the exception of Bristolian Philip Hopkins. However, though the sky remained dark, the track started to dry even as the teams changed tyres.

By the time the race started, the track was close to dry again and it seemed as though Hopkins had made an inspired decision. As the track continued to dry, Hopkins got quicker and quicker while the other drivers started to struggle as their wet tyres overheated. Drivers like Juan-Pablo Montoya, who had pushed hard in the early laps, now began to fall back as their tyres faded.

Into the lead after a measured opening stint went Jamie Davies but Ralph Firman was closing in. However, at Village, Paula Cook had spun her car out of the race and the car was abandoned on the grass on the outside of the track.

April 14 1996	
Formula 3 meeting	
British Formula 3	Jamie Davies (Dallara F396)
Dunlop Rover Turbo Cup	Jeremy Cotterill
Unipart Mini Seven	Phil Manser
Unipart Mini Miglia	Stewart Drake
National Saloons	Michael Woodcock (Escort Cosworth)
Mini Allcomers	David Abbott (Mini Miglia)

Hopkins was, by now, on a charge but lost control at Village and as he spun, his car clipped the parked car of Cook. In a frightening accident, his Dallara flipped over and over but Hopkins was largely unscathed as the race was stopped to deal with the incident. By now, about half of the scheduled race distance had run and the remaining cars sat on the grid awaiting a restart. In this situation, parc ferme conditions applied and no work could be done to the cars and, with the track now dry, the Avon tyre technicians declined to give their approval for a restart due to the condition of the wet racing tyres on the cars. Their concern was that the tyres could fail if the race restarted on a dry track and so Davies was declared the winner of an unusual race.

The Touring Car package arrived in early May for the first of two visits during 1996. It was the season of the Frank Biela and Audi A4 steam-roller but it nearly went badly wrong when Frank crashed heavily at the Complex in qualifying after losing control on oil dropped by team-mate John Bintcliffe! 'We had one broken engine and one smashed car,' remembers Audi Team Manager John Wickham.

With Sunday as a day-off, the Audi team worked wonders to rebuild the car after the 100mph impact and used the facilities of a local Audi dealer to prepare the car in time for Biela to win the first race on Monday. Then, even more impressive was his charge from the back of the grid to third place in the second race. Less fortunate was Gary Ayles who went head-on into the Chicane barriers in his Andy Rouse-run Nissan Primera. He escaped with whiplash and bruising. When the series returned over the August Bank Holiday weekend, Biela wrapped up the title with a second and a third place in rounds 21 and 22 of the 26 race calendar. At the same meeting, young Dane Kristian Kolby was confirmed as Formula Ford champion.

'Thruxton has been very good to the Audi Touring Car team and Frank Biela tied up the championship there in 1996. When Frank came to the UK for the first time in

Frank Biela (Audi A4) leads the Touring Car pack into the Complex, May 1996. Photo: Empics.

1996, he thought a lot of circuits were dangerous. He thought Thruxton was crazy, but he loved it!' says Wickham. For the former BARC Competitions Manager, it was particularly fitting that the team he now managed should clinch the Touring Car crown at what he could rightly claim to be his home circuit.

May 4/6 1996
British Touring Car meeting

Auto Trader British Touring Cars	Frank Biela (Audi A4)
Auto Trader British Touring Cars	Jo Winkelhock (BMW 320i)
Slick 50 Formula Ford	Kristian Kolby (Van Diemen RF96)
Formula Vauxhall Junior	Luciano Burti
Formula Vauxhall Junior	Tim Mullen
Formula Renault Sport	Darren Turner (Van Diemen RF96)
Formula Vauxhall	Peter Dumbreck
Ford Credit Fiestas	Jason Minshaw
Classic Touring Cars	Roly Nix (Chevrolet Camaro)
Renault Spiders	Jason Plato

A one-day meeting in late July was headlined by British Formula 3 and the increasingly-popular Privilege Insurance GT Championship. However, the meeting was not a success for the normally pace-setting McLaren F1-GTR of Ian Flux and Texan Jake Ulrich. 'Unfortunately, we couldn't test and the set-up of the car was absolutely

June 30 1996
Brooklands Raceday

URS Classic Formula Ford 2000	Tony Hancock (Van Diemen RF82)
Thoroughbred Sports	Joe Ward (TVR Griffith)
Formula Saloons	Pete Stevens (Vauxhall Carlton)
BOSS Formula	Nigel Smith (Reynard 92D)
Group 4 Trophy Race	Stuart Graham (Alfa Romeo T33/3)
ERF Intermarque	Malcolm Hamilton (Jaguar E-Type)
Ace Sports/Saloons	Nigel Reuben (Lotus Elan)
Classic Sports	David Methley (Marcos GT)

July 28 1996
Formula 3 meeting

British Formula 3	Juan-Pablo Montoya (Dallara F395/6)
Caterham K Series	Justin Keen
Pirelli Porsche Cup	Richard Finney (944 Turbo)
Privilege Insurance GT	Thomas Erdos/ Cor Euser (Marcos LM600)
Caterham Vauxhall	David Walton
Esso VW Vento VR6	Matt Johnson

hopeless. In the Can-Am Lola in Thundersports we were pulling about 178mph up to the Chicane and I thought we'd pull more in the McLaren. As it turned out, the car was so bad through Church that we only got to about 167mph up the hill. It just wouldn't ride the bumps. It was like driving a pogo stick! That's all right through the Complex or the Chicane but not at Church and Goodwood,' reckons Flux. The race was won by the Marcos LM600 of Cor Euser and Thomas Erdos.

August 24/26 1996	
British Touring Car meeting	
Auto Trader British Touring Cars	David Leslie (Honda Accord)
Auto Trader British Touring Cars	Rickard Rydell (Volvo 850)
Formula Vauxhall Junior	Andrew Kirkaldy
Slick 50 Formula Ford	Mark Webber (Van Diemen RF96)
Slick 50 Formula Ford	Jacky van der Ende (Mygale 96)
Formula Renault Sport	David Henderson (Ermolli FRS96)
Ford Credit Fiestas	Gareth Downing
Formula Vauxhall	Stuart Moseley
Classic Touring Cars	Roly Nix (Chevrolet Camaro)
Renault Spiders	Scott Lakin

September 15 1996	
Festival of Motorsport	
Swire Renshaw Super Coupe	Ian Churchill (VW Polo G40)
BMW Challenge	Peter Challis (M5)
Caterham Scholarship	John Aylott

In September, the Thruxton Festival of Motorsport was held to cover all types of action with cars, motorbikes and trucks on the same programme. A good crowd arrived to see some close and varied racing, with the car action headed by a round of the BMW Challenge. Wrapping up the season was a Championship Finals meeting on October 13th but, without Formula 3, it was a low-key meeting. Local star Adrian Cottrell made it a good day by scoring a pair of wins in the final rounds of the BARC Renault Clio Championship and two seasoned campaigners also took wins that day: Malcolm Jackson (K Sports 1600) and Don Hardman (BRC Formula Ford 1600) both had more than 20 years of racing behind them.

October 13 1996	
Championship Finals meeting	
Modified Production Saloons	Gerry Cain (Rover SD1)
Morgans	Matthew Wurr (+8)
Porsche Classic	Pat Jennings (911RS)
Renault Clio	Adrian Cottrell
Renault Clio	Adrian Cottrell
Formula Renault 1700	Justin Cadman (Martini MK63)
RDS Automotive K Sports 1600	Malcolm Jackson (Mallock MK20B)
BRC Formula Ford 1600	Don Hardman (Reynard 92FF)

The 1997 racing calendar took on a rather different look to previous seasons. The 12 days of racing were allocated to just eight events, four of them two-day events selected to attract the maximum possible crowds to the circuit. It was a simple commercial decision by the BARC to gain the best return from the rare days of racing allowed.

'As a circuit, we have to try and keep an infrastructure which allows the circuit to run the type of events we wish to run, but we have to do that on the income from 12 days,' explains Dennis Carter. 'If we ever have more days available, the nature of that will change again. It is so important to the BARC as a club to maximise the income from the circuit to support the Club. I'd like to think we may be able to increase circuit usage and that is a constant discussion. We've not given up on that.

'Since the High Court order was put in place 25 years ago, the level of noise generated by motorsport has come down. There is a lot to be said for continuing the dialogue. We are better neighbours than we used to be. The relationship with the local authority is very good. They are very supportive of 99% of the things we do,' reckons Carter.

'The major change has been a move to a more permanent type of arrangement. To begin with, Thruxton was always based on temporary buildings. We've tried to move away from that and construct buildings of a higher standard. And, of course, some of this you do merely to stand still as people's expectations of facilities increase. We've invested a lot of money. The continued support of land-owner Henry Pelham has allowed the Club to make that investment and his role in the on-going development of Thruxton has been vital.

'Our intention is to retain Thruxton with international status and to continue the improvement in facilities. It is very important to us that we never stand still. I feel that, in years to come, there will be pressure to slow the circuit down. Its a very quick circuit. My own feeling is that we should try and resist that, as it is one of the last truly flowing circuits. It has a character all of its own and overall, the safety record of Thruxton is very good.'

Headlining the '97 programme was a brace of Touring Car meetings to be run over the early May and August Bank Holidays. A round of the highly-popular Motor Cycle News British Superbike Championship drew in the two-wheel enthusiasts in July and a month earlier Thruxton shuddered as the FIA European Truck Championship contenders arrived. This was the first FIA International meeting at Thruxton since the final Formula 3000 race in 1985.

Topping and tailing the season were three one-day national car meetings, two of them Formula 3 meetings. The 12th day of race action was a Production TT Motorbike meeting on Easter Monday.

The only club meeting of the 1997 season was the March season opener when a new local talent emerged. Southampton's Peter Clarke was only 17 when he won the BARC Formula Renault Championship and among his rivals was another youngster just starting out. Charles Hall had his first ever car race that day and impressed onlookers with his handling of a Tatuus RC96 Formula Renault as he chased race winner Clarke. Andover's Ray West made it a good day for local fans by winning the Modified Production Saloon Car race in the Opel Manta he prepared in his workshops at the circuit.

March 16 1997	
BARC meeting	
Modified Production Saloons	Ray West (Opel Ascona)
Classic/Historic Saloons	Alec Hammond (Jaguar MK2)
Formula Renault	Peter Clarke (Van Diemen RF96)
Autotecnic BMW Challenge	Colin Wells (M3)
Post Historic Touring Cars	Peter Brown (Triumph Dolomite Sprint)
URS Classic Formula Ford 2000	Steve Nichols (Van Diemen RF82)
Group One Touring Cars	Graham Scarborough (Ford Capri)

April 13 1997	
Formula 3 meeting	
Autosport British Formula 3	Jonny Kane (Dallara F397)
Formula Vauxhall	Luciano Burti
Supersports 200	Neil Riddiford (Mallock MK32)
Porsche Cup	Johnny Mowlem (993)
Tomcat Turbos	Geoff Prince
Porsche Classic	Paul Edwards (911SC)

The April Formula 3 race will long be remembered for an incident that happened on the slowing down lap. During the closing stages, Frenchman Nicolas Minassian was fending off Jonny Kane in the lead battle but it all changed as they came up to lap the slower car of Michael Bentwood. David Addison was the commentator at the Complex that day, and had a birds-eye view of the remarkable situation that developed.

Ralph Firman (Dallara F396) en route to winning the British Formula 3 Championship. Photo: Paul Jackson.

'In the closing laps, Kane was gradually reeling Minassian in. As they went through Noble and started to set the cars up for Goodwood, Minassian was getting worried by Kane who was looming large in his mirrors. Bentwood was in front of them and pulled to the left hand side of the road but, unfortunately, he also lifted off. Minassian, who had been concentrating on watching Kane in his mirrors, came barrelling up behind Bentwood and had to lift, which allowed Kane to get past the pair of them up the inside and very close to the marshals' post.

'Minassian had led for nineteen and a half laps of a 20-lap race and was absolutely hopping mad. As they came out to the Complex on the slowing down lap, Kane was waving to the crowd as he was delighted. Minassian was also waving away but he was very unhappy! Towards the Complex he pulled up alongside Bentwood and showed that he wasn't pleased by gesticulating at the slower driver,' recalls Addison.

'Going out of Cobb, Minassian got ahead and forced Bentwood to slow down. They both got slower and slower and ran out onto the concrete apron before the cars stalled as they were now going so slowly. Minassian leapt out of the car and rushed over towards Bentwood who was completely baffled by it all. Eventually, Minassian slapped Bentwood on the side of his helmet before the marshals managed to restrain Nicolas.'

The stewards of the meeting had little option but to ban Minassian from racing for 30 days and during that time he missed two Formula 3 races. Sadly, had it not been for that momentary loss of control, Minassian may well have beaten Kane to the title.

May 4/5 1997
British Touring Car meeting

Auto Trader British Touring Cars	Frank Biela (Audi A4)
Auto Trader British Touring Cars	Gabriele Tarquini (Honda Accord)
Slick 50 Formula Ford	Daniel Wheldon (Van Diemen RF97)
Formula Renault Sport	Marc Hynes (Tatuus RC97)
Formula Vauxhall Junior	Antonio Pizzonia
Ford Credit Fiestas	Graham Jennings
ICS Classic Touring Cars	Andy Bacon (Chevrolet Camaro)
Vauxhall Vectra SRi V6	Julian Westwood
Renault Spiders	Bryce Wilson

June 7/8 1997
European Truck meeting

BARC/MGOC Class A	Mick Mercer (Midget)
BARC/MGOC Class B	Colin Simpson (Maestro)
Bridgestone Ginetta G27s	Suzi Hart-Banks

The first Touring Car meeting was held over the early May Bank Holiday and while Touring Car victories went to Frank Biela (Audi A4) and Gabriele Tarquini (Honda Accord), many will best remember the meeting for a destructive accident at the start of the Vauxhall Vectra SRi V6 race. A chain-reaction incident off the grid left several cars badly damaged, notably that of Brazilian Cesar Gauterio who barrel-rolled along the top of the barriers at Allard.

Over the August Bank Holiday weekend, the Touring Car circus was back at Thruxton and, though the Renault pairing of Alain Menu and Jason Plato was now setting the pace, the Audi squad came good with Biela and Bintcliffe taking a win each in changeable conditions.

August 23/25 1997
Touring Car meeting

Auto Trader British Touring Cars	Frank Biela (Audi A4)
Auto Trader British Touring Cars	John Bintcliffe (Audi A4)
Slick 50 Formula Ford	Jacky van der Ende (Van Diemen RF97)
Formula Renault Sport	Marc Hynes (Tatuus RC97)
Formula Vauxhall Junior	Doug Bell
Ford Credit Fiestas	Gareth Downing
ICS Classic Touring Cars	Roly Nix (Chevrolet Camaro)
Vauxhall Vectra SRi V6	Flavio Figueiredo
Renault Spiders	Bryce Wilson
Renault Spiders	David Shaw

The season closed with the final British Formula 3 race of the season and that meeting allowed Minassian to make amends for his earlier indiscretion. While Kane drove a measured race to second and made sure of the title, Minassian won convincingly. The other highlight of the meeting was a titanic showdown for the conclusion of the Unipart DCM Mini Seven Challenge. Steve Bell, Dave Braggins and Phil Manser all had a chance of winning the title but Bell held a slight advantage. As the pack dived into the Chicane for the final time, Bell was able to ease back and keep out of trouble, knowing that fourth place was enough to make certain of the title. While young Rob Cullum flew the kerbs in typical Mini style, Manser beat Braggins to the line to win the race by a fraction, but the title had gone to Bell.

October 12 1997	
Formula 3 meeting	
Autosport British Formula 3	Nicolas Minassian (Dallara F397)
Unipart Mini Seven	Phil Manser
Unipart Mini Miglia	Bill Sollis
Trigard VW Vento VR6	Simon Graves
National Saloons	Toni Ruokonen (Honda Integra R)
Formula Vauxhall	Justin Wilson

And so the curtain fell on another season of racing, the 30th since Thruxton first opened on March 17th 1968. In those 30 seasons, the circuit witnessed many great performances from many great drivers. But it had also proved a unique challenge to the legion of club racers who had done battle on the demanding sweeps of the Hampshire track. Invariably, the racing at the circuit is fast, close and exciting and many races have only been finally resolved in a nail-biting, last-lap lunge into the Club Chicane.

Many improvements had been made over the years to the circuit and its facilities, but the track remained faithful to the original layout that had first been dug out during the winter of 1967.

The outright lap record

Date	Driver	Class	Car	Time	Speed
17/3/68	Philip Tose	F3	Brabham BT18	1m27.2s	97.27mph
15/4/68	Jochen Rindt	F2	Brabham BT23C	1m16.0s	111.60mph
7/4/69	Jochen Rindt	F2	Lotus 59	1m14.0s	114.62mph
30/3/70	Jochen Rindt	F2	Lotus 69	1m14.0s	114.62mph
9/8/70	Frank Gardner	F5000	Lola T190	1m13.6s	115.24mph
9/8/70	Peter Gethin	F5000	McLaren M10B	1m13.6s	115.24mph
12/4/71	Ronnie Peterson	F2	March 712M	1m13.4s	115.55mph
1/8/71	Frank Gardner	F5000	Lola T300	1m12.2s	117.47mph
3/4/72	Ronnie Peterson	F2	March 722	1m11.6s	118.46mph
23/4/73	Jean-Pierre Jarier	F2	March 732	1m11.2s	119.12mph
23/4/73	Jacques Coulon	F2	March 732	1m11.2s	119.12mph
23/4/73	Carlos Pace	F2	Surtees TS15	1m11.2s	119.12mph
18/8/74	Vern Schuppan	F5000	Lola T332	1m11.0s	119.46mph
31/3/75	Brian Henton	F2	March 752	1m11.0s	119.46mph
31/3/75	Jacques Laffite	F2	Martini MK16	1m11.0s	119.46mph
26/5/75	Ian Ashley	F5000	Lola T400	1m11.0s	119.46mph
19/4/76	Jean-Pierre Jabouille	F2	Elf 2J	1m10.88s	119.66mph
11/4/77	Brian Henton	F2	Boxer PR276	1m10.67s	120.02mph
29/5/78	Geoff Lees	British F1	March 781	1m10.41s	120.46mph
16/4/79	Marc Surer	F2	March 792	1m09.11s	122.73mph
7/4/80	Brian Henton	F2	Toleman TG280	1m09.04s	122.85mph
20/4/81	Marc Surer	F2	March 812	1m08.00s	124.73mph
12/4/82	Johnny Cecotto	F2	March 822	1m07.37s	125.90mph
27/3/89	Roland Ratzenberger	British F3000	Reynard 88D	1m04.44s	131.62mph
16/4/90	Pedro Chaves	British F3000	Reynard 89D	1m04.43s	131.64mph
11/8/91	Dave Coyne	British F3000	Reynard 90D	1m03.66s	133.23mph
26/9/93	Phillipe Adams	British F3000	Reynard 91D	1m02.75s	135.16mph

The Formula 2 race winners

1968	Jochen Rindt (Brabham BT23C)	**1978**	Bruno Giacomelli (March 782)
1969	Jochen Rindt (Lotus 59)	**1979**	Rad Dougall (March 782)
1970	Jochen Rindt (Lotus 69)	**1980**	Brian Henton (Toleman TG280)
1971	Graham Hill (Brabham BT36)	**1981**	Roberto Guerrero (Maurer MM81)
1972	Ronnie Peterson (March 722)	**1982**	Johnny Cecotto (March 822)
1973	Henri Pescarolo (Motul M1)	**1983**	Beppe Gabbiani (March 832)
1974	not held	**1984**	Mike Thackwell (Ralt-Honda RH6/84)
1975	Jacques Laffite (Martini MK16)	**1985**	(Formula 3000 race)
1976	Maurizio Flammini (March 762)		Emanuele Pirro (March 85B)
1977	Brian Henton (Boxer PR276)		

Thruxton Circuit Map

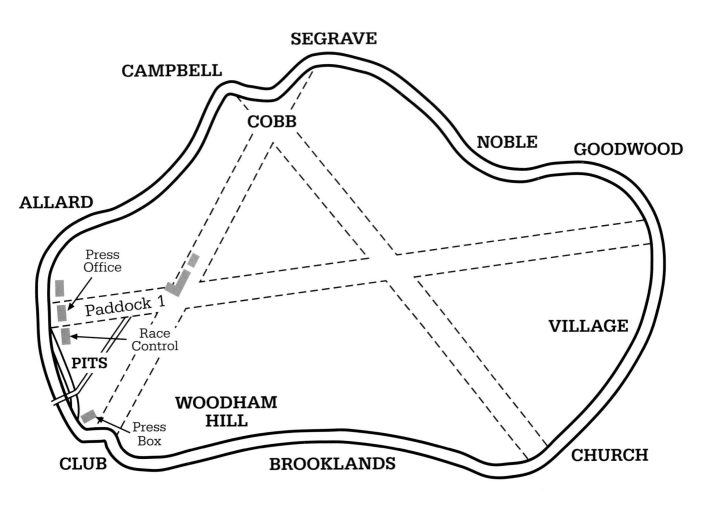

APPENDIX 3

The Formula Ford 1600 lap record

Date	Driver	Car	Time	Speed
19/5/68	Richard Mallock Brian Sharp Ian Foster	Mallock U2 Merlyn MK11 Merlyn MK11	1m33.4s	90.81mph
6/7/69	Liane Engeman	Pringett Mistrale	1m31.8s	92.39mph
30/8/69	Ian Taylor	Dulon LD4C	1m30.6s	93.62mph
21/9/69	Bryan Sharp	Merlyn MK11	1m30.2s	94.03mph
14/6/70 14/3/71	Syd Fox Peter Lamplough Tony Brise	Macon MR8 Palliser WDF2 Elden MK8	1m29.2s	95.08mph
18/4/71 25/4/71 2/5/71	John Trevelyan Richard Mallock Rod Jackson	Crossle 20F Mallock MK9B Titan MK6	1m27.8s	96.60mph
6/6/71	Andy Rouse Richard Mallock	Dulon LD9 Mallock MK9B	1m27.4s	97.04mph
22/8/71	Jeremy Gambs	Lotus 61M	1m27.2s	97.27mph
30/7/72	David Ferris	Merlyn MK20	1m26.8s	97.71mph
28/8/72 31/10/76 21/11/76	John Stevens Derek Warwick Kenny Gray	Merlyn MK17/20 Hawke DL15 Royale RP24	1m25.4s	99.32mph
29/10/78	Kenny Acheson Michael Roe	Royale RP26 Van Diemen RF78	1m25.3s	99.43mph
8/11/80	Rob Tennant	Royale RP26	1m25.20s	99.55mph
13/11/82	Andy Wallace	Van Diemen RF82	1m25.03s	99.75mph
30/5/83	Andrew Gilbert-Scott	Lola T642E	1m24.8s	100.02mph
11/3/84	John Pratt	Reynard 84FF	1m23.98s	100.99mph
29/3/87	Alain Menu	Van Diemen RF87	1m22.0s	103.43mph
25/5/87	Dave Coyne	Swift FB4	1m20.89s	104.85mph
18/10/87	Alain Menu	Reynard 87FF	1m20.59s	105.24mph
16/10/88	Jose Cordova	Reynard 88FF	1m20.01s	106.00mph